Literature of the Global Age

Literature of the Global Age

A Critical Study of Transcultural Narratives

MAURIZIO ASCARI

McFarland & Company, Inc., Publishers
Jefferson, North Carolina, and London

LIBRARY OF CONGRESS CATALOGUING-IN-PUBLICATION DATA

Ascari, Maurizio.
　Literature of the global age : a critical study of transcultural narratives / Maurizio Ascari.
　　　p.　　cm.
　Includes bibliographical references and index.

　ISBN: 978-0-7864-5959-9
　softcover : 50# alkaline paper ∞

　1. Postmodernism (Literature)　2. Transnationalism in literature.　I. Title.
PN98.P67A83　2011
809.3'048 — dc22　　　　　　　　　　　　　　　　2011009260

BRITISH LIBRARY CATALOGUING DATA ARE AVAILABLE

© 2011 Maurizio Ascari. All rights reserved

No part of this book may be reproduced or transmitted in any form or by any means, electronic or mechanical, including photocopying or recording, or by any information storage and retrieval system, without permission in writing from the publisher.

Cover images © 2011 Shutterstock

Manufactured in the United States of America

McFarland & , Inc., Publishers
　Box 611, Jefferson, North Carolina 28640
　　www.mcfarlandpub.com

For Franca

Table of Contents

Preface and Acknowledgments	1
Introduction	5
For a Planetary Culture	7
Transcultural Narratives	11
Through the Green Line	14
Around Postmodernism	17
After 9/11	21
Beyond Postmodernism	25
The Dialectics Between Words and Reality	30
Narratives of Responsibility	33
Morals as Transgression	37
1. Julian Barnes, *Flaubert's Parrot* (1984)	41
Relics of the Past	41
Rethinking History	44
The Language of Parrots	46
Avatars of Truth	49
2. Magda Szabó, *The Door* (1987)	52
Behind the Door	53
Emotions, Thought and Ethics	55
An Epic of Emotions	56
Against Orthodoxy	59

From Ethics to Aesthetics	62
The Tragedy of Betrayal	63

3. Abraham B. Yehoshua, *Mr. Mani* (1990) 66
    Back to the Bible 68
    The Shadow of the Akedah 72
    Looking for a Father 75
    Escaping from History 76
    The Other Within 79

4. Ian McEwan, *Atonement* (2001) 82
    The Dangers of the Imagination 83
    Eroticism and Forgery 86
    Night into Nightmare 88
    War Hells 89
    Criminal and Mourner 90
    A Book on Books 92

5. W.G. Sebald, *Austerlitz* (2001) 95
    Narratives of Exile 96
    Architectures of Suffering 98
    Mirroring Lives 102
    Ghosts of Memory 104
    On the Verge of the Abyss 107

6. Haruki Murakami, *Kafka on the Shore* (2002) 110
    Rewriting the Enigma of Oedipus 111
    Life on the Shore 113
    The Possible Story of Miss Saeki 116
    Nakata versus Johnnie Walker 118
    Into the Labyrinth 120

7. Jonathan Safran Foer, *Everything Is Illuminated* (2002) .. 124
    One Novel, Two Narratives 126
    Heart of Darkness 129
    Beyond the Tragic 131
    Blindness and Insight 134
    Postmemory Novels 136

8. Azar Nafisi, *Reading Lolita in Tehran* (2003)   139
    Back to Tehran   139
    Life in Black   141
    The Politics and Poetics of Identity   143
    Narratives of the Iranian Diaspora   146
    A Heated Critical Debate   148
    Language and Democracy   151

9. Conclusion   154
    Traveling with Mr. Bean   154
    Bearing Witness   157
    Inner Frontiers   162
    Narratives and Remediation   163
    Grasping Complexity   165

Notes   167
Bibliography   181
Index   197

Preface and Acknowledgments

The story of this book is far from linear. It was originally rooted in two experiences which often trigger a process of personal evolution — traveling and reading. It was in Cyprus, in 2004, that I first came into contact with what is commonly labeled as a *green line*, an armistice line between two territories. A green line is literally a no man's land, a stretch of ground that is interdicted. In terms of space it separates two ethnic groups or communities or nations which have been at war. In terms of time it hopefully separates war from reconciliation, but reconciliation needs an effort, for it takes energy to rebuild mutual confidence and to re-establish dialogue.

My first experience of what might be regarded as a political and cultural fault line — since the Christian Greek–Cypriot and the Muslim Turkish–Cypriot communities front one another on the two sides of the Cyprus green line — prompted me to read several books, not only about the near East but also other 20th-century conflicts. My aim was to try to understand what had escaped me as I wandered from one side of the line to the other, entering functioning churches and mosques, and also dilapidated buildings which had once served as places of worship, with a strange feeling — part elation, part dismay, mostly awe. Experiencing this green line alerted me to the need to reconceive culture not only in a supranational way — as my studies had taught me — but also in a planetary way, so as to create a supracultural container, just as the concept of the sacred includes religions in the plural.

My travel impressions, combined with my reading, translated into a series of talks I gave on books such as Yehoshua's *Mr. Mani* and Nafisi's *Reading Lolita in Tehran*. Then the idea of a volume came to my mind. Its original title was *The Classics of Tomorrow*, since in my eyes these works have captured such important aspects of our time. For months I discussed my hypothesis with colleagues and friends. As a result, the volume underwent a complete rewriting and was published in Italy under the title: *La sottile linea verde: romanzi contemporanei tra oriente e occidente* (2009, *The Thin Green Line: Contemporary Novels between the East and the West*), but I felt that my research was not over.

To test my approach even further, I started giving talks on the subject of world literature and intercultural understanding, this time in English and in international contexts, such as a seminar entitled "Questioning the European Identity/ies: Deconstructing Old Stereotypes and Envisioning New Models of Representation" (University of Bologna, May 15, 2009) and a research workshop (University of Cardiff, Research and Graduate School in the Humanities, October 26, 2009). In response to the stimuli I was offered by my new interlocutors — including the American publisher McFarland, whom I contacted with a proposal — my project changed again, and the result is the present volume.

I regard the labored genesis of this work both as a sign of its *experiential* quality — for it has been subject to a constant evolution alongside my own — and also as the progressive unfolding of my original motivation, namely the need to communicate my critical response to a series of works, as I did first in the context of a lecture room and then in writing, to reach a wider audience. Therefore, in my critical analysis I have aimed, whenever possible, to render the sense of reading as a process — a quest for meaning which entails false inferences and adjustments of perspective — in order to underline the performative dimension of this interaction, which makes something happen, provoking inner change in readers.

In an article on the public role of writers and intellectuals, Edward Said discussed the increasing separation between academic discourse and public space, indicating the "generally hermetic, jargon-ridden, unthreatening combativeness" of the former as the cause of the "marginalization of the humanities."[1] This work is an attempt to bring the discussion of literature back into public domain, without renouncing the most useful analytical tools that academic thought has developed, but also without losing the sense of literature as a cultural practice that produces meaning in a social, political, historical context. Far from being parasitic and self-centered, an act of criticism should be a way to make literary works live, to invite readers to return to a novel or memoir or a poem or a play with different eyes, or to address it for the first time if destiny has not brought them into contact with it before. If I achieve this result, I will regard myself a fortunate man.

To conclude, I should add that the longer I live, the more I realize that writing a book is a collective rather than individual effort, even when only one person signs it, for every book bears the traces of innumerable conversations and exchanges with colleagues and friends and family, and even with strangers. I will therefore list here — in alphabetical order — some of the persons who have helped me find my way: Silvia Albertazzi, Giorgio Amitrano, Alessandra Calanchi, Riccardo Campi, Maria Teresa Cassini, Alessandro Castellari, Remo Ceserani, Daniela and Guido Fink, Vita Fortunati, Gilberta Golinelli, Rossana Guffanti, Maria Hadjipavlou, Christopher P. Hood, Stephen Knight, Simona Mambrini, Rita Monticelli, Jean-François Plamondon, Tilde and Alberto Schön, Stephanos Stephanides, Dominique Vittoz, Tadahiko Wada, Michael Webb, and Franca Zanelli Quarantini.

I feel that my wife, Franca, deserves special thanks for taking my place in real life while I was losing myself in the labyrinth of words, and for welcoming me with a smile of complicity when I came back from outer space.

Introduction

"What Is a Classic?" is the title of an address T.S. Eliot delivered before the Virgil society on October 16, 1944. In this seminal text — which significantly was written while Europe was devastated by World War II[2] — Eliot redefined the classic in a transcultural way, contrasting the "relative classic," which achieves distinction within a single language, with the "absolute classic," which is such "in relation to a number of other languages."[3] I have long been intrigued by this definition, which emphasizes the communicative power of literature, its ability to cross linguistic and cultural borders, contributing to the creation of an *ecumene*, i.e., a supranational community. Of course Eliot was intent on providing a conflict-torn Europe with a common cultural basis to rebuild upon the ruins:

> We need to remind ourselves that, as Europe is a whole (and still, in its progressive mutilation and disfigurement, the organism out of which any greater world harmony must develop), so European literature is a whole, the several members of which cannot flourish, if the same bloodstream does not circulate through the whole body.[4]

This image is redolent of previous biological metaphors — such as that of Christ as the head of the Church or the medieval theory of the body politic — that emphasize inter-relatedness and mutuality. Moreover, while drawing a parallel between the political and cultural wholeness of Europe, Eliot not only emphasized the role of literature in ensuring the well-being of this supranational body, but also hinted at future forms of "world harmony," i.e., at the creation of a planetary *ecumene*.

Needless to say, we are still striving after this ideal, which is far from attained. As a group of scholars including Sheldon Pollock and Homi Bhabha argued introducing a volume on *cosmopolitanism*, a concept which is central to the current debate on citizenship and globalization[5]: "Cosmopolitanism is yet to come, something awaiting realization."[6] Yet, fostering a condition of *world citizenship*— based on the idea that "each human being has responsibilities to every other,"[7] in Kwame Anthony Appiah's words — seems the only way to achieve political balance and sustainable development in harmony with Gaia. Appiah, who is a philosopher, sees *conversation* as the key to this attitude of mutual recognition "across boundaries."[8] Therefore I think that, following Eliot, we should take very seriously into account the performative power of literature to cross cultural barriers and weave a network of connections, for in a way all good works of literature are transcultural, like classics, as is proved by the importance translation has had over the millennia in the development of human civilization.

Recognizing the long-standing role of literature as a mediator between ethnic groups and/or nations — and its inherent power to contrast a logic of exclusion based on difference, insofar as literature invites us to empathize with characters, abandoning the shell of our own ego — should not obscure the specificity of our cultural situation. As we know, the turn of the millennium has been marked by an acceleration and intensification of previous cultural phenomena, and the contexts in which literature is produced and consumed have changed dramatically in the last few decades due to the process of globalization. As we shall see, contemporary literature may be deemed as transcultural due to several factors, including the fact that many contemporary authors are themselves in-between cultures. According to John Pizer, "Transnational literature written by bilingual and bicultural authors" is not only calling into question "the very notion of discrete 'national' literatures," but it is also "helping to redefine the very principle of world literature."[9]

Following in the footsteps of Wolfgang Welsch, I have opted for the term *transcultural* because it goes beyond the intercultural and multicultural perspectives in the deconstruction of the 18th-century concept (Herder) of single cultures, proving both descriptively more attuned to present reality and projectually more open. As Welsch clarifies, both interculturality and multiculturality, in their effort to establish communication and coexistence between communities whose culture they basically continue to regard as coherent, fail to challenge the traditional view of cultures as "spheres or islands."[10] On the other hand, transculturality takes into account both "the inner differentiation" of modern cultures and their "external networking"[11] due to global migration and communication. As Welsch writes, "Cultural conditions today are largely characterized by mixes and permeations."[12] Our identities are indeed hybrid, and it is increasingly difficult to describe something as entirely foreign or entirely our own. The editors of a recent volume on transculturalism put the liberatory power of this concept in a nutshell when they claim: "Whereas culture may have the capacity to free us from the dictates of nature [...] the merit and capacity of transculture is to free us from the conventions and obsessions of culture itself."[13]

Starting from these premises, I wish to clarify that I will use the term *transcultural narratives* to exemplify both the conditions that currently preside over the creation and circulation of literature, and the ideological frameworks we utilize to interpret them. As regards the subtitle of this study, I will comment on it by quoting David Damrosch, in whose eyes "world literature is not an infinite, ungraspable canon of works but rather a mode of circulation and of reading."[14] Of course, the eight texts I will discuss as case studies to exemplify the theoretical issues presented in this Introduction are definitely not meant as the foundation of a canon. What we need today are tools rather than lists.

Far from proving homogeneous in terms of politics and poetics, these works — ranging from 1984 to 2003 — trace a diachronic cultural itinerary that will hopefully enable us to assess what I regard as a cultural shift — a change in cultural perceptions and preoccupations that has taken place at the turn of the century and that, in my eyes, invites us to reassess the category of postmodernism. At the same time, these eight books all look backwards — albeit in different ways — toward some of the great historical events that marked the period between the 1940s and our present: World War II and the Holocaust, the Cold War and the communist regimes, the Arab-Israeli conflicts and the Palestine question, the Iranian Revolution. Starting from these diversified historical contexts, these volumes enable us to meditate on the big issues — concerning conflict, memory, trauma, identity and responsibility — we face in our lives, individually and collectively. Reading these works of fiction, which distill quintessential aspects of the human experience, has been for me a highly rewarding *humanitarian* exercise, if I am allowed this play on words.

For a Planetary Culture

Today's critical and theoretical discourses on literature not only relate texts to the wider domain of culture but also investigate new cartographies. In the second half of the 20th century, postcolonial criticism/theory has striven to overcome the binarism *us/them* that had characterized the colonial order, in an attempt to advocate cultural hybridization, to give voice to the memories of subalterns, and to shed light on the conflicts that were provoked both by colonial expansion and by the subsequent migratory fluxes. Nations, their foundation myths and national consciousness were deconstructed in seminal works such as Benedict Anderson's *Imagined Communities* (1983) and *Nation and Narration* (1990), a collection of essays edited by Homi Bhabha. Gender studies have likewise helped to detach the study of literature from the container of the nation, considering literature as a cultural representation and a determining factor of identity in its multifaceted formations.

As a result of these and other concomitant factors, the concept of literary canon — as a list of foundational texts on which national literature and identity rest — is no longer a viable tool to study contemporary culture, whose dimension can rather be described as *planetary*. At various levels, institutions have operated to substitute the restrictive notion of a national canon with a wider scope that corresponds to the complexities of our present. As Stephen Greenblatt and Giles Gunn remarked in their groundbreaking *Redrawing the Boundaries* (1992), the new fields of study that developed in the second half of the 20th century disrupted the traditional approach to literature as based on *close reading*— an approach whose object was "to train students in the analysis of the principal works of the literary canon."[15] The profession of literary studies has undergone a process of thorough refashioning, and the new theoretical imperative has been the idea of *breaching the boundaries*— both on a political and on a cultural level, including the boundaries between disciplines themselves. Suffice it to think of the popularity that prefixes such as *inter-*, *trans-*, *multi-* and *cross-* have recently enjoyed in combination with adjectives such as *national*, *racial*, *ethnic*, *cultural* and *disciplinary*, to name but a few.

Moreover, already in the 1960s, scholars in social sciences and cultural anthropology had started to debate the issue of globalization, which became of common interest in the 1980s and has subsequently come to polarize public opinion (pro/anti). According to Roland Robertson, globalization "refers both to the compression of the world and the intensification of consciousness of the world as a whole."[16] The recent economic crisis has once again made us (painfully) conscious of the fact that the world has become a single system, although of course this increased interdependence does not imply an harmonious integration, but rather entails a variety of effects — the rise of conflicts and fundamentalisms on the one hand, the progressive relativization of local/national cultural practices and ensuing forms of syncretism and creolization on the other. Our perception of globalization oscillates between the conceptual poles of chaos and order. What matters, however, is that when we deal with issues ranging from economics to the military, religion and ecology we feel increasingly obliged to take a global perspective to grasp the whole extent of the problem and develop appropriate solutions.[17] Likewise, when we deal with culture, we should be aware of the fact that the total exceeds the sum of the parts, so to speak. As Ulf Hannerz claimed, "More than ever, there is a global ecumene. The entities we routinely call cultures are becoming more like subcultures within this wider entity."[18]

In the last few decades, the development of comparatism has also contributed to a vision of literature as a system of genres and themes which are characterized by a transnational circulation.[19] Starting from the idea of *Weltliteratur* as conceived by Goethe,[20] Franco Moretti has recently proposed to refound comparatism — enlarging its horizons beyond Euro-America — so as to render it suitable for an epoch in which literature is "a planetary system."[21]

As George Steiner remarks, Goethe regarded *Weltliteratur* as a means to advocate an enlightened cosmopolitanism against "the Teutonic verbiage and archaicizing fervour of the new German philology and historiography."[22] Studying other languages and traditions is a means to fight against chauvinism and intellectual isolation. In this respect, Goethe is an important reference point, also as the author of the *West-Eastern Divan*, a collection of poems that celebrates the encounter between the East and the West. This is why when David Barenboim and Edward Said — respectively a Jewish-Argentinian and a Palestinian — decided to create a youth orchestra in 1999, in order to favor the dialogue between young people coming from Israel and from the neighboring Arab countries, they chose to call it the *West-Eastern Divan*.

At the turn of the century an increasingly closer dialogue has been sought out between literary criticism and theory on the one hand and cultural studies, translation studies, multiculturalism, semiotics and social sciences on the other. This exchange between disciplines has been instrumental in implementing a comparative view of literature on a planetary scale. This is proved by texts such as *Death of a Discipline* (2003) by Gayatri Chakravorty Spivak, whose biography is in itself a manifesto of our present, since this theoretician of feminism and postcolonialism is of Bengalese origin and teaches both in the United States and in India. According to Spivak, only a planetary perspective enables us to overcome the dialectic between identity and alterity that opposes peoples and cultures, for planetary thought associates the concept of alterity to the indefinite that is external to the planet.[23]

I believe that to embrace a truly planetary perspective in our attitude to contemporary culture we need to reassess the value that the concept of postmodernism still has as an intellectual tool. For postmodernism is after all a Euro-American phenomenon (and theoretical construct),[24] whose planetary dimension has possibly been overrated. Of course I am not claiming that other levels of analysis — which are internal to the cultural containers of single nations, of Europe as a whole or of Euro-America — have become superfluous, but I believe that in order to grasp the complexities of our present the gaze of critics should embrace its objects from different distances, with a zoom effect. As Moretti himself writes: "There will always be a point where the study of world literature must yield to the specialist of the national literature, in a sort of cosmic and inevitable division of labour."[25]

Although the planetary character of contemporary culture invites us to expatiate on various literatures, crossing the borders between Euro-America and the rest of the world, this wide comparative attitude also implies a major consequence, that is to say, renouncing — at least in some cases — the opportunity of experiencing texts in the original language. I am aware of the risks that reading a text in translation entails, and I agree with Moretti that to embark on this venture we have to abandon the practice of close reading, which is inevitably linked to a restricted canon of texts, in order to adopt the practice of *distant reading*,[26] which enables us to study literature as a system, working on themes, tropes and genres.

As I underlined while discussing Goethe's attitude, the election of a critical point of view on the territory of literature also entails a political stance. After all, as Greenblatt and Gunn argue, "Literature is not entirely separable from either interest or ideology," although "it is not reducible to those either."[27] Thus while in the 1990s many scholars were growing interested in the planetary and the global, others took a defensive stance, reasserting the importance of Western culture.

The so-called *canon wars* were ignited by books such as Allan Bloom's *The Closing of the American Mind* (1987), which defended the role of Western classics within university curricula against the attempt of multiculturalists to open up reading lists so as to include texts by women and minorities. A few years later Harold Bloom, another strenuous advocate of the Euro-American cultural identity, opposed his purely aesthetic view of literature — a "post-Emersonian version of Pater and Wilde" — to the prevailing view of literature as "an overt crusade for social change."[28]

Thanks to its conservative ideological outlook, *The Western Canon* (1994) achieved the status of an international best seller. Bloom's scathing criticism was leveled at *the school of resentment*—an assortment of critics who had been guilty of listening to the sirens of Marxism, feminism, multiculturalism, deconstructionism, new historicism and semiotics, proving oblivious to the appeal of aesthetic criticism, which Bloom regards as exempt from ideological prejudices.

Although the sacred flame of art that animates Bloom compels respect, his polemical vein was ill directed. Moreover, although the project to delineate a Western canon still commands admiration in its titanic ardor, it risks being translated — in terms of reception if not of intention — into an act of political closure, in support of those who wish to trace a neat border between the cultural identity of the Western world and the rest of the world. Drawing a parallel between Bloom's "dismissive aestheticism" and Samuel Huntington's thesis on the clash of civilization, Edward Said asserted that both thinkers "radically misapprehend" what makes cultures and civilizations interesting—"not their essence or purity, but their combination and diversity, their countercurrents, the way that they have had of conducting a compelling dialogue with other civilizations."[29]

Transcultural Narratives

On the shelves of bookshops virtually all over the Western world, volumes which have ripened in faraway locations vie for the buyers' attention with European and American books, influencing the taste of the reading public. But in most cases those faraway narratives bear in themselves the traces of the influence of Western culture. This pervasive dynamic of exchanges — between cultures at large, but also between genres and media — induces us to rethink culture on a planetary level, also in relation to the composite human landscape of contemporary societies, which are in themselves the result of huge and diversified migratory fluxes.

Indeed, the various linguistic and cultural declinations of contemporary novels are often rooted in the hybrid identities of their authors, as is shown by the works I am discussing. The Japanese Murakami has spent much time in the United States, and his role as "cultural mediator"[30] has been emphasized by critics. The Iranian-born Azar Nafisi studied in Great Britain and in the United States, where she currently lives. The father of Abraham B. Yehoshua — who was born in Jerusalem to a family of Sephardi Jews — was an orientalist who spoke Arabic fluently. Moreover, in the 1960s the writer himself spent a few years in France. Jonathan Safran Foer is a

Jewish American. W.G. Sebald was of German origin, but spent most of his life in Great Britain, where he taught at the university of East Anglia, although he kept writing in his native language. Julian Barnes explains his love of things French as follows: "Both my parents taught French; I went to France with them on holiday; I read French at school and university; I taught for a year at a Catholic school in Rennes,"[31] although this smooth account leaves out — as he claims — the anxiety that was inherent in his early experiences of crossing the Channel.... Even McEwan, whom one may be tempted to regard as essentially British, actually spent his childhood in Singapore and Tripoli. The case of the Hungarian writer Magda Szabó is trickier, but *The Door* arguably crosses the cultural borders of Hungary due to the role ancient myths and literature play as counterpoint to the main action.

As Homi Bhabha wrote, culture is increasingly produced in interstices, within societies that are hybrid also on a linguistic level.[32] Given this, we should not be surprised to realize that contemporary authors confront the issue of translation not only because of the transnational dissemination of their books, but already during the creative process, as is shown by Sebald's considerations on his choice to write in German:

> I have lived in this country far longer than in Bavaria, but reading in English I become self-conscious about having a funny accent. Unlike Conrad or Nabokov, I didn't have circumstances which would have coerced me out of my native tongue altogether. But the time may come when my German resources begin to shrink. It is a sore point, because you do have advantages if you have access to more than one language. You also have problems, because on bad days you don't trust yourself, either in your first or your second language, and so you feel like a complete halfwit.[33]

The in-between position of many contemporary writers produces a two-sided effect: on the one hand of strength, since it opens up perspectives; on the other of weakness, since it implies a less confident relation with the language(s) they utilize in their writing. Characteristically, *L'Analphabète* (2004, *The Illiterate*) is the title Agota Kristof — an author of Hungarian origin who fled to Switzerland after the Soviet repression of 1956 — has chosen for an autobiographical text she wrote in French, like her novels. In this linguistic memoir Kristof describes her difficult relation with the foreign languages life compelled her to learn — German, Russian and French itself.[34] This brings us to the condition of the subject in the present cultural phase, which Zygmunt Bauman defined as *liquid modernity*. Due to factors such as migrations and forms of distant communication, we live in societies where the relations between individuals, their communities and their jobs are destructured, and identities are increasingly flexible.[35]

Our interrelated and dynamic present has been analyzed by Arjun Appadurai in *Modernity at Large* (1996), in which the scholar highlights the peculiarities of a world where spectators and images are in circulation at the same time, and where artworks are experienced collectively. According to Appadurai, until recently artworks and media had been unjustly regarded as belonging to the escapist dimension of fancy, whereas they belong to the active and performative realm of the imagination, which is capable of exerting an action on reality: "It is the imagination, in its collective forms, that creates ideas of neighbourhood and nationhood, of moral economies and unjust rule, of higher wages and foreign labor prospects. The imagination is today a staging ground for action, not only for escape."[36]

Of course the ability of contemporary writers to engage in public debates should not be mistaken for a return to old forms of realism, since alternative modes of representation likewise consent to interact with reality in a performative way. As W.G. Sebald asserted, realism "functions only if it goes beyond its own boundaries," and Sebald transgressed the boundaries of realism by veering towards the "allegorical."[37] Szabó and Yehoshua are likewise interested in the allegorical, while authors such as Foer and Murakami tackle important issues nonchalantly blending realism, fantasy and myth.

It is thanks to their ability to trigger the imagination, opening us to alternative worldviews, that narratives exert an action on reality and translate into political acts. Narratives are indeed capable of crossing the fault lines between cultures and societies, bridging the gaps, overcoming suspicion and prejudice, contrasting the logic of opposition that often stems from emotional dynamics, also due to the amplifying effect of the media. In *Geopolitics of Emotions* (2008), Dominique Moïsi draws our attention to the impact emotions such as fear, humiliation and hope have in international relations, associating fear with the Western world, humiliation with Muslim countries and hope with Asia. In a world where the quest for identity has replaced ideology as the engine of history and media amplify all important events, emotions count more than ever.[38] We should not forget that emotions are currently investigated by diverse disciplines in relation to ethics and memory. Suffice it to mention volumes such as *Destructive Emotions* (2003) — where Daniel Goleman dialogues with the Dalai Lama on "what Buddhists call the Three Poisons: hatred, craving, and delusion"[39] — or *The Ethics of Memory* (2002), where Avishai Margalit studies the relation between memories and emotions.

Martha Nussbaum's study of the connection between emotions and the law should also be kept in mind. In *Hiding from Humanity* (2004) the scholar analyzes the role of disgust in the exclusion, subordination or criminalization of groups such as homosexuals, women and Jews, as well as the role of shame and humiliation in marking the boundary between normalcy and deviancy. According to Nussbaum, "Law without appeals to emotion is virtually unthinkable,"[40] and although we tend to associate laws with rational wisdom and balance, they actually rest also on "a roughly shared conception of what violations are outrageous, what losses give rise to a profound grief, what vulnerable human beings have reason to fear."[41]

With their investigation into the human, narratives are capable of exploring also the emotional dimension of conflicts, offering an important point of view on those recent events — such as the war in Afghanistan, the Gulf wars, 9/11 and global terrorism — that loom large in the collective imagination. Although the immediate consequences of these events manifest themselves in specific places, their psychological, political, economic and cultural repercussions are felt on a global scale. They are inescapable, and we must find a way to cope with them in a critical way.

Through the Green Line

As we have seen, the concept of boundary has become central in contemporary culture. A huge body of theoretical works concerning borders, frontiers and boundaries has in fact been produced in the last few decades, notably exploring the relationship between boundaries and conflicts. Scholars from different disciplines — from anthropology to history, literature and philosophy — have shown an increasing interest for this category, often focusing on the permeability of boundaries as contact zones, also in an attempt to disprove the traditional view of a boundary as a line that delimits two homogeneous areas.[42] Starting from this general issue, let us focus on the particular kind of boundary from which this book originated.

What is a green line? I only had a rather vague idea of what this meant until I visited Nicosia to take part in a conference on "Cultures of Memory/Memories of Culture" in February 2004[43] and was confronted with an entirely new kind of urban landscape. What I knew in theory became part of my actual experience. The Greek-Cypriot section of the city, where I was staying, was divided from the Turkish-Cypriot section — and still is — by a buffer zone that ran through the houses. The interplay between the *real* and the *symbolic* was stunning. Some of the barricades on the Greek-Cypriot side, for instance, had been painted in the colors of the Greek flag. Let me remind you that the flag the Republic of Cyprus adopted in 1960, after gaining independence from the United Kingdom, is absolutely neutral, for it includes neither blue (Greece) nor red (Turkey), and displays the shape of the island itself, together with colors — such as white and olive green — that stand for peace.

The green line was established in 1964, when the commander of the international peace force drew a green cease-fire line on a map of Cyprus. The green line became impassable after the July 1974 invasion of Cyprus by Turkey and was reopened in April 2003, when some crossings were created. I will never forget Nicosia, with the UN blue berets and the checkpoint that had been opened in Ledra Street a few months before, a gap in the barrier that had divided the two halves of the city for 30 years. And I will never forget the emotion I felt when I crossed the checkpoint and found myself on the other side, where everything was the same and everything was different. I had an eerie feeling that the fault line between the East and the West runs there, between the abandoned houses of the old city of Nicosia, an urban *no man's land* that is a paradox in itself, for the density of the city population on both sides contrasts eerily with the ghostly character of that stretch of territory.

Yet, the Cypriot green line was not the first to be traced, for a green line surrounding Israel had been created already in 1949, after the 1948 Arab-Israeli War. The Israeli green line is associated with a more recent boundary, the Israeli WestBank barrier, an eight-meter high wall that only partly corresponds to the 1949 armistice line, for it extends into Palestinian territory. For these reasons, its opponents argue that this is an attempt to illegally annex Palestinian land. A similar barrier divides Israel from the Gaza strip.

Since I am interested in the symbolic and cultural relevance of real places, let me remind you that many a commentator has drawn a parallel between this wall and the Berlin wall — an association that came once again to the fore on the occasion of the visit of Pope Benedict XVI to Israel and the West Bank in May 2009. If we wish to analyze the emotional impact of this wall on the Western public, we should keep this association between Jerusalem and Berlin in mind, for it brings the West Bank barrier closer to the heart of Europe. As the Pope — whose German origin also plays a role in this geopolitical and geocultural scenario — remarked during the speech he pronounced in the refugee camp of Al Aida: "In a world where more and more borders are being opened up — to trade, to travel, to movement of people, to cultural exchanges — it is tragic to see walls still being erected."⁴⁴ As we know, Israel and the occupied territories had already been visited by Senator Barack Obama in July 2008, and in October 2009 President Obama was awarded the Nobel Peace Prize for preferring dialogue and negotiations "as instruments for resolving even the most difficult international conflicts."⁴⁵

Unlike the green line in Cyprus, of whose existence many are oblivious, the Israeli green line is regarded as an issue of planetary import. A third green line existed in Lebanon between 1975 and 1990, during the Lebanese civil war. Its name does not refer to pencil or ink color, but rather to the foliage that grew in the urban areas that were abandoned during that war.

These reflections have brought us to distant lands. Green lines put us in touch with both local conflicts and international politics, for in these cases the two dimensions are inter-related. Let me add that the tangible reality of green lines triggers a deep emotional response. The solidity of concrete walls is disheartening, while the small urban jungles one sees in these tormented cities have a melancholy poetry about them. Hoda Barakat, a French writer of Lebanese origin, captured the eery quality of the Beirut green line in a novel entitled *The Tiller of Waters* (1999), where this surreal post-urban landscape plays a major role since the protagonist finds refuge in that primitive oasis, which in his eyes takes on a salvific value as a site of regeneration:

> Raised in these narrow alleys, I no longer knew whether the medlar tree whose fruits had now been nourishing me for weeks had stood near the Antabli fountain for as long as the souq had been a souq, or whether it had grown and born fruit in my absence ... in the concerto of this Garden of Eden that the Lord had set aflame to conquer the destruction, to obliterate it and triumph over it. To return sovereignty to the soil.⁴⁶

In the eyes of Westerners, who witness these political, social and military events from a distance, through the filter of the media, these near-Eastern green lines have become bigger and bigger, until they may look impossible to cross. These boundaries have indeed acquired a powerful symbolic value as the fault lines separating two civilizations which are often perceived or represented as hostile — the Judeo-Christian world versus the Muslim world. At least, this is how the situation in the Near East is depicted by those who believe that we are faced with a clash between competing and mutually exclusive civilizations. Samuel Huntington's seminal essay on the *Clash of Civilizations* (1993, 1996) comes to mind in this respect. Various causes may induce certain sectors of public opinion to advocate this theory — such as fear and suspicion, or political and economic vested interests. As a result, some fringes of society emphasize the element of distance. Instead of working to turn the green line into a permeable contact zone, they regard the conflict between the West and the East — two Eurocentric categories that are after all vague and relative — as virtually inevitable.

On the other hand, many writers are fighting against that fault line — whether they were born in those territories or come from afar. In February 2009, after the Gaza bombings, Japanese author Murakami Haruki visited Israel to receive a literary prize, although many of his fellow countrymen had tried to discourage him from doing so. His gesture was strongly symbolic. In the talk he gave when he accepted the prize — which is awarded to those writers who defend the freedom of the individual in society — Murakami powerfully evoked our sense of impotence, only to restore our faith in the power to act. After claiming that "we are all human beings, individuals transcending nationality and race and religion, fragile eggs faced with a solid wall called the System," the writer reminded us that "we must not allow the System to take on a life of its own. The System did not make us: We made the System."[47] According to Murakami, "If we have any hope of victory at all, it will have to come from our believing in the utter uniqueness and irreplaceability of our own and others' souls and from the warmth we gain by joining souls together."[48]

Around Postmodernism

In the conviction that contemporary literature is a primary tool in the effort to foster intercultural understanding, I intend to study it as a representation of experience, as a laboratory where the relation between the human and the surrounding world is analysed, experimented with and redefined. Since traditional generic labels do not fully capture the kind of writing I aim to discuss, I will adopt the term *life narrative*,[49] which spans not only a variety of received literary genres, ranging from the novel to the memoir and biography, but also recently developed hybrid forms such as graphic novels, graphic memoirs[50] and autofiction.[51] The term *life narrative* encapsulates the idea that narrative is grounded in experience, both one's own and other people's. It evokes not only the liberating power of fiction, with its ability to create alternative worlds, but also the documentary and performative dimensions of confession[52] and testimony — two ethical acts which are connected with truth and reconciliation, notably in a post-conflict environment.

As a critical concept, *life narrative* calls our attention to the individual, with his/her complex web of affiliations and allegiances. Like Murakami before him, Ian McEwan has also won the Jerusalem Prize. In the acceptance speech he gave in February 2011, McEwan has reasserted the value of the novel — "a form that is plural, forgiving, profoundly curious about other minds, about what it is to be someone else."[53] Narratives can help us escape the danger of narcissism and recover the meaning of life, which can be grasped in its entirety only if we acknowledge the other, as Emmanuel Levinas argued.[54]

Yet, before embracing a planetary perspective to study contemporary novels in their *performative* dimension, I need to gauge my theoretical instruments by reassessing the space and time coordinates of postmodernism — a Euro-American phenomenon which has undoubtedly disseminated all over the world (suffice it to think of the vast variety of literatures and cultures in English), but which has not penetrated all cultures in the same ways and at the same time.

The term *postmodernism* indicates a philosophical, aesthetic and literary attitude whose creative impetus and political momentum were associated with a critical reappraisal of the myths of modernity that Western societies inherited from Renaissance Humanism, Enlightenment and Positivism. Foremost among these is the presumed objectivity of science, which was presented at the end of the 19th century as the engine of a technological and social progress that was identified as the utmost good. The disaster of the 20th-century World Wars has sanctioned the failure of the line of development European civilization had undertaken, showing the dark visage of science, technology and rationality itself, which were implicated in totalitarian ideologies and in their irrational frenzy of destruction.

In very broad terms, as Linda Hutcheon writes, postmodernism translates into statements that are "self-conscious, self-contradictory, self-undermining"[55]; that is to say, it relativizes every absolute, paradoxically questioning its own deconstructive and relativist attitude. Postmodernism is marked — in Lawrence Cahoone's words — by "pluralism and indeterminacy," "a new focus on representation," "an acceptance of play and fictionalization,"[56] and the rejection of "the illusory nature of any unified self."[57] Other items could be added to this list, such as the crisis of historicity and the decline of ideologies.[58]

Of course it is easy to ironize on this loss of fundamentals, which emphasizes the multiplicity and limits of the human — presenting every form of knowledge as situated, therefore partial — and possibly inviting to forms of nihilism, since if we assume that every view of the world has the same value we may be tempted to infer that no view has any value. This is at least the caricature of postmodernism that its detractors offer, but if it is true that postmodernist thought may drift towards the liquid, its best expressions support a culture of complexity in which the acceptance of the other and the assertion of the self coexist on the unstable plane of difference, whose balance can be preserved only within a high civilization that ensures tolerance and respect.

What I wish to underline is that still in the 1980s postmodernism — as the cultural expression of late capitalism — was far from a global phenomenon, both on a creative and on a critical/theoretical plane.[59] This is proved by a comparison between Julian Barnes's *Flaubert's Parrot* (1984) and Magda Szabó's *The Door* (1987), which were published at a few years' distance in two countries that were then divided by the cold war — the United Kingdom and Hungary. As we shall see, Barnes's novel is typically postmodernist, not only because it contaminates the novel with the essay, proving playfully irrespectful of conventional genres, but also because one of its central concerns is the relation between the original and the copy, a stance which is linked to the interest of postmodernist writers and architects for intertextuality and citations.[60] While Barnes is an acrobat of literature, who embraces a deconstructive attitude towards traditional culture, wallowing in irony and subtlety, albeit without forgetting the human element, Szabó's novel is less experimental but deeply *political*—in an apparently subdued tone, without clamor, but with all the force of a parable — and also evokes the abysses of tragedy and myth. In this respect, *The Door* reminds one of other novels that were written in Eastern Europe, such as Christa Wolf's *Medea* (1996), which turns antiquity into an instrument to criticize the recent past.[61]

Europe has deeply changed between the 1980s — when Barnes and Szabó wrote on opposite sides of the Iron Curtain — and the present, thanks to the fall of the Berlin Wall and the enlargement of the European Union towards the East, due to the inclusion of various countries that formerly belonged to the Soviet Bloc. Unsurprisingly, the debate on the identity of the continent is rampant, and the definition of "post–Western Europe," has been coined to indicate a supranational political entity whose center of gravity has shifted from the Atlantic to the Mediterranean, and whose Eastern borders coincide with the coasts of the Black Sea.[62] In this post–Western Europe not only is the Orient closer, but the relationship between center and periphery has changed, also due to the policies the European Union has adopted toward minorities, following the principle of unity in diversity.

In an epoch of rapid evolution, in which the European atlas has been deeply redesigned and in which the European space is marked by a proliferation of micro-contact-zones between intra- and extra–European cultures that have been brought into contact by migrations, life narratives constitute a fundamental instrument to understand our present and plan our future. Life narratives explore not only our world but the way in which we look at it. They explore the act of narrating as a quest for meaning, in an attempt to come to terms with what strikes us as tragic or baffling and inscrutable, with our sense of loss and our inability to cope. These narratives often investigate the present through the past, since without memory there is no identity and no future. This is of course true not only on an individual level, but also on a collective one, since divided memories — those of people who have experienced a conflict from opposite sides — risk replicating, if they are not elaborated, the vicious circle of destruction.

I believe that postmodernism is mutating into something different not only because of the increasingly close encounters between cultures that were formerly distant, but also because of the in-depth reassessment of the past — notably of the 20th century — that marked the Western world in the 1990s. As we shall see, contemporary narratives are often characterized by a high level of technical sophistication, which frequently translates into multiple narrative levels — stories that intertwine or are enclosed one within the other, like Chinese boxes. Yet, alongside these complex techniques of montage, these narratives reveal a strong political engagement, in an attempt to tackle both the great historical issues that still weigh on our collective memory — starting from Nazism and the genocide of the Jews — and the great issues of our present, such as the Palestinian question and the Iran regime.

Life narratives are instrumental to a reflection that brings us into contact with the shadows of history. It is probably in this form of engagement that postmodernism found its accomplishment and also experienced a transformation, since its playful experimentations, its investigation of epistemological processes, or representational strategies, and of ontology itself have become functional to the exploration of other issues which are felt as more cogent, such as the coexistence of cultures, reconciliation, and the political import of the imagination, under the aegis of a new faith in the power of words to turn into action as a result of their impact on readers. To sound this hypothesis, I will first briefly hint at the debate on postmodernism that has marked the turn of the millennium.

After 9/11

The idea that postmodernism ended on September 11, 2001—a date that was close to the watershed of the millennium and therefore endowed with a strong symbolic power—is tempting. Although no cultural shift can be so sudden, on that day something changed, either in reality or in our perception of it. Two catastrophes circumscribe postmodernism in the collective imagination. On the one hand the Shoah, of which Auschwitz has become the emblem; on the other the terrorist attacks on the twin towers in New York, which have obliged us to question the relation between the West and the rest of the world.

According to Jean-François Lyotard, Auschwitz marked the end of the project of civilization, freedom and progress that characterized modernity, which was therefore left unachieved.⁶³ In *The Postmodern Condition* (1979) Lyotard suggested that the plan to exterminate the Jews was conducted with such managerial efficiency that it retrospectively cast a shadow on the Western concept of reason and on the Enlightenment itself, one of the Great Narratives (together with Idealism and Marxism) on which Western civilization had been grounded between the 18th and the 20th centuries. 9/11 compelled us to face new imperatives, while our keywords suddenly became obsolete, unsuitable to guide us towards the future. Islam became closer in geographical terms and more distant in cultural terms. The specter of a conflict of civilizations—which was evoked by many—made us feel powerless. The *doves* suddenly realized that they were unprepared to face an encounter that risked becoming a conflict, while the *hawks* believed that the time to fight was now.

In 1993 Samuel Huntington published an article that was republished three years later in book form as *The Clash of Civilizations and the Remaking of World Order* (1996). Discussing the geo-political order after the end of the Cold War, Huntington argued that due to the decline of ideology the world was reverting to a previous pattern of conflict between competing civilizations, that is to say, between divergent cultural and religious identities. After listing eight major civilizations—Western, Confucian, Japanese, Islamic, Hindu, Slavic-Orthodox, Latin American and African—Huntington claimed that "the most important conflicts of the future will occur along the cultural fault lines separating these civilizations from one another."⁶⁴ Significantly, given the neo-conservative agenda that underlies this text, Huntington grouped Israel together with the predominantly Christian West. This view of global politics, however, is simplistic both because it does not fully take into consideration the hybrid character various cultures have achieved in the course of the 20th century and because it minimizes the clashes that routinely occur between countries that are close in terms of both geography and culture.

In 2004, Akbar S. Ahmed—who had authored *Postmodernism and Islam* in 1992—reassessed Huntington's theses in the aftermath of 9/11 with the aim to argue that "postmodernism lay buried in the rubble on that fateful day."[65] While the fall of the Berlin Wall, in 1989, had apparently decreed the failure of the Great Narratives that had marked Cold War, 9/11 brought the totalizing ideological projects back again. The challenge to postmodernism therefore came from the political world, as embodied by George W. Bush and Osama bin Laden, whose monolithic view of the world not only demonized the *other* as an enemy, but also imposed an absolute orthodoxy and uncritical allegiance on correligionaries and compatriots, stigmatizing dissent as treachery. The election of Barack Hussein Obama—who is an African American and a Christian whose father's family belongs to Islam—has broken this scheme, although the recent past keeps weighing on international politics.

The Gulf wars, the war in Afghanistan and 9/11 engendered a climate of distrust between the East and the West, resulting in a variety of effects. The term *occident*—which is in itself relative and changing, like its correlative *orient*—has recently acquired new meanings. While Edward Said's works—starting from *Orientalism* (1975)[66]—compelled us to become aware of the imperialist implications that characterized the Western gaze on the *orient* as a cultural construction, at the beginning of the new millennium the attention of the Western cultural world—notably of the media—has focused on the Eastern gaze towards the *Occident*. This new critical and historical attitude is exemplified by the eloquent title of *Occidentalism: The West in the Eyes of Its Enemies* (2004). In this controversial book Ian Buruma and Avishai Margalit explore aspects of anti–Americanism/anti-Europeanism such as the hostility towards cities intended as places of license and sin; the bourgeoisie as the expression of a mercantile and anti-heroic society; the rational approach to knowledge, with its utilitarian and anti-Romantic connotations; and finally secularization, which has partly excluded religion from the public sphere.[67]

While at the end of the 20th century in the Western countries— which are increasingly agnostic, if not atheistic, and definitely materialistic—religion was regarded by many as a cultural phenomenon belonging to the past, with the new millennium faith has found a new centrality in political speeches and in the collective imagination, not as a personal choice, but as a cultural and political coordinate. Even the rather intransigent atheism of books such as Daniel C. Dennett's *Breaking the Spell* (2006) results from this climate of intolerance and from this emphasis on religion as belonging to the public sphere.[68] The evolution of Western societies towards a secular and tolerant pluralism has been questioned by the spectacular clash between two airplanes and two towers in the heart of the New York Financial District, that is to say, at the core of the global financial system. Speed and verticality, two powerful symbols of capitalism and of the American way of life, have been turned one against the other.

The terrorist attacks of 9/11 are at the root of a new form of cultural industry, which has developed in various directions. On the one hand, these events have been conducive to a renewed interest in the contemporary East and its conflicts. I am thinking, for example, of the Afghan writer Atiq Rahimi, who has spent many years in France, and who published in French works such as *A Thousand Rooms of Dreams and Fear* (2002) — on the Soviet invasion of Afghan — and *Le retour imaginaire* (2005), where a bombarded Kabul is evoked by means of words and photographs. I am also thinking of best sellers such as *The Kite Runner* (2003) and *A Thousand Splendid Suns* (2007) by another Afghan writer — Khaled Hosseini, who expatriated to the United States. Azar Nafisi's *Reading Lolita in Tehran* (2003) — a controversial book which has been stigmatized by some as an instance of neo-orientalism, spreading stereotypes in support of the U.S. military campaigns in the Middle East — also comes to mind.

Of course I am not claiming that 9/11 triggered this trend, but that it nurtured it. Near East conflicts, for instance, were already at the heart of various late-20th-century novels, such as the moving and complex *Gate of the Sun* (1998), where the Lebanese Maronite Christian Elias Khuri — who is the editor of the cultural supplement of a Beirut newspaper — recounts the life of Palestinian refugees in the camp of Shatìla, contrasting it with the memories of their home country. I have already mentioned *The Tiller of Waters* (1999), where the French-Lebanese writer Hoda Barakat describes a devastated Beirut. In this novel, an underground cloth-store metamorphoses into a magic place, enabling the protagonist to escape the painful reality of internecine war. The list would be much longer, for late 20th-century conflicts and the ensuing migratory fluxes have changed the geography of contemporary literature, bringing the condition of the Near and Middle East to the attention of Western readers. Actually, many of these novels and memoirs have seemingly been written as a function of the Western public, an element we should not underrate when we assess their ideological components.

Moreover, 9/11 is unequivocally at the root of another fictional trend, which critics have labeled as the *9/11 novel* or *post-9/11 novel*. Some of these books deal directly with the terrorist attacks on New York. That is the case of Jonathan Safran Foer's *Extremely Loud and Incredibly Close* (2005), Jay McInerney's *The Good Life* (2006), Don DeLillo's *Falling Man* (2007), Art Spiegelman's graphic novel *In the Shadow of No Towers* (2004) and Martin Amis's "The Last Days of Muhammad Atta" (2008). Others revisit the attacks tangentially, without explicitly mentioning them. Suffice it to think of Michael Cunningham's *Specimen Days* (2005), Salman Rushdie's *Shalimar the Clown* (2005) and John Updike's *Terrorist* (2006) — which deal in various ways with the threat of terrorism in the United States — or of Ian McEwan's *Saturday* (2005), which opens with the image of an airplane burning in the sky. Although readers later discover that this fire was simply due to a technical problem, the main character immediately connects it with terrorism, also because on that day — February 15, 2003 — a great public rally against the incipient Iraqi war is taking place in London, where the story is set. One cannot but agree with Michiko Kakutani when she claims that this book "reverberates with post-9/11 anxieties and fears."[69]

Mohsin Hamid's *The Reluctant Fundamentalist* (2007) is particularly interesting, due to its literary quality, its subject and the hybrid identity of its author, since Hamid is of Pakistani origin, grew up in the States and finally moved to London in the summer of 2001. In 2003, Hamid described himself as a wanderer who has "no more choice but to drift than does a dandelion seed in the wind."[70] The novel is presented as a long monologue during which the main character Changez — who is of Pakistani origin, but who obtained a degree at Princeton (like his author) and subsequently enrolled in the army of finance — tells an American about his life and the change of direction that brought him back to Lahore, where the conversation is taking place. 9/11 plays a major role in the personal history of Changez, since it suddenly turns his multiple belongings into a source of conflict, due to the attitude of suspicion Americans develop towards the Arab world. Because of this new climate, the hero starts wondering and worrying about the role he is playing within the global economy and comes to regard himself as a janissary at the service of American imperialism. In the course of the novel we are faced with Changez's reluctance to accept the economic fundamentalism of the United States rather than the religious fundamentalism of Islam, and this produces an effect of estrangement on Western readers. The political dimension is intertwined with a love story between the hero (whose name allegorically hints to change) and a girl from New York whose name is Erica. The play on words between *Erica* and *Am-erica* is apparent, and this figure soon takes on allegorical connotations as the personification of a broken American dream.⁷¹

As we can see, the collective trauma of 9/11 was elaborated in a variety of literary works, but what counts most is the impact this event had on the conception itself of the novel. As Chris Cleave remarked:

> It is as if expectations of books have risen after Sept. 11. The world today is to the pre-Sept. 11 world what falling glass shards are to a window, and the job of a novelist is to describe the new view through those glittering fragments. Yet somehow we expect writers, while they're at it, to show us how to glue the window back together: to give us meaning, hope, and even happy endings. It is extremely demanding and incredibly unfair.⁷²

Beyond Postmodernism

After 9/11 a certain kind of postmodernism — with its jocular manner, its ostentatious irresponsibility, its deconstructive frenzy — suddenly appeared frivolous against the enormity and terrible novelty of this tragedy, which was immediately replicated on every television screen throughout the world. As Eric W. Rothenbuhler wrote: "On the morning of 11 September 2001, an act of war against civilians in a place at peace scrambled the categories of culture, cognition, and communication."⁷³ Along with the dust of the twin towers, a new craving for reality spread across the West.

This does not mean, of course, that we should simplistically associate postmodernism with a general lack of engagement. Suffice it to think of what Linda Hutcheon labeled *historiographic metafiction*,⁷⁴ which was often inspired by the attempt to give voice to those who had been previously silenced or whose story had been told by their oppressors, in the wake of intercultural encounters that were marked by the asymmetries of military and economic power. Indeed, to assess the political impact of postmodernist fiction we should take into account its intersection with postcolonial fiction in works such as Salman Rushdie's *Midnight's Children* (1981) and J.M. Coetzee's *Foe* (1986). Revisiting the canonical works of the Western tradition — or *writing back* from the margins of the former Empire to the Center, according to the phrase Rushdie coined in 1982⁷⁵ — has enabled postcolonial authors to rediscuss the ideological premises of those colonial texts that had constructed otherness to legitimate domination, and therefore to achieve a new form of agency.⁷⁶

While postcolonial novels combine technical awareness with deep motivations, already in 1984 the postmodernists' lack of engagement was stigmatized by Marxist scholar Fredric Jameson, who described postmodernism as "The Cultural Logic of Late Capitalism."[77] In his analysis of Western culture after World War II, Jameson underlines the fall of the barriers between *high* and *low*, and the creation of a close circuit between artworks, media, advertising and the market, in connection with a new interest for commodities and consumerism. As a consequence, art has lost its Utopian drive — that is to say, all faith in its ability to change the world — and has been reduced to a hedonistic game, a celebration of the present with its commercial and media icons.

Jameson attacks postmodern eclecticism, whose various forms — from architecture to literature and cinema — favor a nostalgic revisitation of the past, devoid of "genuine historicity."[78] In his eyes, postmodernism has commodified the past as a repertory of forms, in the absence of any critical attitude, while an authentic historical reflection cannot but deal with the past in its depth, exploring its *otherness* in order to achieve a better understanding of our present. Moreover, Jameson regards the postmodern society of the *simulacrum* — in which representation prevails over reality — as the correlative of late capitalism in its post-industrial stage. Postmodern culture should therefore be considered as "the internal and superstructural expression of a whole new wave of American military and economic domination throughout the world,"[79] i.e., the product of American imperialism.

Twenty-five years later, Jameson's essay still commands respect, but in this quarter of a century many things have changed, and some sectors of culture have evolved in the direction of a dialectical relation with the past. While one cannot but agree that in the postmodern period the barriers between high and low have crumbled, this refashioning of literary genres has not implied the lowering of novels to the lowest common denominator of mass products. The nostalgic form of pastiche, for instance, has far from replaced the more critical form of parody.[80]

In a 1998 article Linda Hutcheon remembered she had devoted a fair amount of energy to demonstrating that "the 'postmodern' has little to do with nostalgia and much to do with irony," explicitly contrasting Jameson's theory. In the same article, however, she also admitted that she had undervalued "the very real and very uneasy tension between postmodern irony and nostalgia."[81] Briefly, even the major theorists of postmodernism find it difficult to evaluate the relative importance of irony and nostalgia in late–20th-century culture. Moreover, while Jameson stigmatized nostalgia as an expression of conservatism and an instrument of marketing (let us think of the so-called *heritage industry*), other scholars have chosen to study it as an approach to the past that is alternative to history, insofar as it is linked to the emotions and the body.[82]

We should also remember that the last few decades have been marked by a crisis of traditional historiography, whose claims of scientific objectivity have been deconstructed both by the theoretical reflections of Hayden White and Dominick LaCapra and by the advent of new hermeneutic categories such as *witnessing, memory* and *trauma*, by means of which scholars approach past conflicts within a transdisciplinary perspective.[83] As Andreas Huyssen reminds us, "Memory discourses of a new kind first emerged in the West after the 1960s in the wake of decolonization and the new social movements and their search for alternative and revisionist histories,"[84] destined to explode in the 1980s, in relation to the debate on the Holocaust, and in the 1990s, after the genocides in Ruanda, Bosnia and Kosovo. Starting from this scenario, Huyssen discusses the paradigmatic function the Holocaust has acquired as "a universal trope for historical trauma."[85] A major factor that has influenced both the recent debate on memory and the archival acquisition of recorded testimonies is the awareness of the fact that we are approaching the time when all the eyewitnesses of the Holocaust will be dead.[86]

Today's culture unceasingly explores and problemizes the relation between history, historiography, the cultural representation of the past (by means of novels, films, graphic novels...), testimony and autobiography, in connection with memory, trauma, the subjectivity of knowledge and the multiplicity of points of view. All this induces one to rediscuss Jameson's approach to the present, without denying its heuristic import.[87]

Moreover Jameson was not the only thinker who denounced the political complicity between postmodernism and capitalism. In 1996, Terry Eagleton — another Marxist critic — launched a new attack on Western culture with *The Illusions of Postmodernism*, where he stigmatizes the postmodernists' distrust of the concepts of truth, reason, identity and history. According to Eagleton, this refusal to confront *great narratives* is at the basis of the complicity between postmodernist thought and the capitalist system, which has prospered thanks to this ideological indeterminacy.

To understand this debate, we should remember that postmodernism results from the crisis of modernity and that its political import has been connected with its deconstructive approach. Postmodernism has redefined the myths and institutions of modernity, bringing to the fore alternative narratives, based on the respect of human rights, the fight against identity discriminations linked to race, gender and sexual preference. The fight against apartheid, the affirmative action and equal opportunities movements are all examples of a political action that is rooted in a new view of the human, which has been both ideologically supported and mediatically disseminated by postmodernist culture. Yet it is hard to deny that postmodernism has been aligned with the system from an economic point of view.

The relation between postmodernism and the political economic circuit is at the heart of several studies,[88] notably of Antonio Negri and Michael Hardt's *Empire* (2000). According to the two authors, globalization has involved an increasing loss of sovereignty on the part of nation states, which exert an ever smaller influence on the fluxes of money, technology, labor and goods. This has led to a new world order, which is no longer marked by the aggressiveness of traditional imperialism, but by a political balance that is functional to the needs of global capital. In the global perspective of the Empire — as Negri and Hardt define this state of things — even the most relevant ideological aspects of postmodernism, such as the celebration of identity differences, have but a weak political meaning and are perfectly compatible with the logic of a global market:

> Many of the concepts dear to postmodernists and postcolonialists find a perfect correspondence in the current ideology of corporate capital and the world market. The ideology of the world market has always been the anti-foundational and anti-essentialist discourse par excellence. Circulation, mobility, diversity, and mixture are its very conditions of possibility. Trade brings differences together, and the more the merrier![89]

While some scholars have underlined the political shortcomings of postmodernism, others are dissatisfied with the label itself. In the year 2000, Zygmunt Bauman chose to call our present *liquid modernity*, contrasting the rigidity and boundedness of solids with the volatile nature of fluids, whose shape changes with time. Although Bauman claims that modernity was liquid from its inception, he acknowledges that this process has achieved an unprecedented dimension in our recent past, obliging us to rethink concepts such as *emancipation*, *individuality*, *time/space*, *time* and *community*.[90] *Pseudo-modernism* is the label Alan Kirby has devised to describe our present, which is marked by the conflict between different forms of fanaticism, as well as by the proliferation of ignorance and anxiety. According to Kirby, "Pseudo-modernism was not born on 11 September 2001, but postmodernism was interred in its rubble."[91]

In *The Mourning After: Attending the Wake of Postmodernism* (2007), Josh Toth and Neil Brooks likewise define our present as "a period of mourning" that marks "the dissolution of the postmodern episteme," adding that "this emergent epoch seems to 'mourn' the apparent loss of the very idealistic alternatives that postmodernism strove to efface."[92] Although the two scholars recognize that "the most obvious marker of a new cultural dominant must certainly be the terrorist attacks in New York [...] and the culture of fear they initiated," they retro-date the beginning of this cultural shift, arguing that "a particular *work of postmodern mourning* began sometime in the early nineties [...] and that a new form of realism had begun to emerge in its wake."[93]

As Toth and Brooks claim, the bell announcing the death of postmodernism has been tolled over and over again by commentators since the mid-1990s, as is shown by a long list of volumes,[94] starting from the seminal *The End of Postmodernism: New Directions* (1993), edited by Heide Ziegler. This varied critical and theoretical output has been recently analyzed by Stephen J. Burn (*Jonathan Franzen and the End of Postmodernism*, 2008), who not only expands on the "growing dissatisfaction critics and writers felt with postmodernism in the early 1990s,"[95] but goes to the core of the debate by claiming that the different meanings this term has "in different disciplines and contexts" are "attached to different chronologies."[96] As a result, while "many novelists and critics have already posited the end of literary postmodernism, to a social theorist concerned with the logic of late capitalism, postmodernism might show few signs of weakening."[97] Yet, Burn concludes that "there are too many different attempts to map a route beyond postmodernism in too many different disciplines in the mid-1990s to dismiss such efforts as entirely untimely or entirely misguided."[98]

Although the question of chronology is thorny, due to the multifaceted character of postmodernism, surfing on the Internet suffices to show that the end of postmodernism has become a trope both to explain current crises and to invoke regeneration. When Jean Baudrillard died in 2007, Matthew Beaumont wrote an obituary entitled "Baudrillard and the end of postmodernism: what next,"[99] while another article discusses the election of President Obama as a departure from the entropic decline of postmodernism under the Bush administration.[100] Even the credit crunch crisis has been explained by André Glucksmann in terms of self-referentiality, since "the financial bubble, piling credit on top of credit, got rich on self-affirmation," gradually eliminating the "principle of reality."[101] Glucksmann concludes that "it would be a good thing if fear of a universal crisis allowed us to burst the mental bubble of postmodernism."[102]

Of course the fact that a certain number of texts debate or even proclaim the end of postmodernism does not suffice to turn this perception (or wishful thinking on the part of some) into a fact. What it indicates, however, is a growing restlessness and dissatisfaction. Several scholars feel the need to develop new conceptual tools to grasp the contemporary world, as is shown also by the expression *post-postmodernism*, which has however little meaning, and seems rather a provisional solution, until a new *ism* becomes a catalyst of cultural energies. Looking for a name that embraces the present cultural phase is not my aim, but I share with others the feeling that the term *postmodernism* has lost its edge. And I believe that at the beginning of the new millennium we feel even more strongly the condition of incertitude that Homi Bhabha described in 1994 as "a sense of disorientation, a disturbance of direction."[103]

The Dialectics Between Words and Reality

To understand our present it is often useful to investigate our past. Let us therefore look back to Oscar Wilde, whose introduction to *The Picture of Dorian Gray* (1891) enunciated revolutionary concepts such as: "There is no such thing as a moral or an immoral book," or "It is the spectator, and not life, that art really mirrors."[104] These maxims condense principles of the aesthetic movement such as the non-referential character of art, that is to say, the rift between art and reality, emphasizing the role of the reader in the interpretative process, in order to shift upon him the *ethical responsibility* of the text as a signifying entity, while the writer acknowledged only an *aesthetic responsibility* for the form he/she had created. At the end of the 19th century Walter Pater and Oscar Wilde, the theorists of *art for art's sake*, identified music — whose language is self-referential — as the pivot of their system of correspondences between the arts. This aesthetic approach was subsequently pursued by modernist writers such as Katherine Mansfield, Virginia Woolf and Irène Némirovsky. Today the critical world is well aware of the fact that modernism was indeed rooted in the aesthetic movement, although this genetic link was undervalued due to the rhetoric of decline that marked the *fin de siècle*.

By detaching the novel from reality, breaking the chain that according to the traditional view of literary communication united reality to reality (reality — writer — text — reader — reality), Wilde intended to free literature from the constraints of public opinion, denying its function as a vehicle of the commonsensical values associated with State and Church. Modernists shared this anti-conformist attitude, either in the attempt to achieve an unconventional understanding and representation of human experience (Joyce) or to denounce a condition of communicative impasse and loss of meaning (Beckett). This emphasis on the distance between author and reader, which was often related to a formalist view of the text, filtered from modernism to postmodernism, assuming a more markedly existential character since the condition of uncertainty of the postmodernist subject embraces not only the sphere of epistemology, but also that of ontology.

The importance that reception theory, aesthetic response theory and more generally the act of reading acquired in the post-structuralist landscape between the 1960s and 1970s — thanks to the works of Hans Robert Jauss, Wolfgang Iser, Umberto Eco and others — testifies to the fertility of Wilde's approach to literary communication. While the concept of authorial intention was increasingly devalued, the creative aspect of the reader's interpretation was conversely emphasized. As regards self-referentiality, postmodernist writers often experimented with the text's ability to create *possible worlds*,[105] often in the attempt to reveal the constructedness of narratives, thus simultaneously inviting and deflating the illusion of reality and the suspension of disbelief. As we can see, postmodernism asserted itself against mid–20th-century realism also by rediscovering its roots in turn-of-the-century aesthetics, which it re-elaborated in the direction of complexity, exploring the ludic potentials of narratives, the labyrinths of language, the claustrophobic enigmas of self-consciousness and the unstable nature of the real.

Thomas Pynchon's *The Crying of Lot 49* (1966) is one of the founding texts of postmodernism. When I was at the university, I too got lost — together with the novel's main character, Oedipa Maas — in the American metropolis of San Narcisso, a self-referential place without any center or ultimate meaning. The proliferation of delirious clues that Oedipa discovers, during her quest to solve the postmodern urban mysteries she faces, seems to point to a secret society whose name is *WASTE*. The text dramatizes the entropic experience of postmodernity, where the excess of information is conducive to the loss of informative value. Everything amounts to nothing. At the end, readers feel they are in a dead-end position. San Narcisso is a hall of mirrors, and I have no doubt that Pynchon counted on the interpretative cooperation of readers, for whom he created a well-polished reflective surface, ultimately leaving them the responsibility of locating a meaning within this disturbing and labyrinthine fictional world.

The emphasis on self-referentiality and the tendential nihilism that mark *The Crying of Lot 49* testify to important aspects of postmodernism, but reducing postmodernism to its more experimental, hyper-rational and skeptical expressions would be a biased account of this period. While texts such as John Fowles's *The French Lieutenant's Woman* (1969), with its alternative endings, and Italo Calvino's *If on a Winter's Night a Traveler* (1979), with its proliferation of beginnings, subverted the traditional structure of plot, providing subsequent writers with influential models of self-reflexive narratives, the connection between postmodern and postcolonial brought to the fore the political value of literature. Following the example of novels such as Jean Rhys's seminal *Great Sargasso Sea* (1966), which offered a politically charged rewriting of Charlotte Brontë's *Jane Eyre* (1847), many late-20th-century authors utilized fiction as a tool to fight those mechanisms of discrimination and control — in terms of race, gender and class — which were implicit in the social and cultural practices of the past.

The shadow of the Holocaust also provided postmodernist authors with a deep motivation to write, as is the case of Georges Perec, who was born in France from parents of Polish-Jewish origin and grew up as an orphan, since his father died as a soldier during the war, and his mother died in Auschwitz. While Perec's interest for crossword puzzles, verbal games and archives — as well as his membership of the *Oulipo* group, a "Workshop of Potential Literature" which also included Raymond Queneau and Calvino — reminds us of the more experimental aspects of postmodernism, his works are also the vehicles of deeper meditations on life and history.

La Disparition (1969), which has been translated into English as *A Void*, is a lipogrammatic novel in which the letter e never features. This absence is replicated at plot level, since the novel investigates the disappearance of a character, named Antonio Vowl in the English version. Yet, far from simply indulging in linguistic juggling, here Perec is actually elaborating a complex trope for the disappearance of Holocaust victims. Likewise, his semi-autobiographical work *W, or the Memory of Childhood* (1975) presents two parallel narratives, focussing respectively on the author's own experience and on a dystopian island that becomes a figuration for concentration camps. As the writer himself acknowledged, at the origin of his need to write there is his parents' silence, due both to their disappearance in his early childhood and to the subsequent lack of memorial traces.[106]

As Burn claims, "If it is impossible to anatomize the wide scale end of postmodernism it is possible [...] to ask which strands survived and which died as postmodernism approached the millennium."[107] A critical attitude toward the past has proved a key element in the renewal of postmodernism. As we have seen, Jameson and Hutcheon — two of the best-known theoreticians of the movement — have explored the tension between irony and nostalgia, two different ways of relating to the past, the former critical and innovative, the latter emotional and escapist. The life narratives I will discuss delineate yet another way of relating to the past, since they focus not only on the connection between history, memory and trauma, but also on individual responsibility, dramatizing failure, incomprehension and betrayal. What is more, they explore in various ways the reparatory potential of writing.

Narratives of Responsibility

In his inaugural speech on January 20, 2009, President Obama greeted the advent of "a new era of responsibility,"[108] foregrounding a word that calls to mind the challenges of ecology and sustainable development, of solidarity and social justice. Literally, *responsibility* indicates the ability to *respond*, that is to say, to act or decide in response to an event or a situation. We tend to associate responsibility with care, while the relation between responsibility, memory and guilt — both one's own guilt and somebody else's — is more complex, for what action can atone for evil? In the narratives that we will discuss, words are offered as a ritual of purification, as a meditation on the errors of the past that triggers a process of personal development.[109]

The Door opens with a heartrending avowal of guilt. The text is presented as the account of a crime, a tragic confession since it confronts us with the involuntary — but no less terrible — betrayal of love:

> Once, just once in my life [...] a door did stand before me. That door opened. It was opened by someone who defended her solitude and impotent misery so fiercely that she would have kept that door shut though a flaming roof crackled over her head. I alone had the power to make her open that lock. In turning the key she put more trust in me than she ever did in God, and in that fateful moment I believed I was godlike — all-wise, judicious, benevolent and rational. We were both wrong: she who put her faith in me, and I who thought too well of myself.[110]

The irreversible character of guilt — which is linked in this case to misunderstanding and to the breaching of a limit — translates into trauma, into the recurring, obsessive visitation of a dream. The creature that the protagonist loved and betrayed comes back every night, like a ghost that resurfaces from the unconscious of somebody who has no self-compassion. At the end of this narrative, the dream occurs once again, unchanged, and the key turns uselessly in the door lock at the heart of this oneiric figuration. The message may seem desperate, but in the course of our reading many things have happened in our minds, fully justifying the creative impulse from which this story originated — a story where the distance between the author, Magda Szabó, and her narrator, Magda, is virtually erased.

I have chosen to contrast this volume with Barnes's text, where the author hides behind the scenes and plays with the volatile relation between writing and reality, ironizing on the proliferation of simulacra and on the processes of mythopoesis, although in the ending the biographical quest at the heart of *Flaubert's Parrot* turns out to be rooted in the narrator's life, and its cerebral, often comic élan veers toward the pathetic. Reading Barnes and Szabó remains however a profoundly different experience, since *The Door* evokes the power of passions to vehicle an ethical message of much greater import, regarding the contrast between personal loyalty and social norms. This choice is related to the fact that *The Door* was written in a communist country, not in the consumerist and liberal societies where postmodernism developed. And yet we find the same ethical concerns in subsequent novels by English and American authors. In these works, the return of ethics is often associated not only with the daring formal experiments that have characterized postmodernist aesthetics, but with the memory of the Holocaust and of World War II.

We know how important the field of *memory studies* has become in recent years, also due to the progressive disappearance of Holocaust survivors and witnesses, and therefore to the necessity of recording and discussing the memories of eyewitnesses before those who deny the Holocaust can take advantage of this. Our present attitude to the Holocaust is encapsulated by Marianne Hirsch's concept of *postmemory*, which "describes the relationship of the second generation to powerful, often traumatic experiences that preceded their births but that were nevertheless transmitted to them so deeply as to seem to constitute memories in their own right."[111] *Postmemory fiction* deals with the legacy of mid–20th-century traumatic events in an attempt to achieve a sense of personal connection with them. Postmemory narratives are marked both by affection and by engagement, that is to say, by the desire to turn words into action, and I believe that the question Hirsch puts in a recent essay — "Can the memory of genocide be transformed into action and resistance?"[112] — has already been answered by works such as Art Spiegelman's *Maus: A Survivor's Tale* (1986-91) and W.G. Sebald's *Austerlitz* (2001), the two case studies Hirsch discusses.

I also wish to mention the growing critical and theoretical interest for the cultural representations of trauma, which Laurie Vickroy defines as "a response to events so overwhelmingly intense that they impair normal emotional or cognitive responses and bring lasting psychological disruption."[113] Being well aware of the risk of immersing readers in a sterile "quagmire of victimization," Vickroy argues that the critical analysis of *trauma fiction* should conversely enable us to reconsider the "potentially ethical function of literature,"[114] calling our attention to the fact that "trauma narratives critique culturally dominant views of identity and marginality and resist suppression of traumatic events."[115] This brings us back to the late–20th-century collective historical and philosophical reflection on the Holocaust, which has helped contemporary authors both to go beyond those aspects of postmodernist relativism that were closer to hedonism and nihilism, and to reassert the importance of ethics.

As we shall see, the German expatriate Sebald chose to go back to the Holocaust — the absolute evil at the heart of the 20th century — taking a difficult path, halfway between documentary and fictional writing. Sebald made his tension towards the real apparent both by disseminating the text with photographs and by adopting a first-person authorial narrator. At the same time, he constructed *Austerlitz* as an overt allegory, insisting on the simultaneous symmetry and contrast between the narrator and the title hero, who respectively embody the progeny of perpetrators and of victims.

The Jewish American Jonathan Safran Foer deploys a similar strategy in *Everything Is Illuminated* (2002). Part of the book is written by Jonathan — an alter ego of the author who narrates in the third person his imaginative reconstruction of a Jewish past that is otherwise irretrievable — while the other is written in the first person by the Ukrainian Alex as a memoir and letters addressed to Jonathan. As we can see, Foer not only represents himself as a character, partly writing the novel from inside, but chooses to shed light on the heart of darkness of Western history utilizing the imaginative power of words, filling the blank at the heart of the *final solution* and giving full substance to what survives only as a series of personal and place names.

Like Foer, Ian McEwan conceives *Atonement* (2001) as a narrative that has been written by its protagonist to expiate her guilt. Briony uses her talent for storytelling — an ambivalent power, given the tragic results it produced in combination with her childish prejudices and drives — to evoke an alternative version of reality, in which life prevails over death. Also Murakami's *Kafka on the Shore* (2002) — which borders on magic realism — investigates the relation between responsibility and the imagination, mentioning the negative exemplum of Adolf Eichmann. The Holocaust is entwined with the tormented events that accompanied the creation and the history of the state of Israel in Abraham B. Yehoshua's *Mr. Mani* (1990), whose narrative structure is articulated into five monologues. Yehoshua chose to imprint these monologues with the character of orality, since his speakers address an interlocutor, who is however silent or whose answers are not reported in the text. Finally, *Reading Lolita in Tehran: A Memoir in Books* (2003), expounds its critique of the Khomeini regime through a first-person narration that foregrounds the autobiographical character of the text.

The ethical import of these hybrid works translates into recurrent discursive strategies. These narratives of responsibility may take the form of memoirs (*Reading Lolita in Tehran*), of novels bordering on memoirs (*The Door*), or of novels that contain inset life narratives. Thus in *Flaubert's Parrot* the fictional narrator's attempt to write an unconventional biography of Flaubert actually amounts to an effort to explore his own life and the death of his wife. In *Mr. Mani* five fictional narrators relate their own life stories together with those of others. In *Atonement* we become acquainted with a character who has written a novel that turns out to be a confession and yet goes beyond the truth of facts to explore the compensatory power of fiction. *Austerlitz* combines the authorial narrator's attempt to write the history of the title hero with his own life story. *Kafka on the Shore* juxtaposes two life narratives. One is told in the first person and in the present tense by the hero, emphasizing the character's agency, while the other is told in the third person and in the past tense. *Everything Is Illuminated* features the author in the process of writing a mythical novel, and a fictional character who is writing a memoir in which the author appears as a character.

On the one hand these texts underline their experiential matrix, aiming to bridge the gap between fiction and reality. On the other, they aim to preserve the freedom that the novel consents compared with autobiography, which entails more rigid referential conventions, and they also refuse to abide by the dictates of realism in order to explore the power of words to conjure up alternative interlacing worlds.

By using a definition such as *narratives of responsibility*, I do not aim to circumscribe a literary subgenre, such as *trauma fiction* or *Holocaust fiction*, but rather to indicate a trend whose defining element is its performative dimension — the relationship it posits between author and readers, who are called to respond — both cognitively and emotionally — to their ethical and aesthetic complexity. On a cognitive level, these narratives invite their readers to embrace what Kalí Tal describes as the mission of the cultural critic, i.e., a deconstructive attitude, challenging "the assumptions upon which any communal consensus is based."[116] On an emotional level, they invite readers to empathize with characters, creating a bond. As a result, readers are invited to appraise the historical background of these life narratives — be they pivoting on distant or recent events — with an attitude that is very different from the two poles of the postmodernist attitude to the past, the critical distancing of irony and the uncritical projection of nostalgia.

Narratives of responsibility present us with an important model for reading in the age of globalization because they explore conflicts and traumas, infusing us with a renewed faith in language as an instrument of mutual understanding, atonement and reconciliation. They also provide us with precious psychological tools, inviting us to relate to others, keeping the borders of our ego permeable. And they remind each of us of the necessity to take an active role in the formation of one's own moral outlook, alerting us to the risk of uncritically accepting the collective assumptions that go under the label of "common sense"[117] as if this term was unequivocally synonymous with wisdom.

Morals as Transgression

In *The Terrible Power of a Minor Guilt* (1998) Abraham B. Yehoshua remarks: "It has been difficult in recent years to find in written critiques of novels, stories, plays or even films a direct reference to the moral issues raised by the work."[118] In an attempt to explain why contemporary literature removes moral conflicts, Yehoshua lists various reasons: the development of psychological explanations of human behavior, which attenuates the individual sense of responsibility; the role of the law, which delimits licit and illicit forms of behavior; the spreading of the media, which deals with new moral issues less insightfully but with more immediacy than literature; the idea that art must be judged on a formal/aesthetic level; and finally the fear that an ethical reflection on art may be conducive to new forms of censorship. These questions cannot of course be neglected, but Yehoshua comes to an important conclusion: "Morality is not some far-off shining star suspended in the sky of our lives. It is omnipresent; it can be found everywhere that human beings are conducting interpersonal relationships."[119] I agree with these words, although I do not believe that ethics have disappeared from the discourses of/on literature and culture, for in the more than ten years that separate us from Yehoshua's essay, ethics have achieved a new centrality.

A wide range of titles could be cited to prove this. Part of Yehoshua's essay has been republished in a reader entitled *Ethics, Literature, Theory* (2005) which opens with these words by Wayne C. Booth: "During the last fifteen years or so, there has been an explosion of interest in questions about the ethical effects of reading literature."[120] This confident statement is a far cry from that which opens a similar reader published in 1998, *Rene-*

gotiating Ethics in Literature, Philosophy, and Theory: "This volume starts from the perception that in 'advanced' literary circles for most of the 1970s and 1980s, few topics could have been more uninteresting [...] than the topic Ethics and Literature."[121] The thought of Emmanuel Levinas has proved central to this rediscovery of an ethical approach to literature, as is shown both by Robert Eaglestone's *Ethical Criticism: Reading After Levinas* (1997) and Andrew Gibson's *Postmodernity, Ethics and the Novel: From Leavis to Levinas* (1999), but Martha Nussbaum's seminal *Love's Knowledge* (1990) should also be mentioned.

Discussing the link between literature and ethics today does not imply going back to the traditional view of the novel as the vehicle of a predefined morality that is shared by the majority of people, in other words embracing those prejudices that Oscar Wilde deconstructed — as we have seen — over a century ago. On the contrary, we should consider a life narrative as an individual ethical statement, an assumption of responsibility on the part of the author.

To understand this view of ethics, I wish to refer to the philosopher Umberto Galimberti, who traces the development of Western ethics in its various stages and proposes a new model: the ethics of the wanderer, who adheres, at every step, to the changing landscapes he/she encounters.[122] Freed from the constraint of a final destination, the wanderer inhabits the present. His nomadic perspective entails a view of the ethical act as "an absolute choice concerning present events."[123] In Galimberti's eyes, ethics do not offer preconceived answers, but originate from the confrontation with an ever-changing context, permanently refounding themselves thanks to an ongoing dialogue between present and past.

The complex ethical relation between the individual and society is analyzed by Zygmunt Bauman in *Modernity and the Holocaust* (1989), where the sociologist explores those bureaucratic systems of authority in which individual morality is incapacitated through obedience, conformity and distance from the ultimately evil results of a process. When an individual is involved in a chain of actions the responsibility of which seems "essentially 'unpinnable,'" a mechanism of "*free-floating responsibility*"[124] occurs. Refuting the notion that morality has a social origin, Bauman claims that discriminations and persecutions are rooted in society at large, while the individual is often obliged to fight against these collective forms of deviance. Drawing on the thought of Emmanuel Levinas, Bauman has developed a view of morals as based on individual responsibility rather than on collective ethics, and in his conversations with Keith Tester (2001) he states again: "Clearly, then, moral acts meant *breaching* rather than *following* the socially designed and monitored norms."[125]

The novels we are going to examine invite individuals to rediscover their own sense of responsibility, even when this means opposing the current ideology and morals. This is the attitude of Emerence, the virtually mythical character Szabó created in *The Door*— a woman who directs her unconditional charity towards every suffering human being, from Jews to German soldiers. In *Everything Is Illuminated*, on the other hand, Alex's grandfather is trapped in the dilemma between self-preservation and responsibility, and it is only at the end of the novel that his grandchild Alex becomes able to achieve a responsible manner of behavior, by opposing his own violent and unenlightened father. In *Kafka on the Shore* another adolescent embarks on a quest for self-knowledge which entails a conflict with an obscure paternal figure. Interestingly, both in Foer's and Murakami's novels this generational conflict is linked to the ambivalent heritage of World War II.

As we can see, these novels tackle delicate and important subjects. They become meeting places, where experiences and projects can be elaborated intersubjectively. And they are all the more intense insofar as their authors' imagination answers collective needs, not solipsistic instances. Contrary to the skepticism, if not the nihilism, of postmodernism, as exemplified by Derrida's theory of *différance*, which hypothesizes a perpetual deferral of meaning, that is to say, a game of mirrors both on the side of composition and on that of interpretation, Raoul Eshelman's theory of performativity advocates a holistic view of communication, rediscovering the relation between author, text and reader, and underlining the artifact's ability to trigger change. Through the analysis of contemporary novels, films and architectures, Eshelman delineates a new aesthetics, replacing the deconstructive aloofness of postmodernist irony with a renewed adhesion to the artwork, a process of affective identification, an acceptance of the coordinates of the artifact — in short, an attitude that the critic condenses in the term *belief*.[126]

Also the Marxist critic Terry Eagleton devotes a chapter of *After Theory* (2003) to "Morality," discussing the tendency of theoreticians of culture to mistake morality for moralism and to derubricate ethics as a body of rules that simply restrict behavior. Against this reductive view of the human, which privileges the political over the personal, Eagleton rediscovers the concept of morality precisely through the fictional representation of moral choices: "To grasp morality as a great novelist understands it is to see it as an intricately woven texture of nuances, qualities and fine gradations."[127] In the works of Henry James — an author Eagleton repeatedly mentions — we do not find preconceived norms, but a deep investigation into human behavior, which cannot be effected "by abstracting men and women from their social surroundings."[128] Morality is not a set of preconceived norms that are mechanically applied to situations, but an individual choice, which is always made here and now.

So, let us read literature in this time of complexity and plurality, of incertitudes and conflicts, when the nostalgia of orthodoxy and dogma can find us unprepared on a variety of fronts: that of religious fanaticism, but also those of atheism and scientism, of materialism and fascism,[129] for both the voice of God and the silence of God can turn into a weapon against the human. We live in a time when the curiosity that is born of desire and the freedom that is born of money can easily disperse in the rivulets of shopping in a mall — a time when we run the risk of forgetting that democracy is a precious treasure, which we should never take for granted. Narratives are here to complicate our life, to project us out of ourselves and make us feel — with a surprise that is ever renewed — how much joy and how much pain run hand-in-hand with the sun and the clouds around this small planet from dawn to dusk every day.

1

Julian Barnes, *Flaubert's Parrot* (1984)

Due to its jocular attitude to tradition, *Flaubert's Parrot* (1984) is a perfect example of postmodernist irony. It does not take anything seriously and turns critical playfulness into a method, in an attempt not only to deconstruct the conventional approach to biography, but to investigate the "possible worlds" that narratives create as well as the complex referential relation between language and reality.[1] Barnes's quintessentially postmodernist text goes so far as to undermine its own aesthetic premises, as is proved by a long list of precepts addressed to future writers, which culminates in this passage:

> There shall be no more novels which are really about other novels. No "modern versions," reworkings, sequels or prequels. No imaginative completion of works left unfinished on their author's death. Instead, every writer is to be issued with a sampler in coloured wools to hang over the fireplace. It reads: Knit Your Own Stuff.[2]

"Knitting Their Own Stuff" is precisely what postmodernists, who are possessed by the demon of intertextuality, do not intend to do, and *Flaubert's Parrot* itself participates in this postmodernist trend, due to its symbiotic relation with Flaubert's works.

Relics of the Past

Flaubert's Parrot is still an atypical book, and it looked even more so when it was published, in the mid–1980s. When he conceived this virtuosistic set of variations on the theme of biography, Barnes aimed to unsettle his readers' expectations, choosing a circuitous approach to his subject, as is clear right from the beginning:

> Six North Africans were playing boule beneath Flaubert's statue. Clean cracks sounded over the grumble of jammed traffic. With a final, ironic caress from the fingertips, a brown hand dispatched a silver globe. It landed, hopped heavily, and curved in a slow scatter of hard dust.[3]

This sketch of contemporary life is far from irrelevant, since the six North Africans are playing in Place des Carmes in Rouen, where a statue of the author can be seen. Moreover, we are informed that the statue we see today is not the original one, which was carried away by the Germans in 1941, together with the railings of the cathedral, possibly to be turned into army-cap badges. These notations exemplify the digressive nature of the text and its emphasis on the investigation of the eccentric, of what — being at the margins — has been less explored and can actually prove more revealing.

Barnes himself explains his unconventional attitude to biography through a metaphor: "the idea that a great novelist lies in a sort of unofficial burial mound — something Anglo-Saxon or Egyptian — and there is always an entrance to it, through which it was taken in, and then he was buried and the entrance was sealed up."[4] The biographer's enterprise consists in penetrating — like an archaeologist — inside the edifice, retrieving the body and the objects that surround it, and finally recreating the writer "backwards, from that moment of burial."[5] Yet, mainstream literary archaeology does not satisfy Barnes, who wonders: "What happens if you sink in tunnels at lots of different unexpected angles into the burial chamber? Perhaps this will tell us something about him and his work that something sequential and conventional won't?"[6]

It is owing to this indirect approach that the book takes shape. The North African boule players stand for our present, the social context in which Flaubert's memory lives. The statue — which had been created to resist through time, but which actually succumbed to war — reminds us of the events that may obstruct the transmission of cultural memory, and the contrast between the vulnerability of the statue and the solidity of words is easy to trace. Barnes underlines this with irony, reminding us of the fact that Flaubert "died little more than a hundred years ago, and all that remains of him is paper. Paper, ideas, phrases, metaphors, structured prose which turns into sound,"[7] while most of the material traces of his existence have been cancelled.

Those who have made a literary pilgrimage to Rouen know that the city on the banks of the Seine is a bustling industrial center, and moreover that it suffered extensive war destruction. In close proximity to a Renaissance edifice or a Gothic church — such as the cathedral, which Claude Monet repeatedly painted in order to capture the play of sunlight on its facade — one sees a modern building or a viaduct. The *quais* are hectic highways, and the river is bordered by factories and port structures. Rouen is neither solely devoted to beauty nor inclined to a timeless poise. Flaubert's house in Croisset — a city suburb — was demolished a few years after the death of the author to make way for an industrial complex to extract alcohol from cereals. Reflecting on the disappointment in store for those who look for tangible signs of Flaubert's presence, Barnes introduces a major issue:

> Why does the writing make us chase the writer? [...] Why aren't the books enough? Flaubert wanted them to be: few writers believed more in the objectivity of the written text and the insignificance of the writer's personality; yet still we disobediently pursue. The image, the face, the signature; the 93 per cent copper statue and the Nadar photograph; the scrap of clothing and the lock of hair. What makes us randy for relics?[8]

Perhaps for those who were born in Catholic countries — and are therefore accustomed to the reverence surrounding religious relics — it is easier to understand this aspect of literary cult. A relic is a catalyst — not only a proof that something happened (provided it is not fake) but something that puts you in touch with someone. Saint Francis's walking stick makes you feel close to the Saint due to a mystic virtue which is associated with the body rather than with the spirit. We know that Saint Francis rested his hand on that stick. Should we regard this as an inferior form of religion that is close to superstition? Or as a legitimate form of cult that is based on the emotions? We face the same problems when we visit Shakespeare's birthplace in Stratford, the Brontë parsonage in Haworth or Goethe's house in Weimar. Are we intrigued by these sites because we are trying to assess the influence of the environment on genius? Or do we hope to sense a presence that may linger there?

Henry James devoted a short story ("The Birthplace," 1903) to the predicament of a cultivated and sensitive keeper of Shakespeare's birthplace. At first Morris Gedge enthusiastically accepts this coveted job, but soon he painfully realizes that the whole place is a vulgar mise-en-scène, a collection of objects that have little to do with the poet. The anecdotes he tells over and over again to the crowds flocking to the shrine have no firm basis, but it is precisely in the sancta sanctorum — the birth room, where there is neither furniture nor stories to tell—that the protagonist has a revelation. That emptiness becomes charged with meaning, and Gedge finds a way to reconcile the opposite tensions that are tearing his soul apart—the desire to know and the actual impossibility to do so. Gedge then turns his guided visits into a spectacle, a form of art—an openly fictional ritual that is animated by the flame of literature. Bringing description and anecdote to excess, presenting himself virtually as an eyewitness, Gedge paradoxically retrieves the sense of his intellectual honesty and of his mission. What he previously despised as a mercenary and falsified hagiography has become an allegory celebrating the triumph of words over reality.

Rethinking History

In his book, Barnes is looking for a similar kind of consummation, for he also begins from the awareness that the truth of life is impossible to grasp—no matter how much hard data we possess—and opts for invention. Indeed, *Flaubert's Parrot* is at the same time a biography, a work of criticism and a novel, the narrator of which—Geoffrey Braithwaite—is a retired physician and a widower whose children live far away and who fought in the North of France in 1944. By entwining the life stories of Flaubert and Braithwaite, Barnes multiplies the time levels on which his work is structured—the present of Braithwaite's act of writing, the recent past of his journey on the traces of Flaubert, the remote pasts of World War II and of Flaubert's life—until our backward movement in time brings us to the events depicted in the Bayeux tapestry, celebrating William the Conqueror's victory at Hastings in 1066, which tapestry is preserved not far from Rouen, close to the shores where the D-Day invasion took place.

One may wonder what the Bayeux tapestry has to do with Flaubert, but Barnes's hybrid work demands a dose of patience, which it repays with both narrative entertainment and critical wisdom. After taking us to two apparently unrelated scenes of war—first to June 6, 1944, when the allied forces invaded continental Europe from the French coast, and then to the Norman invasion of England, nine hundred years before—Barnes offers us a few lines that deserve our attention: "Both events seemed equally strange: one too distant to be true, the other too familiar to be true. How do we seize the past? Can we ever do so?"[9]

This reflection is central to our understanding of *Flaubert's Parrot*, which can be regarded as part of a wider cultural current that was aimed at deconstructing the claims of objectivity that history as a discipline made between the 19th and 20th centuries. In his seminal *Metahistory* (1973) Hayden White argues that historians cannot avoid interpreting the textual and documentary traces of the past by means of present ideological coordinates and that when they narrate the past they inevitably utilize rhetorical tools.[10] Historical writing is actually related to literary writing, for it entails both tropes and a creative element. We cannot achieve an "innocent" knowledge of the past. Even as authoritative a word as *tradition* was deconstructed in the late 20th century by Eric J. Hobsbawm and Terence Ranger, whose *The Invention of Tradition* (1983) analyzes the symbolic rituals by means of which a community restates — in a largely fictitious way — its sense of continuity with the past.[11]

In the same period, the problems concerning historical knowledge were investigated by those postmodernist narratives that Linda Hutcheon labels as *historiographic metafiction*. As the Canadian critic remarks, these novels express the skeptical attitude to history that has developed as a result of the theoretical works of Hayden White and Dominick LaCapra,[12] calling to question "our confidence in empiricist and positivist epistemologies."[13] Hutcheon, however, underlines the contradictory character of postmodernism, which she describes as "heavily implicated in that which it seeks to contest."[14] Indeed, postmodernist novelists both enunciate the impossibility of recovering the past and focus all their energies on achieving this impossible feat.

Graham Swift's *Waterland* (1983), which was published only one year before Barnes's book, exemplifies this tendency. The main character is Thomas Crick, a teacher of history who is about to be sacked because this subject is deemed of little utility. To make the situation worse, Thomas's wife, Mary, has been recently hospitalized in a psychiatric clinic. In this situation, Thomas decides to address his students in a different way and instead of teaching them the French Revolution, according to the curriculum, tells them the story of the region where they live — the Fens. That area of East England is marked by a centuries-old fight between human beings and nature, since those low lands, which originated from the deposits of rivers, are subject to the overflow of those same rivers, due to the sediments that continue to fill their beds. In Swift's novel, the dynamic character and the delicate balance of the Fens become a metaphor of literary and historical narration. Each narrative can be regarded as an island of meaning that emerges out of the sea of existence, but narratives may turn into dogmas, thus impeding that flow and change that are necessary to life. According to Swift, history is a fundamental tool to inhabit the world, but it must acknowledge its narrative nature and its inability to capture the essence of reality.[15]

Like other postmodernist writers and thinkers, Barnes too regards the objectivity of history as a myth of positivism, for we cannot understand the past without relating it to our present, that is to say, without rewriting it in our own image to distill a meaning from it that is relevant for us: "History is merely another literary genre: the past is autobiographical fiction pretending to be a parliamentary report."[16] As Umberto Eco remarks, while the modernist avant-gardes broke with the past — risking a communicative impasse, since each artistic language needs to be rooted in tradition — "The postmodern answer to the modern consists in acknowledging that the past [...] must be revisited with irony, not in an innocent way."[17]

This is what Barnes does when he revisits biography as a literary form, not only to make its imaginative component explicit — Virginia Woolf had already described the biographer's task as the art of combining the granite of facts with the intangible rainbow of psychology and ambience[18] — but to reassess the pact of verisimilitude on which this critical enterprise rests. With a self-questioning attitude, Barnes weaves and unweaves the fabric of his plot to create — in Laura Giovannelli's words — a biography that "exasperates and subverts the relations between life and art, author and character(s), history and fiction, configuring itself as an unclassifiable *pastiche* of forms and genres."[19]

The Language of Parrots

Barnes's choice to trace a postmodernist portrait of Flaubert is far from haphazard, since this author has been regarded by many as the father of modernism, due to his pursuit of narrative impersonality. Refusing to adopt an omniscient narrator and to comment on the characters' actions, in *Madame Bovary* Flaubert preferred to rely on sophisticated techniques such as free indirect speech, which renders the limited point of view of a character without authorial intrusions. In so doing, Flaubert anticipated the modernist experiments with narrative perspective, constructing a text that found in the reader's mind its principle of coherence. Flaubert himself enunciated the following oft-quoted maxim: "'The author in his book must be like God in his universe, everywhere present and nowhere visible.'"[20]

This absence of the writer from his work anticipated the interpretative mode that Roland Barthes advocated in his seminal essay on "The Death of the Author," which was published in 1968, a year we associate with the revolt of youth against authority and the past. What the critic refused was precisely the idea of the author as a principal of textual authority, i.e., the assumption that the ultimate meaning of a text coincides with what the writer intended to signify, that is with authorial intention. As Barthes wrote: "We know now that a text is not a line of words releasing a single 'theological' meaning (the 'message' of the Author-God) but a multidimensional space in which a variety of writings, none of them original, blend and clash."[21] This emphasis on the intertextual nature of writing takes us to the core of postmodernism and helps us understand why Barnes chose Flaubert as the subject of his "impossible" biography.

Moreover, Barnes started his career as a lexicographer, and this also helps to explain his sympathy for Flaubert, who authored both a *Dictionary of Commonplaces* (which was published posthumously in the 20th century) and the anti-novel *Bouvard and Pécuchet* (1881), a compendium of universal knowledge reduced to the absurd. Like Flaubert, Barnes is fascinated by the pragmatically efficient but also potentially ironic ways of organizing encyclopedic knowledge.[22]

Flaubert's Parrot is pervaded by linguistic, cultural and imaginative playfulness, and due to its implacably digressive vein reminds me of a computer virus. Specularity and multiplication mark it right from the title, since both Barnes and Braithwaite can be identified as Flaubert's parrot, due to their attempt to rewrite Flaubert's life in a Flaubertian way, underlining the grotesque side of the enterprise, simultaneously evoking and deflating its romantic appeal, playing with emotions in order to deconstruct any suspension of disbelief, making every revelation tinselly. Flaubert's parrot, however, is first and foremost a symbolic object — the parodic literary grail on which the protagonist's quest is focused following his visit to the Flaubert museum in the Rouen hospital, where the father of the writer used to work as a surgeon, where his family lived and where young Gustave grew up. It was in that place that in September, 1981, Barnes — who had been commissioned to write a book on the homes of French writers, which never saw the light — saw the parrot that inspired him to write the book.[23]

The "Musée Flaubert et d'histoire de la médecine" (Museum of Flaubert and the History of Medicine) is deeply consonant with the genius of the author, who delighted in the unexpected combinations of disparate elements. To approach the Flaubert museum, visitors have to go through a series of rooms that remind one of torture chambers, being full of huge bone saws and other gruesome utensils. These are accompanied by a set of engravings that offer graphic descriptions of the operations that were performed on those who had the misfortune to injure an arm or a nose in the course of a battle. This incongruous combination of hospital museum and literary museum would have probably pleased Flaubert, who was portrayed by a caricaturist in the act of dissecting Madame Bovary.[24] Perhaps Flaubert's obstentatious cynicism, his methodical habits and the crude language of certain metaphors he created reveal the influence of a father figure who regarded suffering and the materiality of the body as part of his everyday life.

Among other wonders, this hospital museum houses the stuffed parrot which Flaubert kept on his desk while writing "A Simple Heart," the story of Félicité, who after serving her mistress devoutly for half a century finds herself alone and concentrates all her affection on a parrot named Loulou. When the parrot dies, Félicité has it stuffed and the animal becomes even more precious for her, until on her deathbed Félicité has a vision in which Loulou — like the Holy Ghost — descends from the sky and hovers over her head.

The parrot sheds light on Flaubert's realistic vein, on his necessity to be impregnated with an object in its materiality while his mind was creating. Following a similar mechanism, the parrot takes on a deep meaning also for Barnes's narrator: "I gazed at the bird, and to my surprise felt ardently in touch with this writer who disdainfully forbade posterity to take any personal interest in him."[25] The stuffed bird becomes the instrument of a semi-mystical consonance between Braithwaite and Flaubert, for various reasons. First of all, it is a perfect example of "Flaubertian grotesque,"[26] like the cap young Charles wears at the beginning of *Madame Bovary*:

> This cap was one of those composite headpieces, in which could be detected elements of a fur cap, a lancer cap, a bowler hat, an otter-skin cap, and a cotton nightcap — in short, one of those poor things whose ugliness, even though voiceless, somehow suggests hidden depths of expression, like the face of an imbecile.[27]

I believe that Flaubert enjoyed describing this hopelessly amorphous object. What is certain, he put a lot of energy into rendering Charles's opaque ugliness. It is through passages like this that the author conveyed the deep lack of meaning, dignity and coherence that life is capable of — a disquieting revelation that Flaubert fought, or exalted, with irony.

Moreover, Barnes's narrator likes the parrot because this animal — whose main characteristic is that of repeating people's words — becomes an emblem of the loss of meaning that marks the reiteration of language. The parrot's secondhand language is not unlike the sentences Flaubert collected in his *Dictionary of Commonplaces*. Yet, in Flaubert's story Félicité regards Loulou as the image of the Holy Ghost, that is to say, of the logos, and Braithwaite hypothesizes that Flaubert represented himself simultaneously in the servant Félicité, who embodies his personality, and in the parrot Loulou, which embodies his voice.

So far, so good. The narrator's literary pilgrimage seems to have been successful, insofar as he has found a true relic, an object that is capable of putting him into contact with the secular and irreverent saint who is called Flaubert. Things become more complicated when Braithwaite, during his last day in Rouen, visits what remains of the writer's house in Croisset, the Pavillon Flaubert. In fact, although the residence of the author was destroyed, the small building where Flaubert used to write, at one end of the garden, survived, was bought thanks to a public subscription and was finally turned into a museum at the beginning of the 20th century. When the narrator visits the room, he realizes that amidst the strange objects that decorate it — such as an inkstand in the shape of a toad with an open mouth, the golden Buddha that Flaubert kept on his writing desk, and even the tumbler from which he drank just before dying — there is another parrot, which is described by the museum keeper as the original one.

Avatars of Truth

This is the beginning of an investigation that is aimed at identifying the *true* parrot, but in the space of this quest the biography of Flaubert also unrolls, starting from a chapter entitled "Chronology," which is marked precisely by the postmodernist idea that every form of knowledge is relative. If we look at an object from different angles, we see it in different ways; if we relate a fact according to the perspectives of various witnesses or if we adopt alternative strategies of "emplotment" (as Hayden White would say, thinking for instance of the comic/tragic rendering of an event), the result changes not a little. As Allison Lee reminded us, going to the root of postmodernist relativism: "Language creates 'reality,' and language is inescapably plural."[28] Thus Barnes draws up three parallel chronological accounts of Flaubert's life, which delineate the profiles of three entirely different persons. The first enjoys a long series of successes, both in literature and in life; the second goes through a seemingly endless sequence of misadventures and failures; the third describes himself, his writing and his loves by means of metaphors — the core of Flaubert's style — that instead of shedding light on the mystery he embodies, simply clothe it with ever new masks:

> 1875. I feel uprooted, like a mass of dead seaweed tossed here and there in the waves. 1880. When will the book be finished? That's the question. If it is to appear next winter, I haven't a minute to lose between now and then. But there are moments when I'm so tired that I feel I'm liquefying like an old Camembert.[29]

Starting from these three Flauberts, Barnes's narrator ironically meditates on the meaning of the term *biography*. We tend to consider a net as "a meshed instrument designed to catch fish," but we could easily reverse our point of view and consider it as "a collection of holes tied together with string."[30] The same is true for biography, and Barnes does not miss the opportunity to turn this intuition into a parable. In the course of his research, the narrator meets an American biographer who has found a bundle of letters Flaubert wrote to Juliet Herbert, the English governess of his niece Caroline. The letters confirm that Gustave and Juliet were lovers, but instead of handing the letters to Braithwaite, the American biographer burns them because this is what Flaubert asked his mistress to do in his last letter. This episode draws our attention to the invasive relation between biographer and biographee, forcing us to meditate not only on the borders that delimit the public from the private sphere, but also on our need to relate literary texts to the writer's life — a theme James tackled in stories such as *The Aspern Papers* (1888) and "The Real Right Thing" (1900).

The following chapters of *Flaubert's Parrot* deal with a range of eccentric subjects and create an effect of discontinuity in terms of narrative/discursive conventions. These shifting approaches frustrate the expectations of readers, who are constantly obliged to readjust their point of view. In his quest for knowledge, the narrator repeatedly takes circuitous paths in his attempt to overcome the obstacles that prevent him from attaining his epistemological targets. Relativism and excess coalesce in this peculiar literary structure, for the impossibility to recover the ultimate truth about Flaubert engenders a proliferation of avatars of truth, that is to say, of narratives.

Thus in "The Train-Spotter's Guide to Flaubert" Braithwaite discusses the influence of the Paris-Rouen railway — which was constructed by English workers, as Barnes recounted in *Cross Channel* (1996) — on the life of the writer. What connections can we trace between railways and Flaubert? Although Flaubert included railways among the worst products of modernity — together with "'poisons, enema pumps, cream tarts, royalty and the guillotine'"[31] — it was as a result of the inauguration of the Paris-Rouen line in 1843 that he and Louise Colet were able to start their liaison, which was based on secret, brief and sinful trysts at the Hotel du Grand Cerf in Mantes, halfway between the cities where the two lived.

Toward the end of the volume, we arrive at the emotional climax of the novel that is enclosed within this biography. Although we have been told that the narrator is a physician and a widower, we know next to nothing about his wife, until we discover that Ellen Braithwaite committed suicide after a long series of adulterous affairs, like Emma Bovary, the heroine whose initials she shares.[32] While Ellen, with her sexual philandering, may appear as affected by bovarism, her husband identifies with Charles Bovary. As Barnes has remarked: "My narrator Geoffrey Braithwaite is about to tell you a load of stuff about Flaubert because he is unable to tell you the real story he is loaded down by. It will be a novel about emotional blockage, about grief."[33]

Only now do we understand why Braithwaite has developed such an interest in Flaubert, as if the author's experience might shed light on his own life, providing the explanation of an enigma that has been left unanswered by the death of his wife. And yet a reason for Ellen's suicide slowly emerges: "Some people, as they grow older, seem to become more convinced of their own significance," as the narrator meditates; "others become less convinced."[34] With the passing of years, Ellen — who is imprisoned in a marriage that is neither happy nor unhappy — can no longer make sense of her own life. After becoming acquainted with the motives behind the narrator's quest for Flaubert, readers are offered an important reflection: "Books make sense of life. The only problem is that the lives they make sense of are other people's lives, never your own."[35] Books probably cannot make sense of our own lives, but they reaffirm the necessity to look for that sense.

Keeping that in mind, let us go back to the Flaubert biography the narrator is writing and to the twin parrots. At the very end of the book, the narrator discovers that both parrots are actually authentic, since they both come from the museum of natural history in Rouen. When the Croisset Pavillon museum was created in 1905, the curators, who were uncertain about how to furnish that empty room, borrowed a parrot from the collections of natural history. This is also what the curators of the Musée Flaubert did in the aftermath of World War II. The museum of natural history, however, counted as many as fifty parrots, and no one can know for certain which one Flaubert had originally borrowed. With a final twist that provides the perfect finishing touch, truth is everywhere and nowhere, but the quest for truth retains its value. Barnes's narrator may have been unable to locate the authentic Flaubert's parrot, and yet, along the way, he has met the writer, possibly without recognizing him, like the disciples of Emmaus.

2

Magda Szabó, *The Door* (1987)

Some words have no weight. They dissolve like a cloud, leaving nothing behind. Others are slow to sediment and stick to the soul. This is the case of *The Door* (1987) by the Hungarian writer Magda Szabó, a novel that you cannot simply lay down and forget, but that works inside you, corroding your certainties, causing a state of uneasiness. Although at first I did not empathize with the first-person narrator, whose voice seemed so intellectual and self-conscious and dignified, I was wrong. The story is indeed presented as autobiographical, for in this novel Szabó recounted the two decades she had spent in close contact with a woman who entered her life as a housekeeper and little by little acquired an immense role in it.[1]

The novel opens with a recurring dream — disquieting, fraught with anxiety, obsessive. This dream prepares a transition from the present to the past, gauging the emotional relevance these distant events still have — at a deep level — for the person who experienced them:[2]

The oneiric setting is the entrance hall of Magda's building, where she is standing , facing the outer door. She knows that outside there is an ambulance and struggles to open the door. The key turns but the lock does not move[2]:

> In this never-changing dream I am standing in our entrance hall at the foot of the stairs, facing the steel frame and reinforced shatterproof window of the outer door, and I am struggling to turn the lock. Outside in the street is an ambulance. [...] The key turns, but my efforts are in vain: I cannot open the door. But I must let the rescuers in, or they'll

be too late to save my patient. [...] I shout for help, but none of the residents of our three-storey building responds; and they cannot because — I am suddenly aware — I'm mouthing vacantly, like a fish [...] It is at this point that I am woken by my own screaming.[3]

This nightmare dramatizes the narrator's inability to rescue and her impotency in the face of death. In the following pages Magda even describes herself as persecuted by the Kindly Ones, divinities of revenge that preside over the punishment of the guilty. The novel is presented as the confession of a crime, which Magda addresses not to God, who knows the soul of each and everyone, but to her fellow human beings: "I killed Emerence. The fact that I was trying to save her rather than destroy her changes nothing."[4]

The causes of this sense of guilt are clarified only in the last chapters of the novel, which explores the relation between Magda and her eccentric housekeeper, Emerence Szeredás. The housekeeper imposes her rules right from the beginning, for she proclaims that she will accept this job only if the neighbors will give her employers good references. This domestic arrangement is finally agreed upon to the great satisfaction of Magda and of her husband, since Emerence, despite her strange hours and her idiosyncrasies, is an unstoppable working machine, a panzer-model housekeeper. Yet Magda and Emerence soon start hurting one another — when one makes friendly overtures, the other draws back, and they often misunderstand each other's intentions.

Behind the Door

Emerence's intolerance of any compromise with her neighbors and with the authorities has often led her into trouble, although these problems have been solved thanks to the intervention of the lieutenant colonel, a police officer who has become her friend after inspecting her house. Emerence protects her privacy with such a defying attitude that people have grown suspicious, and this is also the case of Magda, whose point of view filters the story. What does the woman conceal behind that door that nobody can cross? The precious crystal and porcelain objects that now and then come out of the flat, full of sweets or other delicacies, seem to indicate that Emerence had set her hands on the goods of a family of Jews, taking advantage of their misfortune. Due to this perception, a dose of despite mingles with Magda's other feelings towards Emerence — a mixture of esteem, perennial surprise and occasional fear — although we later learn that the Grossmanns actually left those objects to the woman out of gratitude, before escaping abroad.

The coexistence between Magda and Emerence is thus an emotional battlefield, where a succession of sallies and skirmishes ends with mutual defeat, but this does not mean that love was lacking. Rather, the book exalts the volatile nature of the Hungarians. Szabó's proud and vehement characters overflow with energy, and they can be as generous as they are revengeful. The book is under the sign of passion — not the passion of Eros, but the passion of the human, that instinctive charge of sympathy or antipathy that conditions, beneath a veneer of civility, every relation. Szabó disseminated her text with revealing clues, such as

> I hadn't thought it through, how irrational, how unpredictable is the attraction between people, how fatal its current. And yet I was well versed in Greek literature, which portrayed nothing but the passions: death and love and friendship, their hands joined together round a glittering axe.[5]

In this novel passion is conducive to tragedy, but then, as Magda meditates, thinking of Schopenhauer: "Every relationship involving personal feeling laid one open to attack, and the more people I allowed to become close to me, the greater the number of ways in which I was vulnerable."[6] It is to avoid being struck once again by destiny that Emerence has locked the door of her flat and of her heart. During her long life, Emerence has indeed suffered repeated traumas, but she is not used to complaining and has reacted to the aggression of the world (not only to violence, but to the pain of losing someone you love) with an effective strategy of survival. She is ready to make gifts to others, but she does not accept any. She enters the homes of her neighbors, but receives them on the threshold of hers.

Emerence works as a caretaker in a small building, and to make extra money she clears the snow for as many as 11 other buildings, overworking herself throughout the winter. She gives her life a meaning by donating herself day after day, but this is not the first image we have of her. On the contrary, Emerence appears at first like a changeable figure — a sort of Janus, whose face easily grows dark, whose anger leaves her interlocutors astonished, whose revengeful character qualifies her as redoubtable.

One of the several talents the author deploys in this book is her ability to change our perception of Emerence little by little, by shifting the meaning of details that Magda at first interprets superficially in an unfavorable way, often relying on somebody else's view of the woman. Thus the author alerts us to the danger of formulating facile and unfounded moral judgments on the basis of unreliable clues that may lead us to misconstrue the motivations of other people's actions.

While initially readers—following Magda—consider Emerence as unpleasantly eccentric, they later discover that her present attitude results from bitter experiences. Incomprehensible reactions, such as her childish terror during storms, acquire a meaning in relation to distant traumas that render this character human and doleful, until the cumulation of the events that marked the life of Emerence (who was born in 1905, while the main action takes place in the sixties and seventies) confers on her an epic stature. Through Emerence, in fact, we cross most of the 20th-century history of Hungary, with its political and social struggles—the harshness of rural life, fascism, World War II, the Stalinist regime of Rákosy (1945–56), the party hypocrisy of communism.

Emotions, Thought and Ethics

With this rich and complex novel, Szabó achieved a major narrative feat. I was aware of this right from my first reading, but I also felt that I could not open the door that led to the book's inner chamber, releasing its ultimate meaning. It was thanks to Martha Nussbaum's seminal *Upheavals of Thought: The Intelligence of Emotions* (2001) that I found the key to open that door. In this study, Nussbaum investigates both the *anti-emotional* prejudice that marked Western philosophy throughout the centuries, and conversely the cultural renderings of emotions in arts ranging from literature to music. At the core of her work is the idea that "instead of viewing morality as a system of principles to be grasped by the detached intellect [...] we will have to consider emotions as part and parcel of the system of ethical reasoning."[7]

According to the scholar, emotions reveal our vulnerability to external events—our lack of control on reality—and this is the reason why, starting from the Stoics, Western thinkers have tried to eradicate them in order to reassert the agency and integrity of the individual. Nussbaum puts this into a nutshell when she claims that "emotions are judgments in which people acknowledge the great importance, for their own flourishing, of things that they do not fully control—and acknowledge thereby their neediness before the world and its events."[8] As a product of the relation between the individual's changing goals and aspirations and the surrounding world, emotions are inherently subjective in their partiality, volatility and ambivalence. Starting from this view of emotions as dynamic, or better tumultuous, and also as revealing the incompleteness of the individual, who exists within a network of relations rather than as a monad, Nussbaum reasserts their importance in relation to phenomena such as cognition and ethics, or thought and value judgments.

To prove that emotions are "richly cognitive phenomena"[9] and to show their ethical import, Nussbaum offers an example of ubiquitous relevance, i.e., personal grief in the face of the death of a parent. Drawing on her own experience, Nussbaum describes the death of her mother in a New York hospital, while she was lecturing in Dublin. This news caused Nussbaum a crushing grief and a deep sense of guilt, due to her absence from her mother's deathbed. This autobiographical passage marks the beginning of Nussbaum's reappraisal of emotions as a fundamental factor in our lives and as a guiding light that directs our ethical judgments. As we shall see, a parallel can be drawn between Nussbaum's theoretical and Szabó's fictional investigations into emotions.

An Epic of Emotions

The Door is a book on emotions intended as an alternative form of cognition. Emerence's moral judgments are actually grounded on the emotions rather than on the abstract principles — be they related to faith or ideology — that other characters profess without having fully interiorized them, and in the end they prove sounder and more insightful than those of her neighbors, including Magda. Szabó's novel is also a heartrending account of the misunderstandings that derive from our inability to relate emotionally to one another, to attune ourselves to others. To analyze the techniques Szabó deployed to represent the enigma Emerence poses, Magda's efforts to come to terms with it, and the conflicts that mark their relation, I will focus on an episode that is central in the novel.

On one occasion Emerence is waiting for a special guest and asks Magda to allow her the use of her dining room to welcome this person suitably. Magda grants this strange request and witnesses Emerence's preparations for a superb banquet, but when the appointed time comes, the guest does not turn up and an impersonal apology is brought in by an intermediary. Given the intensity of Emerence's emotions and the secrecy surrounding her private life, her reaction is typically unpredictable and eccentric, for a dejected Emerence allows Magda's dog to eat the roast she had prepared — right from the princely table where some of Magda's beloved family heirlooms are laid.

When Magda voices her surprise, the episode veers toward the brutal, since Emerence gives vent to her anger by beating the dog. Magda, whose intimacy has been profaned by this incomprehensible psychodrama, strikes back by rejecting the delicious food and expensive wine Emerence has stored in Magda's fridge to thank her and apologize. What Magda does not realize — due both to her inability to empathize and to her own emotional turmoil — is that on that day Emerence has experienced a deep crisis, but the dog, despite the beating it has suffered, has a different reaction: "That animal understood everything. It absorbed information through so many secret antennae, so many mysterious channels."[10]

The role the dog plays within this interpersonal drama is fundamental since — as Nussbaum clarifies in her study — animals share with human beings a capacity for emotions, which also turns into a means of communication alternative to language. While the Stoics believed that neither children nor animals were able to feel emotions, we know that it is precisely in early childhood that our emotional response to the external world is shaped, and also that animals have emotions, as is proved by "a vast cross-disciplinary literature."[11] Indeed, in *The Door*, Viola — as Emerence calls the dog, although it is actually a male — proves able to understand those aspects of Emerence's personality that escape the highly rational and cultivated Magda, who feels more at ease when seated at her typewriter than when she is dealing with fellow human beings.

At the end of this terrible day of conflict — during which Magda has been offended by Emerence and has in turn offended her — Magda cannot fall asleep. Thus she gets dressed and, taking the dog with her, goes to see Emerence. The climax of this event — whose emotional import is rendered by an allusion to Book Six in the *Aeneid*, recounting Aeneas' descent into the underworld — is the reconciliation between the two women, which is not clearly articulated in terms of language, but follows other channels:

> "I'm hungry," I said at last. "Have you got anything left to eat?"
> The smile that — against every logical expectation — lit up her face, was like the sun breaking through steel-gray clouds.[12]

By asking for food at that late hour, Magda undoes the evil spell she cast when she previously rejected Emerence's food. This implicit assertion of trust suffices to re-establish the affective bond between the two women, and Emerence's answer is vehicled by her body rather than by verbal language.

The scope of Magda's visit, however, goes beyond the relation between the two women, since it also involves the mysterious visitor who failed to appear and whose body Emerence symbolically murdered when in her despair she had Viola sit at the table and eat the roast. To have readers grasp the full meaning of this scene, the writer presented Emerence and the dog as "figures from a Greek myth," and the roast itself as "a tangle of viscera, a species of human sacrifice."[13] As the narrator reflects, the person who had failed to keep the appointment "had wounded that most important part of Emerence about which she would never speak, not to anyone. Viola was the unwitting Jason. Beneath Medea-Emerence's headscarf glowed the fires of the underworld."[14] During her night visit, Magda realizes that she has to accept whatever Emerence wishes her to eat, for it is only by that strange ritual — by standing in "for the visitor who had failed to come"[15] — that she can help the woman heal her inner wound.

Only little by little do we discover — with the help of the forward and backward movements of Magda's narrative — that the person in question is a young woman who lives in New York and who should have come to Hungary on business, but her business meeting was cancelled and she thought that "there was no point in coming just to visit the old woman."[16] The practical logic of business is here contrasted with the affective attitude of Emerence, who had actually played a major role in the life of this young American woman, since we discover that it was Emerence who saved the life of this child of Jewish origin when her grandparents — the Grossmanns — committed suicide.

Emerence's act of heroism was moreover accomplished at the price of deep personal humiliation. To save little Eva, Emerence had to pretend that she was her illegitimate child, thus incurring her grandfather's wrath, suffering his savage beating, and falling into disgrace in the eyes of her whole family. Only now do we fully understand the import of Emerence's despair when Eva failed to keep the appointment. The woman will have no other opportunities to visit Emerence. She will actually offer a belated gesture of compensation by visiting her grave and lighting a candle, but the narrator leads us to believe that the ghost of Emerence has not forgotten her, for a sudden wind gust blows the candle.

This episode is emblematic of the novel as a whole because it illustrates the techniques Szabó repeatedly employs to delineate the conflict between Emerence and Magda. The first step of this narrative process is the presentation of an apparently banal event which triggers a disproportionate emotional response in Emerence and consequently Magda's astonishment. Only subsequently — by means of a mosaic of clues that slowly make sense — both Magda and her readers become aware of the distant, often traumatic events that explain Emerence's reaction. Two major timelines intertwine within this process of revelation: the main action — whose significance is explored through flashbacks and flashforwards so as to investigate its motivations and outcomes — and the present reflection on these past events, i.e., the act of narration itself. What enables Magda to render Emerence's life experience, bridging the gap between her own cultivated rationality and her housekeeper's unrestrained emotions, is Greek myth, which conveys a deep knowledge of the human. Mythical references provide the action with a counterpoint that shows the inner resonance — and also the universal value in terms of affective archetypes — of what we might superficially regard as minor crises in the life an uneducated woman of humble origins.

Against Orthodoxy

The Door has that ability to imply — to signify potentially, indirectly, through the inferential processes of readers — that marked the literature of protest of Eastern European countries under communism. We should not forget that the book was published two years before the fall of the Berlin Wall. In recounting apparently irrelevant matters, which pertain to the private life of a woman of no importance, Szabó actually discussed politics, since the life of Emerence is in itself a political manifesto, and we are told that "Emerence was the sole inhabitant of her empire-of-one."[17] This figure combines the most opinionated individualism and the most radical altruism, taking a stance that is alternative both to capitalist hedonism and to Soviet collectivism. Actually, at the core of Emerence's attitude to history and power we find her refusal to ever take sides. As Magda comments, "In her eternal negativity [Emerence] was political."[18]

The woman is not only a dissident in politics but also a heretic in matters of faith. And yet *The Door* is a deeply religious novel, pivoting on the relation between preached and lived words. As Magda realizes from the very first, Emerence "had a sister in the Scriptures, the biblical Martha. Her life too had been a ceaseless round of hard work and giving help to others."[19] Magda cannot understand why a woman who embodies the Gospel so instinctively harbors such a hatred for the Church, and at first she regards this idiosyncrasy as rooted in a curious episode that another woman relates. A few years before, the nearby church received some parcels from Sweden. When Emerence visited the chapel, however, all the warm and useful clothes had disappeared. Only some evening dresses remained, and the charitable ladies who were distributing these gifts gave one to Emerence, thinking that she might sell it. Perceiving this as an outrage, Emerence threw it at the ladies, and from that moment she lost no occasion to give vent to her rancor against God and the Church.

This is the first explanation we are offered, but we subsequently discover that Emerence — who is the daughter of a carpenter, like Jesus Christ — is a Christ-like figure of unconscious purity and boundless dedication, who is foreign to every orthodoxy, be it associated with a party or with a Church: Emerence "refused to believe in God, but she honored him with her actions. She was capable of sacrifice. Things I had to attend to consciously she did instinctively."[20] Emerence, however, is an anarchist. She is perpetually against and does not tolerate any imposition, for she reads every hierarchy of good — be it political or religious — as a hierarchy of power. Her solidarity is with the outcasts, and under the successive waves of totalitarianism that ravage her country she is ready to rescue those who are fleeing under persecution — be they Jews, Russian soldiers or even Germans. What matters for her is the individual, not ideology or faith.

This is why Emerence resists every attempt of the party "educators" to convince her to go back to school. Emerence is suspicious of written words, which unlike spoken words bear no revealing trace of emotions and can therefore be easily utilized to deceive and manipulate. In Szabó's Hungary, language is compromised, being the stuff of political speeches and propaganda. Moreover, the writer draws a parallel between the atheistic message of political institutions and the religious message of the Church. In both cases, words support a written ideology/faith that aims to be univocal and contrasts with the multifarious character of the human. In their monolithical character, ideology and faith tower over single individuals, making them insignificant. For instance, the diffidence of the priest towards Emerence, both before and after her death, proves that he is unable to come to terms with goodness in its absolute alterity, outside any rule.

Emerence is an excessive and unpredictable figure. She is a sort of Great Mother, a creature who is in harmony with the rhythms of nature, who embraces both light and shadow, who is able to accept death — or to give death, out of compassion — but whose true calling is to protect life in every form. This is proved by Emerence's love for stray cats and dogs, notably for Viola, a central character in the novel. On Christmas Day Magda and her husband are coming home from a clinic, for the man is ill, when they find a black puppy which is buried to his neck in the snow. The festive ambience and the severe weather conspire to convince husband and wife that the dog must be brought home as a bizarre Christmas gift. As soon as Emerence sees the puppy, she devotes all her energies to him. Emerence loses no time to adopt the helpless creature:

> She walked up and down the hall with the little dog, wheezing out some old song in her rasping voice, in her own cock-eyed, upside-down, and intensely moving celebration of Christ's birth. With the tightly swaddled black puppy in her arms, she rocked back and forth, a caricature of motherhood, an absurd Madonna.[21]

This scene is interrupted when somebody comes to look for Emerence, since a pipe has burst in the house next door. Emerence's life is a never-

2. Magda Szabó, The Door (1987)

ending run. She does not even have time to sleep properly in a bed, also because her backache prevents her from lying and she prefers to rest in an armchair. When the dog recovers his health, it becomes apparent that he regards Emerence as his true mistress. The name the woman uses to address him is Viola, yet another sign of Emerence's eccentricity, but we later learn that this name is actually close to her heart.

Emerence talks with "her" dog and he answers, barking in a certain way or lifting his paw with an air of intent. The two understand one another perfectly, and we do not find this surprising since Emerence embodies an instinctive form of knowledge, which is mediated by the "heart" rather than the mind. This brings us back to the contrast between action and language, which is central in the novel, whose protagonists — Emerence and Magda — remind us of the Biblical Martha and Mary:

> Now as they were traveling along, [Jesus] entered a village; and a woman named Martha welcomed Him into her home. She had a sister called Mary, who was seated at the Lord's feet, listening to His word. But Martha was distracted with all her preparations; and she came up to Him and said, "Lord, do You not care that my sister has left me to do all the serving alone? Then tell her to help me." But the Lord answered and said to her, "Martha, Martha, you are worried and bothered about so many things; but only one thing is necessary, for Mary has chosen the good part, which shall not be taken away from her" [Luke, 10: 38–42].[22]

Like Martha, Emerence despises Magda's churchgoing and loses no occasion to remind her that clearing the snow or cooking lunch for her husband would be more useful than spending time in a church. Interestingly, while Luke's parable asserts the primacy of listening to the word of Christ on action, the novel problematizes this.

Emerence harbors a deep-seated suspicion of written words. Magda describes her as "an anti-intellectual,"[23] adding that for her those who did not handle tools were "all parasites."[24] Throughout the years she spends in contact with Emerence, Magda strives to assert her right to write, to prove that you can do things with words, but the poetry of this unsolved, tragic novel resides in the contrast between the two women. One can hardly read and write, but is endowed with multiple talents, while the other focuses all her energies on the act of writing. This relation finally proves mutually enriching. Through Emerence, Magda discovers that you can meet God without entering a church and that you can attain deep wisdom without reading books, while Emerence — after observing Magda — develops a sort of tenderness for writing. While at first Emerence is diffident, little by little she starts considering the activity of Magda and of her husband as a children's game. You do not know what good comes of it, but it certainly demands time and energy.

From Ethics to Aesthetics

Emerence questions Magda's ethical and aesthetic coordinates with half-comic, half-pathetic results. To prove her attachment to Magda, Emerence—who is an enthusiastic collector of *objets trouvés*—fills her house with "gifts" whose taste is debatable, such as a garden gnome, a pair of cavalry boots and even the tattered statue of a dog. Fearing a conjugal crisis, Magda moves the gifts to remote parts of the flat, to avoid the fury of her husband, but another crisis is in store, since the housekeeper is not willing to question the value of these objects. When an exasperated Magda claims that the dog is kitsch, Emerence — suddenly curious — asks for an explanation and then reacts to this charge:

> "This dog is fake? [...] "A fraud? Well, hasn't it got everything — ears, paws, a tail? [...] So what if the top of the ear is chipped? You'll take a bit of pottery your friend from Athens dug up on some island and stick it behind glass. Do you have the nerve to tell me that filthy black thing is *complete*?"[25]

With sharp words, Emerence deconstructs the "high" conception of art, advocating an aesthetics of naïvety which is not devoid of strength. It is Emerence's nephew, however, who reveals the logic behind Emerence's gifts when he claims that her taste is "impeccable," only "when she goes looking for presents for the two of you she doesn't buy for the grown-ups. She chooses for two young children."[26]

Another clash between the culturally codified gaze of the writer and the uncultivated but sensitive gaze of the housekeeper occurs when Magda takes Emerence to a film set, in order to initiate her to the "magic of creation."[27] She is in for a bitter surprise. Emerence is disgusted by what she has seen, since the set strikes her as fake, starting from the wind that moves the trees during a love scene: Magda understands that in a faraway time Emerence loved and saw the trees dance. Art is therefore labeled by Emerence as fake, like written words, while truth coincides with life. Through Emerence and Magda, Szabó contrasts the imperatives of action and language, the private and public spheres, the domains of the real and the virtual. The story's tragic ending originates from the clash between two irreconcilable views of the world.

The Tragedy of Betrayal

The final chapters explain the sense of guilt and the need to confess that mark the opening of the book. The first betrayal takes place when Magda, who knows the secret concealed behind Emerence's door, decides to let other people into the flat. Clearing snow from the courtyards, Emerence catches a bad cold and develops pneumonia. Although she is terribly ill, she does not let anybody enter her home. She only accepts the food her neighbors bring to her. After discussing the matter with the two people who are closest to Emerence — the lieutenant colonel and her nephew — Magda sets a trap to enable a physician to visit the ailing old woman.

The consequences of this gesture are huge in relation to Emerence's little world. Her betrayal is absolute. Magda has not only revealed Emerence's secret to the world, but she has proved unable to respect the woman's desire to disappear when she is no longer able to *serve*. Magda has not understood the gesture of love that Emerence made years before toward her friend Polett, whom she helped to die in her old age: "When the sands run out for someone, don't stop them going. You can't give them anything to replace life."[28] These are the words Magda cannot remember at the right time, perhaps because her faith prevents her from doing so, perhaps because she is unable to go beyond common sense and common feeling.

Yet this is not the last act of betrayal that marks the novel. The illness that strikes Emerence after serving Magda and her husband for twenty years coincides with the award of a prestigious literary prize which marks the crowning of Magda's career and the opportunity to break the silence that the regime previously imposed on the author. Cancelling the trip Magda is scheduled to make to Athens to participate in a conference would fuel the rumor that the regime actually prevented her from expatriating, and therefore risk an international crisis. It is the public sphere that prevails over the private, but Magda's course of life clearly contrasts with that of Emerence, whose compassion for the individual has always come before any other consideration.

Despite her daunting appearance, we finally discover that Emerence's life has been planned on the twin principles of loving and giving, although in her powerfully sensitive soul unrequited love may easily turn into hate. She is "St. Emerence of Csabadul, the madwoman of mercy, who asks no questions but rescues all alike."[29] In the novel's bitter ending it is the people who surround her who are finally revealed as mean — what is more, understandably so, for they are all striving to survive.

Soon after Emerence has been hospitalized, her friend Sutu offers to take her place as a caretaker. The people who live in the building disdainfully refuse the idea, but after the death of Emerence it is her friend Adélka who succeeds her, and for a bitter irony of fate it is Sutu whom Magda employs as a housekeeper. In this corrosive novel it is Emerence's best friends who actually profit from her death, and in the eyes of Magda they are no less culpable than herself. Indeed, *The Door* deals with the inexorability of mourning and the impossibility to accept loss, giving vent to a sense of guilt that takes on vaguely pathological and definitely existential connotations.

The tragic magnitude of Magda's regrets is clearly not the only "excessive" aspect of this emotionally overflowing short novel, where Emerence—whose name means *venerable* in Hungarian—acquires a mythological status. Len Rix, who translated the text into English, regards Emerence as the "very soul" of the Hungarian people, with its "oppressed and exploited peasantry."[30] That is why the woman is "invested with all sorts of mythical attributes: a Valkyrie, a Madonna, one of the Fates, a little Jehovah, Medea, and so on."[31] In these uncanny pages the nocturnal streets of Pest fade into Virgil's Avernus, while the smell of chlorine in Emerence's flat evokes the depths of Agamemnon's tomb. The story of Emerence is indeed filtered by the gaze of Magda, who rewrites her maid's life in terms of classical culture, but also as a hagiography and borrowing from Balkan folklore. The contrast between the humble reality of Emerence's everyday life and the rhetorical apparatus the writer deployed to describe it is central to this novel, where Emerence becomes a heroine and Magda becomes her singer.

Unlike the cinema-makers Emerence despises, Szabó is actually able to make the trees dance and whisper and cry. The story slowly comes to life, and we shut this book, pivoting on unkept promises and unredeemable mistakes, with a disturbing sense of guilt, realizing that—like Magda—we understood Emerence too late. Our inferences have proved painfully wrong. The character's brusque behavior, her obstinate silences, her irrational fears were actually rooted in hardship and suffering. Emerence had a personal life no one was aware of, and what other people regarded as meaningless episodes actually reverberated in the dark caverns of her mind until they produced heartrending thunders.

Even her plan to build a luxurious crypt for her and her long-dead family members in her native village is revealed to be not a sign of self-aggrandizement, as we originally believed, but the result of her lifelong desire to be reunited with those she loved and lost. Emerence was simply a loyal creature whose affections were strong and whose life had been marked by loss. We are suddenly gripped by a feeling of nostalgia for this woman who finally opened the door of her home with the following words: "And don't you forget that I let you in where I never allowed anyone else. Beyond that, I've nothing else to offer you, because I've nothing else in me."[32]

3

Abraham B. Yehoshua, *Mr. Mani* (1990)

Of Sephardic origin, Abraham B. Yehoshua was born in Jerusalem in 1936 and subsequently taught comparative literature at the University of Haifa. Yehoshua is therefore not a Jew of the Diaspora, but somebody who has experienced the reality of the state of Israel, the formation of which is traced in this volume indirectly through the story of the Manis. This family novel enabled the author to explore themes that are central to contemporary Israeli literature,[1] such as *paternity* and *descendance*, which are related to topical issues like *Jewish identity* and *coexistence with difference*. The target Yehoshua set himself in these pages is ambitious, and it is not easy to discuss *Mr. Mani*, a novel that relies on sophisticated *narrative techniques*, a wide spectrum of *cultural references* and a dense *symbolic articulation* to convey a strong political message. No wonder, since Bernard Horn describes Yehoshua as fitting "into the line of prophets, actively engaged in trying to transform history."[2]

The text is composed of five conversations, which are framed by prologues and epilogues providing us with biographical information concerning the conversation partners. An emotional focus on the present is thus combined with chronological depth. What makes this technique peculiar, however, is the fact that in each dialogue a voice is telling his/her own experience to another person whose voice is unrecorded. In itself, this choice demands readers' patience and ability to cooperate imaginatively, inviting them to fill the gaps, enlivening a conversation that borders on the monologue. Playing with the point of view, in the first four dialogues Yehoshua contrasts younger narrators, whose outlook is more critical, with older interlocutors whose view of the world is more conventional.[3] None of the first four narrators belongs to the Mani family, which is however the object of their conversations, while in the last dialogue it is a Mani who recounts his guilt, a sort of original sin which is destined to reverberate from generation to generation on his descendants.

Moreover, the writer presents these five dialogues in reverse chronological order: the first takes place in the kibbutz of Mash'abei Sadeh in 1982, during the Lebanese war; the second takes us to Heraklion, in Crete, in 1944, during World War II; the third takes us to Jerusalem in 1918, during the British occupation, when the design of a Jewish state in Palestine started to take shape as a result of the Balfour Declaration (November 2, 1917); the fourth opens in Jelleny-Szad, in Poland, in 1899, at the time of the Zionist movement; the fifth, in Athens in 1848. We move from one time to another, from one country to another.

As is apparent, due to the narrative strategies and chronological sequence Yehoshua chose, this text is not easy to read, although patience is sure to be repaid when one deals with Yehoshua's complex forms of creativity. Moreover, to attain the core of this multilayered story, one needs to know other stories. That Jews are great narrators and listeners to stories is proved by the method Freud elaborated, since psychoanalysis is based on the patient's recounting of his outer/inner life story and on the construction of a second story on the part of the analyst. The shadow of Freud looms large over *Mr. Mani*, where Yehoshua — who has been married to a psychoanalyst for half a century — invites readers to an archaeological approach, that is, to dig into the text in order to recover underlying connections and decode recurring symbols.[4] The shadow of another text looms large over this novel — I mean the Bible, to which Jewish literature refers incessantly, although not with a predominantly reverential or citationist attitude, but rather with critical creativity, following an interpretive tradition that prefers argumentation to reiteration.

In dealing with this complex novel, I will privilege some dialogues over others, sacrificing those pages that movingly recreate the ambiences of Jerusalem and render the coexistence between Jews and Palestinians in the city alleys, with the various connotations this difficult neighbor relation has assumed in the course of the 20th century. What I will offer is rather an ideological reading, relating this novel to the Bible, the text on which both the cultural memory and the national identity of the Jews are grounded. This will enable us to meditate on the political stance of Yehoshua with regard to issues such as anti–Semitism, Zionism, the nature of the state of Israel, and the relation between Jewish and Israeli identities.

Back to the Bible

A Biblical pattern informs *Mr. Mani*, the backbone of which is the genealogy of the Mani family:

Eliyahu Mani (1740–1807)
Yosef Mani (1766–1820)
Avraham Mani (1799–1861)
Yosef Mani (1826–1848)
Moshé Mani (1848–1899)
Yosef Mani (1887–1941)
Efrayim Mani (1914–1944)
Gavriel Mani (1938–)
Efrayim Mani (1958–)
Roni Mani (1983–)

As the book of Genesis asserts, the covenant between God and his chosen people rests on genealogy. The story of Abraham centers on God's miraculous intervention, which enabled an old man to engender a nation. Abraham has no children, but the Lord takes him outside, and speaks to him as follows: "'Now look toward the heavens, and count the stars, if you are able to count them [....] So shall your descendants be'" (Genesis 15: 5).[5]

Afterwards, the Lord makes a pact with Abraham, saying: "'To your descendants I have given this land, From the river of Egypt as far as the great river, the river Euphrates'" (Genesis 15: 18). This is the foundation myth of the state of Israel, but what we discover in the following lines is that this is the land of "the Kenite and the Kenizzite and the Kadmonite and the Hittite and the Perizzite and the Rephaim and the Amorite and the Canaanite and the Girgashite and the Jebusite" (Genesis 15: 19–21). The same message recurs in Exodus, where we read: "'So I said, I will bring you up out of the affliction of Egypt to the land of the Canaanite and the Hittite and the Amorite and the Perizzite and the Hivite and the Jebusite, to a land flowing with milk and honey'" (3:17). The territory God chooses as a homeland for his chosen people is not uninhabited, but it is a place where Jews are destined to meet their *others*, although the sacred texts do not specify what the terms of this coexistence must be.

This is a central aspect of Yehoshua's novel, since across the centuries the Mani family shows an irresistible desire to meet the Arabs — those neighbors who yet appear so distant. It is also important to underline that this tension towards one's *other* is rooted in the biography of Yehoshua, whose father was an Israeli orientalist, spoke Arabic fluently and had a deep knowledge of Arab culture.[6] It is definitely no coincidence that Yehoshua dedicated this novel to his father as "a man of Jerusalem and a lover of its past." With a sort of bitter irony, as the cradle of the Jewish, Christian and Muslim religions—that is to say, of monotheisms in the plural, a startling oxymoron, which should make us ponder—Jerusalem is actually a palimpsest that should invite inhabitants and visitors to cross the frontiers between different cultures.

Back to the text: for many years in Jerusalem the Mani family runs "an open clinic" that is "multiethnic, syncretistic, ecumenical,"[7] but in 1982 that building is entirely rented to Orthodox Jews, who are very worried that somebody who is different from them may want to settle there. And yet in 1918—in the aftermath of the Balfour Declaration—Yosef Mani becomes a spy against the English on behalf of Turks and Germans precisely to be allowed to enter the Arab territories and harangue groups of incredulous Palestinians, so as to instill them with a national consciousness than might enable a pacific coexistence with Jews. The story (which is narrated in the third dialogue) is far from lacking humor, since little by little the protagonist develops parallel abilities as a spy and as a prophet of two independent states, which are destined to host respectively Israelis and Palestinians:

> By now too he had his table, and a chair, and a blackboard, and even a glass of water; he stood with the Turkish officers about him and read Lord Balfour's declaration; and then he unfurled a colored map of Palestine that he had drawn himself, with the sea a bright blue, while the Arabs stared at it and failed to comprehend why, if this was their country, it was so small. He pointed to the blue sea, to the Jordan, to Jerusalem, and said, "Awake!" and they looked to see who had dared to doze off; "Get ye an identity," he went on, "before it is too late!"[8]

Although the people of the villages between Ramallah and Nablus get used to this strange fellow and to his inflamed speeches, when Mr. Mani cuts his map lengthways, declaring that the half with the mountains, bordering on the Jordan, is for the Arabs, and the other half is for the Jews, they protest, for they want the sea, too. Mr. Mani, however, has a solution ready for use, and taking another map from his bag, he cuts it horizontally.

Yosef Mani—who has much in common with a previous Yosef Mani, his 19th-century ancestor—is not only the prophet of the tragic situation of conflict and asymmetry that Israelis and Palestinians are currently experiencing, but also an enlightened interpreter of the Balfour Declaration, which reads as follows:

> His Majesty's Government view with favor the establishment in Palestine of a national home for the Jewish people, and will use their best endeavors to facilitate the achievement of this object, it being clearly understood that nothing shall be done which may prejudice the civil and religious rights of existing non-Jewish communities in Palestine, or the rights and political status enjoyed by Jews in any other country.[9]

Keeping in mind the fact that Yehoshua wrote *Mr. Mani* in a context that is marked by the difficult coexistence of Jews and Palestinians in a small territory, and that this problem is rendered in the novel with an effect of historical depth, let us go back to the Bible to focus our attention on other aspects of the story of Abraham.

Since Sarah cannot give birth to children, she advises her husband to unite with their slave Hagar to generate,[10] but once Hagar is pregnant their cohabitation becomes more difficult. The girl grows insubordinate to Sarah — at least this is what her mistress believes — and Hagar finally flees, but the Lord calls her back, and Ishmael is born. Abraham is 86. When he reaches the age of 89, the Lord appears again and reassures him concerning his descendants:

> "I will make you exceedingly fruitful, and I will make nations of you, and kings will come forth from you. I will establish My covenant between Me and you and your descendants after you throughout their generations for an everlasting covenant, to be God to you and to your descendants after you. I will give to you and to your descendants after you, the land of your sojournings, all the land of Canaan, for an everlasting possession; and I will be their God" [Genesis 17: 6–8].

God asks Abraham to circumcise Ishmael, and one year later his wife (Sarah) gives birth to Isaac, who is also circumcised. Abraham is over 100, while his wife is 91.

When Sarah sees Ishmael "mocking" Isaac (Genesis 29: 9), she is afraid and asks her husband to cast out Hagar and her child. At this point religious myths diverge, since Islam also acknowledges Abraham as a patriarch and as the founder of monotheism, but the Bible and the Qur'an offer different — or complementary — versions of his life. After Hagar and Ishmael have been expelled, the Bible focuses on the relation between Abraham and Isaac, whose sacrifice is demanded by God, although the ritual killing does not actually take place. In parallel, the Qur'an tells the story of the sacrifice of Ishmael, which is first demanded and then prevented by God, and which is celebrated in the *Festival of Sacrifice* or *Eid al-Adha*, one of the most important religious holidays in the Islamic calendar:

> And when he reached with him [the age of] exertion, he said, "O my son, indeed I have seen in a dream that I [must] sacrifice you, so see what you think." He said, "O my father, do as you are commanded. You will find me, if Allah wills, of the steadfast." And when they had both submitted and he put him down upon his forehead, We called to him, "O Abraham, You have fulfilled the vision." Indeed, We thus reward the doers of good. Indeed, this was the clear trial. And We ransomed him with a great sacrifice [37: 100–107].[11]

The sacred text of Islam also expands on the relation between Abraham and Hagar and Ishmael, who are abandoned by Abraham in the desert — in the place where the city of Mecca now stands — and soon run out of water and food. Yet, Allah has a spring of water gush from the sand, and subsequently Abraham and Ishmael choose that place as the site of the *Ka'ba*, the sacred edifice that is at the heart of the annual pilgrimage (Haji) to Mecca.

As if the story of Abraham was not complex enough, the Bible offers yet another significant detail on the family ménage of the patriarch, bringing us back to the issue of incest, which is at the heart of Yehoshua's novel.[12] Indeed, in the course of his journeys, Abraham protects himself from rivals by presenting his beautiful wife — Sarah or Sarai — as his sister:

> It came about when he came near to Egypt, that he said to Sarai his wife, "See now, I know that you are a beautiful woman; and when the Egyptians see you, they will say, 'This is his wife'; and they will kill me, but they will let you live. Please say that you are my sister so that it may go well with me because of you, and that I may live on account of you" [Genesis 12: 11–13].

Abraham's strategy, however, produces strange results, since both the Pharaoh and King Abimelech (Genesis 20) fall in love with Sarah, and God has to intervene with revelatory dreams and threats to ensure that Sarah is not obliged to betray her husband.

Still in Genesis, the incest between Lot and his daughters is presented not as a taboo, but rather as a necessary act that engenders two nations. We know that while Lot and his wife are fleeing from Sodom, before God destroys it, the woman turns back out of curiosity, breaking God's prohibition, and is therefore turned into a statue of salt. In the aftermath of this event the two daughters of Lot are alone with their father in a cave where they have found refuge, and after making their father drunk they procreate with him (Genesis 19: 31). This act of incest is not punished by God, but it marks the beginning of two new lineages: the Moabites and the Ammonites (Genesis 19: 36–38).

The embryo of Yehoshua's novel is in these stories, which tell the origin of the Jewish people and seem to anticipate their perennial fight against extinction, against those destructive forces that have menaced it throughout the history of the Diaspora due to the reemergence of anti–Semitism, be it linked with Eastern European pogroms, the Nazi genocide or the tormented life of the state of Israel.

The Shadow of the Akedah

As we have seen, Genesis indicates Jews not only as the chosen people, but also as destined to occupy a territory and a historical time which always involves an encounter with alterity. Moreover, in Genesis, Jews are the recipient of a clear message — survive at any cost, also despite taboos, although God himself, through the sacrifice of Isaac, seems to endanger that descendance that he granted to Abraham. Reviewing *Mr. Mani*, Guido Fink argues that what we find at the heart of the volume is precisely "the Jewish theme of generations and of the difficulty of survival, the terror of *lastness*."[13] The book tackles these issues in a complex way, producing a set of variations on the subject of paternity, survival and sacrifice.

To understand this theme, we should meditate on the ambiguous meaning that the *Akedah* (literally the act of "binding" Isaac, as one would bind an animal in view of its sacrifice) presents in the Jewish tradition as a foundation myth. On the one hand, one may consider this Biblical episode as conveying God's prohibition to sacrifice human beings — in this case, the emphasis falls on the angel who restrains Abraham's hand. At the same time, one may regard the *Akedah* as inviting to martyrdom, to offer one's life for God in an unconditional surrender.[14]

Yehoshua himself wrote an essay to explain the importance the *Akedah* takes on in *Mr. Mani*, focussing on the fifth dialogue of the novel, where Avraham Mani (1799–1861) confesses the obscure guilt on which the Mani dynasty rests. When Avraham goes to Jerusalem, where his son has recently married Tamara, he discovers that Yosef spends his nights in the streets, mingling with the Arabs, whom he regards as Jews "who just don't know it yet."[15] This attempt to obliterate difference leads Yosef to death, since on a snowy night "on the steps leading to the Dome of the Rock, he had his throat slit, madame. He was butchered like a black sheep."[16] Yosef's death occurs on the site of the originary sacrifice of Isaac. Only now does Avraham understand that the marriage has not been consummated, and to ensure his posterity he chooses the path of incest, lying with his daughter-in-law. The dialogue, bordering on delirium, ends with an admission of guilt on the part of Avraham, who feels somehow responsible for his son's death, due to his aversion to Yosef's dream of fusion between Jews and Arabs.

This episode combines the Biblical *Akedah* with other aspects of Abraham's story. As we have seen, the triangle that is made up of Abraham, Sarah and Hagar is the founding myth not only for the Jews, but also for the Arabs, who venerate Ishmael as their forefather. The burial site of Abraham at Hebron is a sacred place both for Jews and Muslims and is the object of deep conflicts.

It is to "our Ishmaelite cousins"[17] that Avraham imputes the death of Yosef, a man whose identity is fluid, who speaks various languages and repeatedly crosses — as other Manis will do in later times — the boundaries between the different communities that reside in Jerusalem. Arnold J. Band sees Yosef's death and his unconsummated marriage as a hint at his homosexuality, but he also acknowledges the political dimension of this story.[18] We are indeed at the core of the symbolic network that underlies the novel. As we have seen, the idea of a pact whereby God grants a land of Israel to his chosen people rests on the *Akedah*, but Yehoshua has this Bible story interact with the story of Isaac and Ishmael — the two sons of Abraham who are at the origin of the Jewish and Arab peoples. The writer thus calls our attention to this missing encounter between two half-brothers, a mythical occurrence which still looms large over the current political conflicts.

As Yehoshua wrote, *Mr. Mani* not only analyzes the historical moments when the opportunity to effect such reconciliation between "half-brothers" was missed, but also intends to emancipate us — by means of catharsis — from the foundation myth of the *Akedah*, the ambiguity of which is singled out by Yehoshua as the source of so much evil, also because — as previously hinted — tradition identifies Mount Moriah, where the sacrifice of Isaac presumably took place, with the Jerusalem hill on which Solomon's Temple was built, and on which both the al-Aqsa Mosque and the Dome of the Rock rise, since this is a sacred place for Arabs, too. Given these facts, it is easy to assess what enormous symbolic power the myth of *Akedah* has, and it is far from surprising that Yehoshua has declared.

> through this novel I wanted to liberate (such an awful presumption) our collective ego from this momentous, powerful, and terrible myth that hovers so portentously over our history and culture. Here is a decisive fact — we built our temple, our holy of holies at the place connected to this appalling story. I wanted to free myself from the myth by bringing it to full realization.[19]

In other words, through *Mr. Mani*, Yehoshua tried to overcome the idea of a covenant between God and the Jewish people as based on the ambiguity of an incomplete gesture. After asserting that "blind loyalty of [Abraham's] kind has subjected humanity to its most horrendous atrocities," the author refutes the intepretation of the Akedah as "a warning to Abraham to abandon the practices of the idolaters who did sacrifice their children," since God actually praises Abraham for his readiness to sacrifices Isaac, without ever reproaching him "for mistaking the essence of the new God he chose."[20]

Yehoshua does not simply criticize the moral validity of *Akedah*, but as a secular thinker he also formulates a hypothesis to explain in anthropological terms how this myth originated. Abraham would have staged the sacrifice to instil Isaac with the idea that he owed his survival to God, in his effort to ensure that his son did not abandon the new faith he had embraced. According to Yehoshua, this might well explain the expression "*Pakhad Yitzhak*—Isaac's dread."[21] Yehoshua's determination to deconstruct the Bible myth is complete, but the political aims of this ideological move—which is substantiated in *Mr. Mani*—remain to be explored.

Adam Katz remarks that Yehoshua considers the *Akedah* as "a symptom of the 'neurotic' condition of exile"[22]—a myth that is deeply linked to the anomalous circumstances in which the Jewish people survived through the centuries in a condition of *diaspora*, identifying *faith* and *genealogy* as the defining factors of its identity regardless of place.[23] This aspect of Jewish identity has been analyzed by Yehoshua in a controversial essay where he explores the fear of persecution that accompanied the Jews for thousands of years, finding its roots in such an early document as the "Book of Esther," which was written centuries before the birth of Christ.[24] In addition, the writer relates the lack of universalism that marks the Jewish religion precisely to the *Akedah*, claiming that Abraham did not regard the new monotheistic religion he had created as addressed to the whole of humanity, but to a particular family, within which—moreover—a cruel selection was operated between Isaac and Ishmael, Jacob and Esau.[25]

Yehoshua not only claims that right from its inception, the Jewish religion is marked by "exclusion," but he associates the culture of diaspora to another aspect of the Bible myth—the Babylonian captivity. What early Jewish history produces is a flexible identity, which enables Jews to survive everywhere, but which also engenders anxiety in Gentiles. Needless to say, Yehosua's aim is not to "justify" anti-Semitism, which he deems as a severe form of cultural deviance, but to understand its roots.

The author regards a liberal form of secular Zionism as the way to cope with this evil. He advocates a form of identity that is related to the land, and in a recent interview he has reaffirmed his conviction that "he owes his own identity to being Israeli, not to Judaism or religion."[26] In another interview Yehoshua has stated that due to the Diaspora the Jews were forced to base their identity on mythology — from the escape from Egypt to the destruction of the Temple — rather than history. Only in the 20th century, after regaining their language and land, have they been able to overcome the fixity of myth in order to face the complexities of history.[27]

As we can see, Yehoshua intends to contribute to this transition of Israel from myth to history. To this end, the writer resolutely distances himself from the "exclusivist" tendencies of a certain Zionism, that is, from every temptation of ethnic purity, conversely regarding the return of the Jews to their land as inextricably associated with their relations with Palestinians.[28] The fusional attitude of Yosef Mani — who constructs Palestinians as Jews who are unconscious of being such — is rooted in the ideological stance of the Canaanite thinkers such as Ben-Gurion and Ben-Zvi, who regarded Palestinian Arabs as "converted descendants of Jews who had remained devoted to the land after the destruction of the Second Temple."[29] While, according to Canaanites, the Arabs of Palestine privileged their loyalty to the land, the Jews chose to be loyal to their faith, losing their contact with the native soil. "Yet now we torture — as Yehoshua remarks — our brothers of old with the afflictions of the occupation."[30] Yehoshua is clearly interested in the symbolic value of the Canaanite theory as an ideological tool supporting a precise political project — the withdrawal of Israelis from most of the occupied lands, the creation of two states and the recognition of an international status to Jerusalem.[31]

Looking for a Father

Having delineated the symbolic architecture and the political message of *Mr. Mani*, I will now analyze the first two dialogues. In the opening conversation Hagar Shilo (whose name is in itself redolent of myth) addresses her mother, Ya'el. Hagar — whose father died in the Six-Day War, when she was a child — attends the university in Tel Aviv, while her mother, who has never remarried, works in a kibbutz. On December 31, 1982, Hagar pays a visit to her mother to tell her that she is pregnant by a young man whose name is Efrayim Mani. The novel therefore opens while the First Lebanon War is being fought. Although this event is in the background, Yehoshua lays great emphasis on it as "a moment at which Israel's founding values were in danger of being ruthlessly subverted."[32] Efrayim has left for the Lebanon front, and since he has repeatedly tried to contact his father, without succeeding, he asks Hagar to pay him a visit.

Thus begins a relation that proves truly important for Hagar, whose mother has often teased her because in her life she kept looking for a substitute of her dead father. Ya'el is a modern woman, who is indifferent to religion and interested in psychoanalytic theories, and she interprets her daughter's behavior as the result of this original trauma. Hagar repeatedly rings at the door of Mr. Mani, but she gets no answer, and when she finally gains access to the flat thanks to a trick, the phone rings. While Mr. Mani is answering, the girl is free to explore the flat, and in the room of his recently deceased mother she sees a stool and a noose. Hagar is terrified at the idea that Mr. Mani intends to commit suicide, perhaps due to his solitude, but we know that the shadow of the *Akedah* looms over the Manis. Hagar feels both the duty and the right to save Mr. Mani in the name of the child she is bearing and of whose existence she informs him.

Although Hagar is not really pregnant, as she later realizes, when Efrayim comes back from the front she sleeps with him again in an attempt to bear a child. Yet, when Efrayim discovers that Hagar is pregnant, he would like to draw back, and it is only due to the intervention of his father that he agrees to acknowledge the child as the latest of the Manis. Although Efrayim is a reluctant father who does not marry Hagar and chooses to study in Great Britain, Mr. Mani repeatedly visits Hagar and her mother at the kibbutz, and even develops a feeling for Ya'el. Hagar has not only found a substitute for her dead father, but it is because of this father figure that she has taken the path of motherhood, since it was her desire for a father that made her wish to conceive.

These complex family links mark in various ways every generation of the Mani family, but alongside the motif of paternity other elements recur from episode to episode, associating distant events. Apparently unmeaningful details such as the snow that repeatedly falls on Jerusalem, the "doll of a Turkish dancer with shiny pants and a fez on her head"[33] that resurfaces in various sections of the book, or the eyeglasses that Efrayim loses at the front in the first dialogue (while in the second dialogue it is a Nazi soldier who loses his own) point to the underlying links that unite the Manis not only to their kin but also to distant persons, even to their enemies.

Escaping from History

This is apparent in the second conversation, which is set in August 1944, during World War II. This section of the novel is marked by the beauty of the Cretan landscape, which contrasts with the ugliness and debasement of war, and draws the protagonist into a time that is antecedent to history. It is on a hill that the conversation between Egon Bruner and his grandmother Andrja Sauchon takes place. Andrja is the widow of an important admiral and since she has not seen her grandson for more than three years, she has found a way to pay him a visit on military ground. Egon is actually not her true grandson, but a sort of adoptive son, whose function is to replace another Egon, whom Andrja and her husband, Werner, had many years before, and who died in World War I. Replicating the Bible story of Abraham and Hagar, Admiral Sauchon resorted to intercourse with a servant girl — Mariette Bruner — to provide his wife Andrja, who was too old to conceive, with another child.

Yehoshua invites us to read Egon's experience in Crete with the Greek myth of Daedalus and Icarus in mind. When Egon — who has been selected as a stretcher-bearer due to his short-sightedness — is parachuted onto the isle of Crete with a stretcher on his shoulders, his commander compares him to Icarus, adding: "But don't forget, Bruner, that your wings are made of steel and won't melt in the sun like his..."[34] This reference to myth triggers Egon's return to Cretan antiquity, which offers Egon a way to escape from the brutality and uselessness of war, as well as from the drive to death that echoes in military slogans: *"Thou shalt not surrender, thy badge of honour is victory or death."*[35]

Crete and the classical world help Egon refute the suicidal destiny both his country and his family have prepared for him. Right from the beginning, we suspect that in the eyes of Andrja the second Egon has to follow the "heroic" destiny of the first. The novel even leads us to think that Andrja actually hates the boy, who is still alive unlike her real son. Indeed, the reason why Andrja arrives on the island where her grandson has been stationed for years — far from the places where danger and glory irradiate their sinister glow — is to bring an order that destines the soldier to the Russian front. Yet, Egon rebels against this death sentence, saving his life thanks to his lucid folly, a paradoxical logic by means of which he strives to overcome the dominant mental structures resting on Nazi ideology.

The two main problems Egon faces are his country's relentless annexation of new territories and its hatred toward Jews. Drawing on the teachings he received from his professor of Greek and Latin, Egon interprets the expansionism of Germany as the aberrant manifestation of a pure desire to revert to classical roots — the same desire which in the century of *Aufklärung*, the German Enlightenment, animated a scholar such as Johann

Winckelmann. Thus Crete becomes the destiny of Egon, who reverses Icarus's myth, surviving the massacre that is in store for his companions thanks to the wind that pushes his parachute far from its target, due to the stretcher he is bearing. Before touching the ground, Egon loses his glasses, but this physical impairment actually coincides with the acquisition of a deeper insight.

In this suspended condition, Egon — who is imbued with the myths of Aryanism — realizes that the deepest dream of the German nation is not only "to drive south" to ancient Hellas, but more precisely "*to exit from history* by hook or by crook, if not forwards then backwards."[36] While most of Egon's compatriots seem bent on escaping from history through a future of death and destruction, Egon aims to bring the German quest to its logical end, by rejoining a time before history.

Paradoxically, he is helped in his itinerary of self-discovery and salvation by a Jew, who will show him the entrance to the Cretan labyrinth, which in these pages is a synonym of safety, while those who abandon Crete are all bound to die, including Andrja. When Egon, walking without his glasses, reaches the palace of Knossos, he meets a man whose profession as a tour guide to the ruins qualifies him for the role of Daedalus in the mythical pattern underlying this episode. The man is actually Yosef Mani, who in the next section of this backward-moving novel appears as the early–20th-century advocate of the pacific coexistence of Israelis and Palestinians under two flags. The eccentric character found refuge in Crete together with his son Efrayim — a fair-haired youth whose presence in the genealogical tree of the Manis suffices in itself to question the concept of genealogy, hinting at non-biological paternity.

To save his son, Yosef gives himself up as a hostage while Efrayim goes home to look for a pair of glasses for Egon. In the meantime Yosef, who speaks both English and German, transports Egon into the past of Knossos, a palace which bears no sign of fortifications and in the frescoes of which there are no weapons, except for a ritual "double-bladed axe."[37] Yosef dies during the night — as if "he needed to atone for some old feeling of guilt, or perhaps to pass it on to me, so that I would have pity on his family..."[38] as Egon subsequently meditates. Mani's father dies to save his son, offering himself as a scapegoat, but he also plays a crucial role in Egon's life, showing him a way out of history, by underlining the fact that in ancient Crete there were no Gods; otherwise the people who lived there "would have learned to write about them...."[39] Thus Egon may envisage the return to a past that preceded the great monotheistic religions.

Together with Yosef Mani, another father figure tightens the knot that binds Egon to Crete. While on his death bed, the German commander who described Egon as a novel Icarus points to him with an ambiguous gesture, half protection and half accusation, which marks him as a deserter. Egon is imprisoned, and in the following months — also thanks to his new glasses — he becomes impregnated with the landscape that is framed by his cell window. In the course of his meditations, Egon understands that the people he met in the ruins were Jews, and once free he starts looking for Efrayim, whose very presence in Crete he regards as a threat: "How could we possibly purify ourselves in the ancient womb of our ancestors [...] with a lot of beastly Jews running around and demanding with their typical insolence to be our partners here too, to share our most primeval myths..."[40]

The Other Within

Egon's dream of a return to the origins is "polluted" by the presence of *otherness* as embodied by the Jew. When Egon breaks at night into the home of the Manis, with his machine gun pointed at them, and abruptly asks Efrayim if he is a Jew, Mani's surprising answer is: "I was Jewish, but I am not anymore... I've cancelled it..."[41] Far from being perceived by the German soldier as a stratagem, this declaration convinces Egon, who is strangely fascinated by it. The episode marks the beginning of a reflection on identity that leads Egon to deconstruct some of the fundamental assumptions of the Nazi regime, starting from the biological interpretation of the concept of race, as hereditary factor. On the other hand, Egon develops an unorthodox concept of race, which he regards as an "allegorical reference" to *nature*: "And what is nature if not character, both human and national, which can be described and changed... Why, didn't Hitler himself speak of *the danger of the Jew in each one of us?*"[42]

After refuting the idea of a biological distinction between races, Egon starts seeing a specularity between Jews and Germans, and we discover that he also toys with the idea of annulling his own national identity: "Suppose there's another Judgement Day, Grandmother, and they'll want to make us pay like after the first war [...] We too will be able to say then, 'We were Germans but we are not anymore ... we've cancelled it...'"[43]

These words are possibly meant by Yehoshua also as a hint at the process of self-criticism on which postwar Germany embarked to elaborate the past and assess the guilt of the fathers, but within the novel they first and foremost express the lucid folly of Egon, who is caught between Nazi ideology and alternative categories of thought. Dissociating identity from biology to consider it as a cultural construct, Egon concludes that a Jew's identity "can exist purely in his own mind, which is why there is reason to believe it can be cancelled there too...."[44] When the Nazis start to search houses for Jews, Egon feels it is the right time to test this theory and also Efrayim's good faith, but he discovers that behind the house of the Mani, a donkey is ready for flight. The equation is simple — if Efrayim flees, he is a Jew, but Egon wants to try him, thus he shoots the donkey and leaves. When he later comes back, Efrayim is still there, while his wife and son have fled, and Efrayim explains that he could not oblige his son to annul his identity, as he had done, since only an adult can make such a choice.

Mani has renounced Jewishness as an individual sacrifice, to ensure that his son may go on living. Efrayim's progeny is not involved in this choice. The pact with God is safe thanks to this strategy. As a result, Egon arrests Efrayim not as a Jew but as somebody who has helped a Jewish woman and child to escape. Efrayim is shut in prison and meet his death on a boat full of Jews which is sunk by the English on the way to Greece, thus becoming yet another Icarus, who drowns in the sea while he is leaving Crete, but he has succeeded in saving his son.

Egon also manages to escape death, since he destroys the order of transfer his grandmother has brought with her, actually condemning him to death on the eastern front. Egon is possibly the most ambivalent character in the novel since he cultivates a personal form of madness that on the one hand alerts him to the collective madness of Nazism, but on the other also prompts him to hate Mani's wife and son, since they belong to a world from which he is ultimately excluded, to the point that he cannot bear "the thought that we'll soon have to leave this place for the swamps and the fog again, and the *they* will continue to look out at this brilliant bay through these ancient, enchanting olive trees."[45]

In a dense essay, Gilead Morahg highlights the courageous political vision that Yehoshua conveys through *Mr. Mani*, where an implicit parallel is drawn between Efrayim Mani, the Israeli soldier we meet in the first conversation while he is fighting in Lebanon, and Egon, the Nazi soldier who is stationed in Crete. The involvement of both characters in occupying forces contrasts with their humanistic background and their humanitarian drive (both perform medical duties). Moreover, Egon's dream to revert to a mythic classical origin paradoxically alludes to the promised land of Zionism, under the sign of a "mythic redemption."[46] As Morahg underlines, the ideological product of this dangerous illusion is a refusal of the other, "an ethos of exclusionary nationalism."[47] Seen in this light, the second section of the novel is a commentary on the background of the previous conversation and works as "an extended exploration of the consequences of Israel's transformation into a nation of conquerors with an evolving culture of occupation."[48]

Egon's concept of identity is pitted against the tension towards otherness that marks the two Yosef Manis — the 20th-century prophet of the two-state solution of the Palestine question, and his 19th-century ancestor, the son of Avraham and his sacrificial victim, who is able to imagine a multiethnic national container whose cohesive factor is place, regardless of the ethnic, religious and linguistic belonging of those who inhabit it. As Morahg remarks, the position of the second Yosef on the Arab-Israeli question "is closest to Yehoshua's own belief."[49] Although I agree with this, I also wish to underline that when Yehoshua was asked what character in *Mr. Mani* most resembles him, he answered that his point of view coincided with that of no character, for a writer must be "flexible, open to changes, mobile."[50]

These considerations bring us back to the *complexity* of this novel, whose aim is to "dislocate" our mind, undermining easy certainties. As Arthur J. Band claims, Yehoshua aims to deconstruct the traditional view of history — as collective and continuous — by portraying individuals who strive to pursue "a degree of personal fulfilment and self-understanding" within "historical circumstances beyond their control or comprehension."[51] Contrasting the suffering of single human beings with the ahistoricity of myth and the crystallized great narratives of written history, the author invites us to conceive cultural and political containers that are open to difference and change.

In *Mr. Mani* Yehoshua takes full advantage of the novelist's prerogative to investigate those contradictory and magmatic dimensions of the individual and collective psyche which can be best captured by means of symbols, without renouncing the opportunity to utilize fiction as an instrument of critical thought in the defense of "world civilization," which both embraces and transcends national perspectives. Morahg puts this concept in a nutshell when he writes that Yehoshua insists "on the ability of literary art to imbue the mysterious with meaning."[52] In so doing, this difficult, engaged and daring novel invites us to reassess the conflicts of our present by looking backward, toward those religious myths that — due to their unquestionable status as religious "truths" — have contributed to the formation of a collective "political unconscious."[53] Only by investigating our attitude to this deeply sedimented layer of cultural assumptions based on "revelation" can we hope to achieve transcultural understanding and to fashion a new planetary ecumene.

4

Ian McEwan, *Atonement* (2001)

The late-19th-century aesthetic of impressionism, the development of psychology and psychoanalysis, and the philosophy of Bergson are just some of the factors that helped change the coordinates of fiction, in preparation for the advent of modernism. Characters became more complex, sometimes obscure, as writers attempted to render their unconscious, thanks to Freudian slips or corporeal clues. The refusal of the traditional omniscient narrator produced texts whose ambiguity and openness were structural. Thanks to a sophisticated use of voice and gaze — from first person narration to free indirect speech and interior monologue — authors offered unreliable or conflicting versions of stories whose essence was virtually unattainable. Instead of achieving a stable interpretative goal, readers fought with ambivalent texts that mirrored the complexity of human relations, perceptions and language. Ford Madox Ford's *The Good Soldier* (1915) is an emblem of this experimentation with subjectivity. In this drawing-room epic, Ford — who was indebted to the sublime uncertainties of James's characters — turned adultery into a pretext to meditate on the impossibility of knowing. Katherine Mansfield's stories — with their virtuosic use of limited point of view — are also typical of the transition between impressionism and the modernist aesthetics of Virginia Woolf and James Joyce.

Although the crisis of realism — that is to say, the refusal of an unproblematic representation of the real — was apparent already in the first half of the 20th century, postmodernism further eroded the coordinates of realism, playing with language's power to create other worlds, but also to deconstruct them from inside. Suffice it to think of John Fowles's *The French Lieutenant's Woman* (1969) with its alternative endings and its repeated authorial intrusions. Fowles's omniscient third-person narrator intertwines his pseudo-realistic narrative with passages where he addresses readers in the first person to reflect on the rules of the game they are playing.

Readers thus learn that what they have just read has happened only in the mind of the main character, and are reminded of the importance of story telling as a self-questioning activity that may actually shape their future, for we unceasingly "screen in our minds hypotheses about how we might behave, about what might happen to us."[1] Elsewhere readers are told that a character who is sitting in a train and staring at the hero is actually the author, who is uncertain about the fate of his creature and settles the question by spinning a florin into the air.[2] Postmodernist authors are not satisfied with building up an illusion of reality. They need to make readers critically aware of the rules and urges that underlie novel-writing as a cultural practice.

These premises help us understand the sophisticated structure of *Atonement* (2001), where McEwan revisits early–20th-century novels with an attitude that differs both from the mimetic concerns of pastiche and from the critical irony of parody. Indeed, McEwan rediscovers intertextuality as a means to achieve metatextuality, that is to say, to meditate on writing intended as an ethical act and to stress the relation between imagination, reality and responsibility. In this text McEwan explores how stories — both those we read and those we "write," also in our inner mind — generate meanings which have a vital impact on our lives. Of course the way we shape our (life) stories has much to do with conventions that are culturally transmitted. This is why the author has been accused by some of looking backward to the past and has been commended by others, such as Geoff Dyer, for his ability to transport the past into the future.[3] As Dyer writes while introducing us to this highly self-conscious novel, which sharply contrasts with the author's earlier gripping manner: "*Atonement* does not feel, at first, like a book by McEwan. [...] Various characters come and go but the novel, at this point, seems populated mainly by its literary influences."[4]

The Dangers of the Imagination

The volume opens with a citation from Jane Austen's *Northanger Abbey* (1818), a parody of late–18th-century gothic novels that has the value of an ironic apologue on the power of the imagination and on the ensuing dangers. Austen's young heroine is a passionate reader of Ann Radcliffe and interprets reality through the filter of these books. Therefore she is ready to consider a secluded house as a site of mystery and a man of daunting personality as a villain. When she is invited to spend a few days at Northanger Abbey, the country house where a friend of hers lives, together with her brother and father, who is a widower, Catherine Morland incurs a series of misunderstandings, for she regards herself as the heroine of a gothic novel. In her self-appointed mission to uncover dark secrets, she even comes to believe that the master of the house has actually killed his wife, but all's well that ends well, and Catherine finally marries the young man she loves.

This intertextual opening prepares us for a certain kind of story, and when we become acquainted with the young protagonist of McEwan's book — Briony Tallis, who is 13 in 1935 and who has just written a play entitled *The Trials of Arabella*—we expect to see her entangled in a broil. We guess that her love for literature and her childish naivety will lead her to misinterpret reality, but with what results? The first part of *Atonement* develops this premise in a mathematical way. It reads almost like a pastiche of modernist novels, for it is through the eyes of different characters that we are shown the small events that take place in the Tallises' country house, and McEwan goes to great length to underline the divergence between the various perspectives.

What strikes us at first is the psychological construction of characters, notably of Briony, a thoughtful and solitary child who is endowed with a lively imagination that she does not know how to control. Briony loves secrets, be they connected with the small tin box she conceals under a floorboard, with her locked diary or with the ciphered writing she utilizes when she fills her notebook. Briony, however, has no real secret to hide, and therefore resorts to fancy. Moreover, Briony has a methodical personality, and her passion for tidiness manifests itself through her taste for miniaturization, which makes her feel she can control reality, as when she plays with the animals of her toy farm.

Although Briony would like to fit every aspect of the surrounding world into her scheme, disorder irrupts into her life due to the divorce between Uncle Cecil and Aunt Hermione, who has fled to Paris with her lover. This is why the three children of the couple—the twins Jackson and Pierrot (who are nine) and their elder sister Lola (a 15-year-old girl whose name reminds us of Lolita)—find refuge at Aunt Emily's. The novel opens on a situation of great expectations, with Briony who is waiting for the cousins to arrive. The girl is not only indifferent to their problems, but she has set her mind on having them perform in the theatrical piece she has written.

It is important to underline that in the past Briony has tried her hand only at short stories and that she has been led to attempt the polyphony of drama precisely because of her cousins. Her life, which has been previously declined in the singular, enters the domain of plurality, but many a problem will stem from this. Briony is thinking only of *The Trials of Arabella*, which she intends to stage in order to celebrate the arrival of her brother Leon from London. This comedy — ending with a marriage — is a message addressed to Leon, for Briony would like him to spend more time at home with her. Arabella is, after all, Briony herself, and Leon is her hero. The child's affections are circumscribed by the family circle, and everything that may endanger it is regarded by her with hostility. Yet, Briony has to face the ineptitude of Jackson and Pierrot, who are incapable of play, and the sophisticated hypocrisy of Lola, who is always ready to manipulate others.

With the second chapter we take on the point of view of Briony's elder sister, Cecilia, who has recently found it difficult to get along with Robbie, with whom she used to play as a child. The son of the Tallises' cleaner, Robbie has just returned from Cambridge with a degree in English, thanks to the financial help of Cecilia's father, but has decided to give up literature for a medical career. As Daniel Mendelsohn remarks, there is a bitter irony in McEwan's portrait of Robbie as "someone who naïvely believes in facts,"[5] for his destiny will be ultimately decided by fancy.

The tension between Robbie and Cecilia reaches its climax when she approaches a fountain to fill a vase with water, and Robbie, in the awkward attempt to help her, breaks it, causing two pieces to fall into the water. At that point Cecilia, without articulating a word, takes her clothes off and dives to retrieve them. The Meissen porcelain is doubly precious since it is the only memory of Uncle Clem, who died in World War I.[6] Behind the squabbles and the embarrassment that oppose Cecilia to Robbie, there is an undercurrent of eroticism, although they are not yet aware of it. A few pages later, however, readers discover that Briony witnessed the scene from a window and that at first she interpreted it as a marriage proposal. Although Briony is ready to grasp the romantic side of a love story that crosses class boundaries, subsequent events prove incoherent with the screenplay she has been mentally writing:

> What was less comprehensible, however, was how Robbie imperiously raised his hand now, as though issuing a command[...]. At his insistence she was removing her clothes, and at such speed. She was out of her blouse, now she had let her skirt drop to the ground and was

stepping out of it, while he looked on impatiently, hands on hips. What strange power did he have over her. Blackmail? Threats?[7]

After Cecilia, wearing only her underwear, has dived into the water, Briony wonders: "The sequence was illogical — the drowning scene, followed by a rescue, should have preceded the marriage proposal."[8] This passage could have been conceived for a manual on creative writing, to illustrate the use of point of view, since the inferences that Briony makes from her observations are all wrong. It is actually Cecilia who is enraged, while it is Robbie who suffers her revenge, although Briony — according to literary stereotypes — imagines Robbie as imperious and Cecilia as passive. The child is jealous of the intimate relation that she perceives between Robbie and Cecilia, as she is jealous of the girls who keep Leon away from her. To make the situation even more complex, we subsequently learn — through Robbie's memories — that three years before Briony threw herself into the water of a canal to be saved by him, and immediately afterwards confessed that she loved him. This episode inspired Briony to write a story where Robbie is portrayed as a humble woodcutter and she is depicted as a princess. Briony's attitude therefore results from a bundle of motivations and moods, including a childish infatuation for Robbie.[9]

Eroticism and Forgery

The hours that precede the summer night — when an involuntary "tragedy of errors" is staged — are charged with erotic tensions that the adolescent characters still perceive in an indistinct way. They are victims rather than protagonists of this burgeoning passion, which frightens them and takes on incestuous connotations. McEwan suggests that the first physical attraction is that which links us to our family members — sisters, brothers, mothers and fathers — and the discovery of the other sex proceeds from this originary drive. Lola, for instance, is intrigued by the arrival of Paul Marshall — a friend of Leon who happens to be a magnate of chocolate — and does not resist the idea of entering his room to have a look around: "On her way out of the room, Lola noticed by the bed a masculine-looking suitcase of tan leather and heavy straps and faded steamer labels. It reminded her vaguely of her father, and she paused by it, and caught the faint sooty scent of a railway carriage."[10] Lola feels disturbed by that object, which puts her in touch with the bodily dimension of both her father and Leon. We should not forget that her parents have just separated and that she is traumatized.

On the other hand, Paul falls asleep immediately after his arrival at the Tallises' and has an incestuous dream in which "his young sisters had appeared, all four of them, standing around his bedside, prattling and touching and pulling at his clothes. He woke, hot across his chest and throat, uncomfortably aroused."[11] It is in the aftermath of this unsettling dream that Paul hears the voices of Lola and her brothers, and after entering the nursery realizes "that the girl was almost a young woman, poised and imperious."[12]

After skillfully delineating the transition between the dream and the erotic encounter, McEwan went on to describe the first interaction between Lola and Paul, evoking the theme of "forgery" which pervades the first part of the novel. The vase Robbie has broken is after all a fake, since it is an 18th-century chinoiserie, and the fountain that provides a background for this little drama is but a copy of the Triton Fountain in Piazza Barberini in Rome. Even the neoclassical temple that decks a little island in the park lake is an architectural pastiche. It is moreover the last relic of the Adam mansion that was burnt in 1880 and on the ruins of which the Victorian neo-baronal country house where the Tallises live was raised. Forgery, or better the imitation of a prestigious model, also marks Lola and Paul, who look for an easy way to acquire cultural capital. Thus when Paul compliments her on her trousers, Lola tells him that she got them at Liberty's on a day she and her mother went to see *Hamlet*, although in fact on that day they saw a matinée pantomime and Lola stained her frock with a drink.

> It was fortunate for her that he too had neither read nor seen the play, having studied chemistry. But he was able to say musingly, "To be or not to be."
> "That is the question," she agreed. "And I like your shoes."[13]

Their relation begins under the sign of mediocrity. Appearances prevail over substance. Paul and Lola, however, love indulging in platitudes, and when he explains that the surrogate (!) chocolate bar he will produce and sell to the army as a ration for the troops will be called *Army Amo*, she answers with worldly nonchalance by conjugating the Latin verb "Amo, amas, amat."[14]

In the meantime McEwan continues to play with his characters' perspective. A chapter is devoted to the perception of Briony's mother, Emily, who is often confined to bed because of her migraine, but who is also endowed with a subtle sensitivity, almost a sixth sense that enables her to guess what is happening elsewhere in the family house. And yet, Emily's faith in her omniscience is ungrounded, and later in the book Cecilia describes her mother as a weak creature, who is incapable of facing the hardships of life. What is certain, Emily will not succeed in preventing the incumbent catastrophe.

Soon the focalization is again on Briony, who has angrily realized that her play will not be staged that night. What she does not know is that other misadventures will take place. Let us leave Briony to her hatred for Lola and proceed to the next chapter, where Robbie is taking a bath and meditating on the events of that day. Robbie harbors a mixture of contrasting feelings. He is proud of his humble origin, but his pride is easily wounded. Moreover, he is convinced that Cecilia tried to humiliate him. Yet, inasmuch as that night he is expected to dine with the Tallises, Robbie decides to excuse himself by writing a letter, although he finds it hard to write because his formal message does not touch on the core of the problem—the sexual attraction he feels for Cecilia. Only after tinkering for a long time with the draft of a letter does Robbie acknowledge the powerful sexual drive that is at the heart of his awkward behavior toward the girl:

> Then, after a few moments' reverie, [...] he dropped forwards and typed before he could stop himself, "In my dreams I kiss your cunt, your sweet wet cunt. In my thoughts I make love to you all day long."[15]

Needless to say, Robbie rewrites his letter to Cecilia, but due to a Freudian slip he finally sends her the first version. What is more, he makes the fatal mistake of confiding the letter to Briony, whose uncontrollable curiosity pushes her to open it.

The events succeed one another with an increasing rhythm. Before dinner, Cecilia and Robbie have a first sexual encounter, which Briony witnesses unseen. Although the child does not entirely understand what is happening, this confirms her sensation of imminent danger. To make things more complicated, in the span of time before dinner a reversal of alliances takes place, due to the sly maneuvers of Lola, who cries on the shoulder of Briony, declaring that her brothers tortured her. Actually, Lola has had a first physical contact with Paul, but she does not know how to mask the marks she bears on her body. Lola is again associated with the instrumentality of lies. Briony not only believes Lola, who immediately achieves the literary status of a persecuted heroine, but chooses her as a confidant to share her secret concerning Robbie's letter. It is here that Lola defines Robbie as a "maniac,"[16] a hasty word that seals his fate.

Night into Nightmare

Everything is ready for the catastrophe. At the end of dinner the Tallises discover that Jackson and Pierrot have disappeared, succumbing to a series of trials too great for their strength—first the separation of their parents, then the punishments they suffered at their aunt's. A search squad is organized. The family spreads in the park to look for the children, but in the darkness a drama takes place in which Briony is involved as a spectator, actress and even authoress, although she does not have the least control of what is happening. When Briony hears Lola crying near the neoclassical temple, and sees a shadow fleeing from the place, she realizes that somebody has tried to rape her cousin, and the name of the culprit soon comes to her lips:

> Everything connected. It was her own discovery. It was her story, the one that was writing itself around her.
> "It was Robbie, wasn't it?"
> The maniac. She wanted to say the word.
> Lola said nothing and did not move.
> Briony said it again, this time without the trace of a question. It was a statement of fact. "It was Robbie."[17]

Michiko Kakutani insightfully defines *Atonement* as "a story about the destructive powers of the imagination."[18] Fiction has already prevailed over fact, and it is too late to avoid disaster. Evil has asserted itself through this unwilling but lethal deformation of the real. Briony has become a victim of her own delusion: she has no questions, but she is ready to provide answers. The following lines describe the ambiguous role of Lola, who is possibly unsure about the identity of her assailant, or perhaps knows all too well that it was Paul, but it is Briony herself who offers her the opportunity to lie, diverting suspicion onto the wrong person:

> Though she had not turned, or moved at all, it was clear that something was changing in Lola, a warmth rising from her skin and a sound of dry swallowing, a heaving convulsion of muscle in her throat that was audible as a series of sinewy clicks.
> Briony said it again. Simply. "Robbie."
> [...] At last Lola turned slowly to face her.
> She said, "You saw him."[19]

Lola's bodily reactions are revealing. At first this girl is the victim of an unforeseen situation, but soon she regains control and with her insinuating tone she strengthens her cousin in her conviction. In the following hours Lola does not even need to lie, for Briony is ready to do so in her place, volunteering herself as the witness of something she saw only in her mind, and thus destroying the love and life of Cecilia and Robbie. This is the immense crime Briony will try to expiate throughout her life. The first part of the novel ends with Robbie's mother who cries desperately while the police van is carrying her son away.

War Hells

The following pages take us to France, during World War II, and exemplify McEwan's interest in the narration of historical events. The hell of war is seen through the eyes of Robbie, who has been freed from jail only to leave for the front, but who is determined to come back home to Cecilia, surviving through the horror that destiny has in store for him in Dunkirk. This section of the novel is a true piece of bravura. Instead of the emotionally charged impressionistic style of the previous chapters, we are offered a terse writing, in an attempt to obtain a powerful adhesion to the real. We are led into a world after the fall, in which the individual is superseded by the collective. Robbie is now wearing a uniform and thinks of his past in these terms: "It seemed another man's life to him now. A dead civilization. First his own life ruined, then everybody else's."[20]

Like other contemporary novels that deal with World War II, *Atonement* is rooted in the war experiences of the writer's father. As McEwan explained: "Many ex-servicemen have found it difficult or impossible to talk about their experiences of war. My father never had any such problems. [...] When I came to write *Atonement*, my father's stories, with automatic ease, dictated the structure."[21] Of course, dealing with events that had such a strong impact on the generation of one's parents implies "a weighty obligation to strict accuracy."[22]

The third part of the novel takes us into a different kind of hell — the hospital where Briony is serving as a nurse, ministering comfort to mutilated bodies and violated souls. Is this to be interpreted as a first form of atonement? Her scarce free time is devoted to writing, which is still her passion. All of a sudden, Briony is struck by an item in a newspaper: five years have elapsed since the events of that fatal night — we are now in 1940 — and Briony learns that Lola, who is twenty, is about to marry Paul. That Saturday morning Briony, after attending the marriage from the back of the church, goes to see her sister Cecilia, whom she has not seen for years, to tell her that she is ready to publicly acknowledge her mistake. Briony faces both Cecilia and Robbie, who has just come back from the front, and accepts their request to visit a lawyer and sign a declaration. Once Briony is out of her sister's house, she realizes with surprise that she is experiencing a condition of serenity, which is however tinged with sadness: "It was her sister she missed — or more precisely, it was her sister with Robbie. Their love. Neither Briony nor the war had destroyed it."[23]

Criminal and Mourner

But is it true that neither Briony nor the war have proved capable of destroying this great love? We discover this only in the last part of the book ("London, 1999"), which brings us to the present. While up

4. Ian McEwan, Atonement (2001)

to now events have been told by an impersonal narrator, now the narrative is in the first person. It is Briony herself who speaks to us on the morning of her 77th birthday to tell us a sad epilogue. She is affected by senile dementia, and the time she still has to atone for her crime is running out. Soon she will be no longer able to control either her language or her mind.

As regards Lola and Paul, who are now Lady and Lord Marshall, Briony met them a few days before. Once again Briony appeared on their path like the shadow of dark memories. Have their lives been haunted by those memories, or have they easily forgotten? Lord Marshall appears to have been involved in every sort of philanthropist activity, and Briony comments: "Perhaps he's spent a lifetime making amends. Or perhaps he just swept onwards without a thought, to live the life that was always his."[24] As in life, so in this novel, reality presents itself as liquid, and our judgments are based on appearances and inferences.

Let us go back to Briony's birthday. We discover that on that night a party will be held in her honor in the Tallises' former country house, which has been turned into a luxury hotel. On that occasion, Briony sees Pierrot, who has become an old man, while Jackson has died, and she is surrounded by their families, as well as by that of Leon. All the descendants of the protagonists of the fatal summer night are gathered for the performance of *The Trials of Arabella*. This is the surprise they have prepared for her. After the play, Briony retires to her room, but instead of sleeping she thinks of the past. Only now do we learn that to atone for the terrible crime of which she was guilty, she has kept writing and rewriting throughout her life a novel that tells those events:

> I've been thinking about my last novel, the one that should have been my first. The earliest version, January 1940, the latest, March 1999, and in between, half a dozen different drafts. The second draft, June 1947, the third ... who cares to know? My fifty-nine-year assignment is over. There was our crime — Lola's, Marshall's, mine — and from the second version onwards, I set out to describe it.[25]

Before publishing this confession, however, Briony will have to wait for the death of Paul and Lola — since from a legal point of view "You may only libel yourself and the dead."[26] The problem is that her life is approaching its end. Only now do we discover that what we read in the second part of the book is again only a story (a fiction within a fiction), which detaches itself from facts according to a law of compensation, since Robbie actually died of septicemia in 1940, and Cecilia was killed in the explosion of a bomb in the same year. Yet, Briony warmly defends her right to reunite the two lovers in this last version of her novel, disparaging the value of a realistic rendering of their life:

> What sense or hope of satisfaction could a reader draw from such an account? Who would want to believe that they never met again, never fulfilled their love? Who would want to believe that, except in the service of the bleakest realism? I couldn't do it to them. I'm too old, too frightened, too much in love with the shred of life I have remaining.[27]

The novel ends with a short circuit between facts and fiction. While in the past of Briony's childhood her imagination prevailed over truth, causing her crime, now that Briony is old her imagination has found a way to compensate for her loss by having the two lovers live together in the realm of the imaginary. Briony has the paradoxical, tragic status of criminal and mourner. She wrecked the life of Cecilia and Robbie, but she is also the one in whose hearts they still live.

We understand only at this stage many aspects of the book that seemed obscure, starting from the stylistic changes that mark its development and actually indicate the various stages in Briony's apprenticeship to writing. The first part of the novel is the product of a juvenile phase of experimentation, while the second and third are the expression of Briony's maturity as an authoress, and the fourth is an example of journal writing. After discovering that Briony has authored the book of which she is the main character, and which therefore acquires the character of a memoir, we are obliged to rethink the whole text not only in terms of contents, but also of form. We realize what a complex narrative strategy McEwan utilized. While the beginning of the novel is redolent of modernism, to introduce us to Briony's first narrative manner, the middle chapters trace her progress toward a more personal form of writing. This self-referential aspect of *Atonement*— which invites readers to peruse the text a second time in the light of the knowledge they have finally acquired — testifies to the technical mastery of McEwan's "late manner." *Atonement* is the work of a virtuoso, and in Frank Kermode words, "the best readers of this book might be Henry James and Ford Madox Ford."[28]

A Book on Books

With this novel on writing, McEwan showed us how the way of telling stories, of representing the world and the human, changed in the course of the 20th century. The intertextual game is here pervasive and goes well beyond the span of the conscious stylistic experiments Briony makes in the course of her career. The broken vase at the core of the scene between Cecilia and Robbie — a vase which is glued back together to simulate its integrity, but which will soon be reduced into fragments — reminds readers of the symbolic object at the heart of James's *The Golden Bowl* (1904).[29]

The summer ambience that marks the opening of the novel, to the background of an English country house, evokes the oppressive heat of the earlier summer L.P. Hartley recounted in *The Go-Between* (1953), which has various similarities with *Atonement*, as McEwan has acknowledged.[30] Both novels stage the conflict between love and class barriers, and in both the tragic climax is triggered by the contact between the sexuality of adults and the volatility of children. Leo, the young protagonist of Hartley's novel, is even more involved than Briony in the adult world that surrounds him. After being invited to spend his summer holidays in the country house of a schoolmate, Leo takes on the role of messenger between Marian, the daughter of the rich family that hosts him, and a man of inferior social condition. Unconscious of his role, but increasingly involved in this love triangle, for Marian has an official fiancé in addition to her secret lover, Leo finally helps to provoke a suicide. The result of this precocious experience of love and death — in which Leo plays at the same time the role of victim and of guilty party — is an emotional block of which the man remains prisoner throughout his life. The book is pervaded by a heartrending longing, an impossible nostalgia, due to the trauma that marked the young protagonist, causing a lack that can be filled only by an act of compassion in the present. Turning once more into a go-between, the protagonist has the chance to reunite what had previously been separated, both in the others and in himself, mending the thread that unites the present to the past, the adult to the child, and that harks back to the world before the fall.

Like *Atonement*, *The Go-Between* is a novel about guilt and redemption, but other similarities link the young protagonists of the two books. Like Briony, Leo courts secrets, through cryptography and a diary, which is protected by a lock, and like Briony Leo tries to impose his will on the world, in his case by means of the black magic he is convinced he can master. Both children trigger imaginative energies that they are not able to control. Briony's experiments with creative writing and Leo's experiments with black magic anticipate the sinister action they are both destined to exert on reality.[31]

Moreover both *The Go-Between* and *Atonement* connect individual and collective trauma to the act of bearing witness. Although the two world wars are largely absent from Hartley's 1953 novel, the main action of which is set in 1900, it is precisely against the specter of these two wars that the final meeting between Leo and an aged Marian takes place. Only now do readers know what message Marian wants Leo to carry to her grandchild — the only living member of her family and the fruit of her illegitimate love — and why Leo is the only person who can accomplish that task of love:

> 'But you can tell him, Leo, tell him everything, just as it was. Tell him that it was nothing to be ashamed of [...]. There was nothing mean or sordid in it, was there? and nothing that could possibly hurt anyone. We did have sorrows, bitter sorrows. Hugh dying, Marcus and Denys killed, my son Hugh killed, and his wife — though she was no great loss. But they weren't our fault — they were the fault of this hideous century we live in, which has denatured humanity and planted death and hate where love and living were.'[32]

The full list of *Atonement*'s literary referents is much longer, as Brian Finney reminds us.[33] McEwan himself has likened Briony to the young protagonist of James's *What Maisie Knew* (1897), commenting that like James he wished to analyze the dilemmas of the child utilizing the wider descriptive resources of an adult narrator[34] — hence his choice to have the story told by a mature Briony, who goes back to her childhood in an attempt to understand her unconscious motivations and to compare her point of view with those of the other actors in this family drama. Robbie has also been likened to Oliver Mellors, the gamekeeper in *Lady Chatterley's Lover* (1928) — a novel Robbie actually mentions — and to Leonard Bast in E.M. Forster's *Howard's End* (1910), while the attempted rape of Lola has reminded readers of Adela Quested's case in *A Passage to India* (1924).[35] McEwan has also drawn a parallel between the first part of *Atonement* and Virginia Woolf's modernist novels (we actually find Briony intent on reading *The Waves*, which was published in 1931), Rosamond Lehmann's *Dusty Answer* (1927) and Elizabeth Bowen's *The Heat of the Day* (1949).[36]

Despite this range of intertextual allusions, *Atonement* is far from an exercise in style, but a novel on the performative power of words, which are capable of making things happen in the real world.[37] Briony is trapped by the invasive vitality of her childish imagination, together with the mesmerizing power of the word *maniac*, which is recklessly pronounced by Lola. McEwan, however, offers us these pages as an act of faith in the redeeming power of words. By detaching themselves from reality, by turning into *lying* — as Wilde would say,[38] in the sense of story or affabulation — words are capable of hurting, but also of healing. The possible worlds they create are perhaps devoid of substance, and yet they are so important in restating our love for life against the devastating force of cynicism and disillusion.

5

W.G. Sebald, *Austerlitz* (2001)

Sebald has been aptly described as "a writer's writer."[1] His prose is dense and vaguely old-fashioned in its meditative elegance, in its love for details and analysis. This is particularly true for his last novel —*Austerlitz* (2001), to which several critical studies have been devoted, expressing admiration but also acknowledging its difficulty.[2] Although Sebald's slow-paced and complex writing may test readers' patience, it also invites them to adopt a critical stance, reflecting and commenting on the text. As Jens Brockmeier remarks, *"Austerlitz* demands a serious reader who follows attentively" not only "a meandering syntax without clear paragraph structure," but also "extensive accounts of very specific details that may or may not contribute to a labyrinthine plot, if we can call it a plot at all."[3]

Moreover, Sebald's works may induce an eerie feeling of melancholy and opaqueness. When I first read his novels, they made me feel vulnerable and devoid of a center, as if my reserves of energy and willpower had been sapped. I could not help identifying with his protagonists, who experience life as an effort to survive after catastrophe, and whose lack of roots entails a lack of future. This persistent aftertaste of alienation was far from pleasant, and I harbored some resentment towards Sebald. Yet, this saturnine mist slowly dispelled once my reading had sedimented and I started to rebuild upon the ruins. In the end I even developed a mixed feeling of affection and sad gratitude for this writer who dared approach the brink of the abyss, thereby instilling his readers with a memorial awareness that is a fundamental value in a post–Holocaust society.

Narratives of Exile

At the beginning of Sebald's books we find a variety of apparently heterogeneous materials — photographs of places, people, objects, but also maps, documents, postage stamps, entrance tickets.... These fragments of past lives and events are narrativised by the author, who commented: "It's one way of making obvious that you don't begin with a white page [...] You do have sources, you do have materials."[4] These words testify to the strong link Sebald pursued between his works and reality, in order to turn his narratives into ethical statements, albeit without sacrificing form. This is why Sebald refused documentary writing, which he regarded as "artless," while he aspired to write "something saturated with material but carefully wrought."[5]

The result is a hybrid text, in which fictional characters and events combine with elements pertaining to different discourses and literary genres. The first is *history writing*— from military to social and cultural history in all its facets. Hard facts are always there in Sebald's works, and we never lose touch with their painful reality, their ontological status as something that happened to our fellow human beings and whose effects still reverberate on our present despite the temporal distance that reassuringly situates them in the past. Artifacts attract Sebald's characters precisely as mediators of memory that bring them into contact with the past, which they find imperative to study. As Sebald claimed in an interview: "Well, the past is what we carry with us. If you want to know where you might be going or where you are likely to be going, you need to know the force lines of the past energies."[6] According to the author, only if you understand "what happened in the earlier part of this century, in the nineteenth and eighteenth century," can you realize that this is "part of your make-up" and that it will ultimately determine "where you will end up or where we will all end up."[7]

Life writing is another important element of Sebald's novels, which are focused on the destiny of single individuals, whose existence they follow before and after the catastrophe of persecution and war, delving into the paradoxical condition of survivors, who live "after an irreparable rupture,"[8] as Efraim Sicher writes. One should also mention the *travelogue*, which Sebald associated with exile, the concomitant issues of marginality and rootlessness, and the ensuing quest for identity. This quest is presented in *Austerlitz* as an alternative to suicide, a destiny that the unfortunate protagonists of Sebald's *The Emigrants* (1992) are unable to escape.[9] Lastly, these books are akin to the *memoir*, for the authorial narrator is omnipresent, either filtering events with his own subjectivity or as a recorder of testimony.

Photographs importantly establish yet another level of intra-textual dialogue.[10] In addition, the mingling of various *languages*— since the German text of *Austerlitz* is interspersed with sentences in French, English,[11] Dutch, Welsh and Czech — mirrors a condition of in-betweenness, calling our attention to the complex forms of belonging that mark the Jewish diaspora as well as the identities of exiles and expatriates.

This multi-layered, ambivalently referential prose embodies what Amir Eshel labels as "semidocumentary aesthetics,"[12] that is to say, the choice to comment on our "immediate historical pasts" not only by contextualizing those events into the wider time span and ideological framework of modernity at large, but also by exploring their significance through figurations. This strategy enables Sebald to connect both with the intellectual dimension of readers and with their emotions, establishing an affective circuit that turns the act of reading into a powerful form of experience. In Sebald's grave and pondering writing, places, people and events trace a design by establishing a network of associations without any explicit comments on the part of the narrator. While reading, we cannot help connecting and drawing inferences, and our growing feelings of uneasiness and oppression slowly take on a special value — not exactly penitential, but rather akin to the elaboration of mourning.

Sebald's life was very different from those of survivors such as Primo Levi and Jean Améry, who went through the horror of camps, bore witness to it and ultimately paid for their consciousness of evil with suicide. Sebald was born in Bavaria in 1944, and in 1966 expatriated to Great Britain, where he taught European literature until his death, in December 2001, due to a road accident. While his characters are often Jews who had to abandon Germany — or other European countries — during the war to avoid the horror of ethnic cleansing, his choice to abandon his native country was free and somehow "belated," but Sebald was definitely unwilling to take part in the collective process of removal of the past that in his eyes marked postwar Germany.

As the writer recounted, due to this "conspiracy of silence," he "had heard practically nothing about the history that preceded 1945" until he was 16 or 17, and it took him "years to find out what had happened."[13] Only when he moved to Great Britain in the 1960s did Sebald become fully conscious of the extent of the massacre and ethnic displacement that the Nazi regime had caused, since "you could grow up in Germany in the postwar years without ever meeting a Jewish person."[14] Once he was on

British soil, Sebald regained contact with that missing component of his native country, that ethnic minority that Germany had disastrously *othered* and persecuted.

Sebald's radical position as a cosmopolitan expatriate — whose "ideal station" would possibly be "a hotel in Switzerland"[15] — enabled him to turn the *heimlich* into the *unheimlich* (literally the *homely* into the *unhomely*), to take the necessary distance and thus see what had once been familiar through foreign eyes. With a highly symbolic gesture — which I am tempted to qualify as a ritual of purification — Sebald embraced the condition of exile that had been imposed on so many Jews and developed the sense of a mission. Writing simultaneously from inside and outside his home country and culture in *The Emigrants*, he explored the in-between position of those German Jews who belonged to that country and yet were construed as *foreign* to it by the Nazis. The author pursued this indirect inquiry into the Holocaust in *Austerlitz*, delving again into the experience of those who had escaped the horror and yet had lost their innocence. As Richard Eder comments, Sebald's determination to break the silence of individual and collective traumas in order to explore the labyrinths of memory turned the writer into a Proust whose madeleine is "poisoned."[16]

Architectures of Suffering

Austerlitz opens towards the end of the 1960s in Antwerp, where the narrator goes "partly for study purposes, partly for other reasons which were never entirely clear to me."[17] Right from the beginning, the actions of the two main characters — the authorial persona and the hero whose story he relates — are presented not as the result of their conscious agency, but as rooted in deeper drives, which moreover combine with an eerie series of coincidences. With marked indifference to the dictates of realism, in his depiction of both psychology and external circumstances, Sebald repeatedly crossed the border between verisimilitude and allegory, turning his characters into tropes and his plotline into a pattern of atonement.

Being plagued by a headache and by "uneasy thoughts,"[18] the narrator finds refuge first at the zoo and then at the Nocturama, where nocturnal animals can be observed in a simulation of their habitat. The living beings that are confined to this realm of inversion live the night during daytime and daytime during the night. The law of tourist attraction prevails over the natural principles of the cosmos, the rhythm of which is grotesquely parodied in this human-made environment. Here the splenetic gaze of the narrator attaches itself to a racoon who sits beside a little stream, "washing the same piece of apple over and over again, as if it hoped that all this washing [...] would help it to escape the unreal world in which it had arrived."[19] At the very beginning of the book, we have already come into contact with a dystopian setting that evokes the experience of concentration camps, which is here presented, however, only obliquely and retrospectively.

As Sebald made clear in an interview, he wished to avoid any melodramatic or sensational approach to "the horror of the Holocaust," which he compared to the head of the Medusa: "You carry it with you in a sack, but if you looked at it you'd be petrified."[20] This myth has been recently explored by Adriana Cavarero, who regards the severed head of Medusa as embodying a horror that is revealed in its effects, since it points both to the dismemberment of the body and to its ontological uniqueness. Reminding us that the term *Gorgon*, which derives from the Sanskrit *garg*, alludes to the emission of a guttural sound, Cavarero remarks that the best-known visual representations of this howl — such as Caravaggio's Medusa — actually render only a heartrending silence.[21] The same stifled cry rises from the camps, which were intended to deprive individuals of their humanity. Exhausted by hardships and privations, "those who have seen the Gorgon represent a degenerated form of helplessness; they can no longer even feel the hurt of the *vulnus* that nevertheless continues to be inflicted on them with methodical perseverance."[22] These are the *Muslims* Primo Levi described as beings who are beyond life, although they have not yet met their death. Sebald deliberately avoided depicting these realities frontally, but while we read *Austerlitz* we feel that horror is never far away, also because that horror — like a radioactive substance — has contaminated the future as well as the past of Europe.

It is from the past that we approach the events of the mid–20th-century. The narrator's itinerary in Antwerp takes him from the Nocturama to the central station, which was inaugurated in 1905. King Leopold of Belgium intended this majestic and bizarre building as a celebration of the new status of colonial power his small country had achieved. In the mind of the narrator, who revisits the memories of that journey years later, the Nocturama and the station strangely coalesce. Moreover, like the animals he saw imprisoned in a reversed world, the railway passengers also appear to him as "somehow miniaturized,"[23] due to the oversized character of the building. With a further leap, the narrator cannot help thinking of these scattered travelers — who wear "the same sorrowful expression as the creatures in the zoo"— as survivors: "the last members of a diminutive race which had perished or had been expelled from its homeland."[24] Coherently with the associative logic that characterizes the novel, the scene is ready for the entrance of the protagonist — Austerlitz, who uncannily resembles, due to his blonde hair, "the German hero Siegfried."[25]

The meeting aptly takes place in the Salle des pas perdus — a place of transit which is framed by a luxurious architectural shell, whose vaguely incongruous decorations exalt "the deities of the nineteenth century — mining, industry, transport, trade and capital."[26] Under the inquiring gaze of Austerlitz — who is presented as a sort of Walter Benjamin[27] or Michel Foucault, always intent on scrutinizing the ideological framework of public architecture — the station takes on a dystopian character despite its opulence. Austerlitz's critical attention is attracted, for instance, by the central position the clock has within the building — a position from which "the movements of all travellers could be surveyed,"[28] while travelers "had to look up at the clock and were obliged to adjust their activities to its demands."[29] This detail enables Austerlitz to call the narrator's attention to the importance that time took on within bourgeois society, in connection with the advent of the railway system.

The standardization of time is indeed a concomitant aspect of the technological progress that in the course of the 19th century enabled humanity to dominate distances by means of railways, setting the ground for 20th-century globalization. Time and space are inseparable in *Austerlitz*, where places are interpolated both with the other places a character has visited — therefore with individual memory — and with the past events those places have witnessed, that is to say, with cultural memory.[30] Thus private and public, individual experience and collective events incessantly intertwine in the book.

The meeting in Antwerp station of the narrator and Austerlitz — two figures whose affinities become increasingly apparent, although they never fully superimpose — marks the beginning of a double itinerary. On the one hand, a counter-history of European civilization between the 19th and 20th centuries is traced, showing the inhuman face of modernity and progress with a Kafkaesque flair for absurdity. On the other, readers are drawn toward the inner dimension of the hero. This conflation of public and private, of rational and emotional, is apparent in passages such as the following, whose full import becomes apparent only when readers come to know the whole story of Austerlitz:

> Austerlitz spoke at length about the marks of pain which, as he said he well knew, trace countless fine lines through history. In his studies of railway architecture [...] he could never quite shake off thoughts of the agony of leave-taking and the fear of foreign places.[31]

As we can see, railways and concentration camps are inextricably connected — albeit metaphorically — already at the beginning of the novel. Yet, this is only the first step of Sebald's approach to the Holocaust, an evil whose magnitude has induced historians and philosophers alike to retrospectively question the whole development of the Western world in the modern period.

Austerlitz embodies this critique of modernity at large. His considerations on station architecture lead him on to military architecture and the technique of fortifications, since "it is often our mightiest projects that most obviously betray the degree of our insecurity."[32] Sebald's digressive style rests on an accumulation of details that slowly shed light on each other, and the disparate subjects that Austerlitz sketches progressively trace an ambitious historical design. Thus the great public buildings that were erected in Belgium at the turn of the century become the emblem of an increasingly organized society, where individuals were caged within immense and chaotic architectural concretions, which actually exceeded their utilitarian function, turning into the emblem of a corrupt and invasive central power.[33] This theory of public architecture as dehumanizing prepares a first revelation, one of the few glimpses of the horror whose shadow looms large over the novel.

Austerlitz's talk on fortifications induces the narrator to visit Fort Breendonk, an early 20th-century building which was conquered by the Germans in 1940 and was turned by them into a penal camp that remained active until August 1944.

Even after studying the plan of the fortress to understand its military logic, the narrator cannot accept that such a "monstrous incarnation of ugliness and blind violence"[34] is actually a product of the human intellect. When we follow the narrator into the entrails of the fort, we suddenly enter the nightmare of camps, where perpetrators and victims cohabited in a small space. In the cell where interrogations took place, due to a combination of disagreeable olfactory and visual sensations, the narrator experiences a resurfacing of his "childhood terrors,"[35] and it is by sharing his sense of nausea that we emerge from this momentary contact with the place where Jean Améry was tortured.

Yet, there is no time for delay in this peripatetic novel, which does not indulge in compassion but continuously displaces its readers. The narrator now brings us to Liège, where he again meets Austerlitz by chance. This time the architectural historian is intent on observing a model town for workers — a project which was rooted in philanthropic idealism, but which unfortunately translated into the practice of accommodating people "in barracks."[36] A few months later, the two wanderers meet again — once again without the least premeditation — in the vicinity of the immense Palace of Justice in Brussels. The 700,000-cubic meter edifice was built in such a hurry that the architect had no time to coordinate all its details. As a result, this "architectural monstrosity"[37] includes rooms with no entrance and staircases which lead nowhere.

The itinerary that Austerlitz and the narrator jointly make through modern architecture is akin to the reflections Zygmunt Bauman offers in *Modernity and the Holocaust* (1989). The sociologist regards the Holocaust not as an aberration of history, but rather as a product of modernity, due to the conjunction of anti–Semitism and the technological-administrative evolution of the West. The Holocaust dehumanized both victim and perpetrator, following a procedure of systematic extermination that was akin to the standardization of industrial production and to the efficiency-driven apparatus of bureaucracy. To analyze the social projects of modernity, Bauman utilizes the metaphor of the gardener, who redesigns nature in order to clear the ground of weeds and let flowers grow. The Holocaust has to be seen in this perspective of social planning, which was totally distorted in terms of ends but was similar to other aspects of progress in terms of means and coordination: "The Holocaust is a by-product of the modern drive to a fully designed, fully controlled world, once the drive is getting out of control and running wild."[38]

Mirroring Lives

Having clarified these implications, let us go back to the novel, We are on board a ferry bound for Great Britain, on which the narrator and Austerlitz have separately reserved a seat. Only now do we learn that Austerlitz teaches in an art institute in London, while the narrator, who is of German origin, has abandoned his home country to live in Great Britain. So far the two characters have communicated in French, but they discover that they both speak English.

At this stage, readers may well be disoriented. Is this intended as a realistic novel or is the author delineating the — possibly pathological — condition of a solitary man who is interacting with a projection of his own mind? The many "coincidences"[39] that mark the relation between these two characters, the affinity of their voices and of their interests seem to indicate that the latter hypothesis is correct, but the photographs that accompany the text tell a different story.[40] When Sebald takes us to Bloomsbury, to visit the office where Austerlitz works, the existence of that room is proved by an image. Although we do not actually know what place it depicts, the picture stands there as a pledge, establishing a bond of trust, inviting us to *believe*. A "fictional pact" is established, and despite the text's ambivalent signals we believe in this visual clue, just as we believe that Austerlitz has focused his studies on the architecture of the capitalist era, notably on "the compulsive sense of order and the tendency towards monumentalism evident in lawcourts and penal institutions, railway stations and stock exchanges, opera houses and lunatic asylums, and the dwellings built to rectangular grid patterns for the labour force."[41]

Now that we have started to understand Austerlitz and his Foucauldian research, and we are taking pleasure in his conversation, he disappears. At the end of 1975, after spending nine years abroad, the narrator decides to go back to Germany, with the intention of settling there. After returning to his native country, his every attempt to communicate by letter with Austerlitz fails, perhaps because — as the narrator subsequently realizes — Austerlitz avoids writing to him from Germany. However, contrary to his plans, only one year later the narrator moves back to Great Britain, but this marks the beginning of a difficult time, characterized by solitude. Thus a new meeting occurs only two decades later, in December 1996, again by chance and again in a station.

In the bar of the Great Eastern Hotel, which was built at the end of the 19th century at the railway terminal of Liverpool Street, the conversation between the two friends focuses for the first time on the past of Austerlitz, who acknowledges that he has spent most of his life building useless inner fortifications to protect himself from a painful consciousness of his origins. Austerlitz recounts that he grew up in Bala, in Wales, as Dafydd Elias, the son of Calvinist minister Emyr Elias. Only as an adolescent, after his mother died and his father became insane, did Dafydd discover that they were actually his foster parents and that his real name was Jacques Austerlitz. This foreign and rather unlikely family name set the character's mind aflame, connecting him to a chain of places and events that cross Europe's geography and history, from the Gare d'Austerlitz in Paris to the village of Austerlitz (now in the Czech Republic), where the French troops led by Napoleon defeated the armies of Austria and Russia, a seminal event in the making of modern Europe.

However, at the end of this long night in the bar of the Great Eastern Hotel we still do not know the hero's ultimate secret, and the two friends decide to see each other the next day. This time their roaming takes them to the Greenwich Observatory, the symbol of the modern conception of time and space. Not only does the clock of the observatory mark the Greenwich Mean Time, but the site of the observatory also marks the 0 meridian, as was agreed in the course of an international conference in 1884, in order to encircle the planet with an ideal grid of lines that would allow it to be measured. Greenwich is therefore the pivot of the 19th- century process of rationalization of time and space — a fundamental stage in the advent of globalization. Yet, time is the very dimension from which Austerlitz seems to be fleeing, since he admits that he has "never owned a clock of any kind,"[42] almost in the hope "that time will not pass away, has not passed away, that I can turn back and go behind it."[43]

Ghosts of Memory

To protect himself from painful memories, Austerlitz has sought refuge in oblivion, but this strategy is useless, like his attempt to stop time by means of photographs and his rebellion against watches and clocks. Being deprived of a past and a future, Austerlitz is condemned to an eternal present in which his identity is perpetually on the verge of annihilation:

> I already felt in my head the dreadful torpor that heralds disintegration of the personality, I sensed that in truth I had neither memory nor the power of thought, nor even any existence, that all my life had been a constant process of obliteration, a turning away from myself and the world.[44]

One of the symptoms of Austerlitz's alienation is his increasing dismay at the idea of writing and even of reading. Austerlitz visualizes language as "an old city full of streets and squares, nooks and crannies,"[45] which has grown up in time and in which — after spending a long time abroad — he is no longer able to find his way back.

It is in this period that Austerlitz starts his nocturnal wanderings, which turn him into a latter-day equivalent of the enigmatic figure E.A. Poe portrayed in "The Man of the Crowd" (1840) as the embodiment of an indescribable and undiscoverable secret. As the beginning of the story clarifies, "It was well said of a certain German book that *'es lässt sich nicht lesen'* — it does not permit itself to be read. There are some secrets which do not permit themselves to be told."[46] Poe's figuration of secrecy reminds us of the condition of trauma, which results in a state of permanent self-alienation, the impossibility to articulate what is at the core of one's identity.

Moreover, Poe's emblematic character — who roams the London streets throughout the night, losing himself in the crowd to avoid solitude — was linked by Marie Bonaparte to the archetype of the Wandering

Jew,[47] a powerful anti–Semitic figuration of the Jewish diaspora. A product of the medieval imagination, this figure was presented as a Jew who had mocked Jesus on his way to crucifixion and had been therefore punished with the curse of eternally roaming the earth, finding no peace. Through this mythical personage, the Jews who chose not to conform to the teachings of Jesus were stigmatized as the progeny of Cain. The many names of the Wandering Jew — Ahasverus, Buttadaeus, Matathias, Isaac Laquedem — point in themselves to his nature as an anti–Semitic trope, standing for the repeated refusal of Jews, generation after generation, century after century, to enter the Christian community, and embodying the concomitant "curse" of diaspora, a condition of permanent exile.

Like Poe's man of the crowd, Austerlitz spends his nights wandering in the urban space, although what attracts him is not the human density of the metropolis, but rather its memorial stratifications, the evocative power of places that have been inhabited throughout the centuries. It is by investigating the collective past that Austerlitz strives to escape his individual destiny as a wanderer who is deprived not only of a destination — we all are in a way — but of the *compass* of his past. Thanks to his self-seeking perambulations, Austerlitz finally manages to articulate the secret that he unconsciously harbors in his chest, reaching the inner repository in which it is preserved. This process of communication between the conscious and unconscious is rendered by Sebald with a technique that borders on fantasy, since unknown voices repeatedly address Austerlitz during his nightly walks, using strange languages:

> It sometimes seemed to me as if the noises of the city were dying down around me and the traffic was flowing silently down the street, or as if someone had plucked me by the sleeve. And I would hear people behind my back speaking in a foreign tongue, Lithuanian, Hungarian, or something else with a very alien note to it, or so I thought, said Austerlitz.[48]

These ghosts can be easily rationalized as inner presences that connect Austerlitz to his forgotten past. Studying fictional representations of trauma, Anne Whitehead reminds us that "the ghost represents an appropriate embodiment of the disjunction of temporality, the surfacing of the past in the present,"[49] since "the traumatic event is not experienced or assimilated fully at the time that it occurs, but only belatedly in its insistent and intrusive return, and hence is not available in the usual way to memory and interpretation."[50] Discussing Sebald's "spectral geographies," John Wylie likewise claims that in *Austerlitz* specters break "the linear sequence of past, present and future,"⁵¹ re-enacting the past in the present, often against the background of places to which they are associated.

Austerlitz repeatedly undergoes the preternatural experience of haunting in Liverpool Street station, and it is precisely in the Ladies' Waiting Room of that station — which is closed for renovation in the 1990s — that Austerlitz is visited by the revelation he has been waiting for. At first, in that silent and empty space, Austerlitz divests himself of his fictitious identity, like an actor who, "upon making his entrance, has completely and irrevocably forgotten not only the lines he knew by heart but the very part he has so often played."⁵² The architectural space is increasingly transfigured while Austerlitz loses himself in contemplation of the light that filters down from a gallery beneath the vaulted roof, until the room becomes the image of an inner space, containing "all the hours"⁵³ of the protagonist's past life, "all the suppressed and extinguished fears and wishes"⁵⁴ he had entertained. In that precise moment three figures materialize. Two of them are middle-aged persons, who are dressed in the style of the 1930s and whom Austerlitz identifies as the minister and his wife. The third is a child sitting on a bench. His legs, in white knee-length socks, did not reach the floor, and but for the small rucksack he was holding on his lap I don't think I would have known him, said Austerlitz."⁵⁵ That rucksack is an eloquent clue for readers, who associate it with Austerlitz's inseparable companion — a rucksack that he has previously described as "the only truly reliable thing in his life."⁵⁶ That rucksack — which is even portrayed in a photograph — becomes the emblem of a rootless figure whose identity is indissolubly associated with traveling and the transitory.⁵⁷

Only inside that abandoned waiting room, in the presence of those ghosts of memory, does Austerlitz realize that he arrived in London — in that very station — half a century earlier. This resurgent image triggers a process of rememoration that enables Austerlitz to reappropriate his true identity, although this process proves far from reassuring, since the man discovers — also with the help of a television documentary — that he came from Prague on one of the *Kindertransporte* that were organized after the *Kristallnacht* pogrom (November 1938). Thanks to this form of rescue, around 10,000 children of Jewish origin reached Great Britain from central Europe in 1938–39.

Sebald was actually inspired to write this novel after seeing a documentary on Susie Bechhofer, who remembered only in her adult age that she had arrived in Wales on one of these trains.⁵⁸ The fact that the woman was born on the same day as Sebald — May 18 — and that she came from

Munich, a city that is close to the author's native town, is possibly at the origin of the specularity between the narrator and Austerlitz. This partial identification between the authorial persona (a descendant of the perpetrators) and Austerlitz (a descendant of the victims and a victim himself) amounts to an assumption of responsibility, an attempt to connect by means of empathy, bridging the gap of indifference and hatred. As Stuart Taberner asserts with regard to Sebald: "From the moment of his birth, his fate as a German was inseparable from that of the Jews murdered by his parents' generation."[59]

On the Verge of the Abyss

Austerlitz's visit to the state archives in Prague at last enables him to reach Věra Ryšanová, who tells him about his parents — Agáta Austerlitzová, who was an opera singer, and Maximilian Aychenwald, of Russian origin, a prominent figure in the Czech Social Democratic Party. Austerlitz was born in a family of cultivated Jewish cosmopolitans, and his own first name — Jacques — is a homage Agáta paid to her favorite composer Jacques Offenbach. Sebald's cultural reference is again far from casual, since the French composer was actually of Jewish-German origin.

Talking in French with Věra — the friend to whom Agáta often confided her child — brings Austerlitz back to the core of his affective tie with that language. The emotional dimension of languages is foregrounded in Sebald's description of the first meeting between Austerlitz, who is merely able to stammer a Czech sentence he has learnt by heart, and the custodian of his childhood.

> *Promiňte, prosím, že Vás obtěžuji. Hledám paní Agáta Austerlizovou, která sde možná v roce devatenáct set třicet osm bydlela.* I am looking for a Mrs Agáta Austerlitzová who may have been living here in 1938. With a gesture of alarm, Věra covered her face with both hands, hands which, it flashed through my mind, were endlessly familiar to me, stared at me over her spread fingertips, and very quietly but with what to me was a quite singular clarity spoke these words in French: *Jacquot*, she said, *dis, est-ce que c'est vraiment toi?*[60]

This marks the beginning of a further stage in Austerlitz's process of self-discovery, focusing on the destiny of his Jewish parents. This inquiry leads him to Terezín (formerly Theresienstadt), a Hapsburg fortress that was turned into a camp during the war. As many as 60,000 Jews were confined in less than a square kilometer, suffering from overcrowding, malnutrition and forced labor. Establishing contact with this place, however, does not prove an instrument of healing, and once back in London Austerlitz plunges again into the abyss. Through his wanderings and researches in European archives, Austerlitz cherishes the idea of finding his mother. He believes he recognizes her in a propaganda film that was shot by the Nazis in Terezín, and in a photo that is kept in the archives of a theater in Prague, but this does not suffice to mend the rent in his soul.

Austerlitz also follows the traces of his father to Paris, but again this quest does not produce a sense of closure. After being told that Maximilian Aychenwald had been interned in a camp near the Pyrenees, the protagonist develops the idea that his father left Paris from the Gare d'Austerlitz, also due to the strange feelings this place triggered in him: — the impression of being "on the scene of some unexpiated crime."[61] Before the narrator takes leave of his friend outside a Métro station, Austerlitz gives him the key to his house in London: "I could stay there whenever I liked, he said, and study the black and white photographs which, one day, would be all that was left of his life."[62] While approaching the end of his apologue, Sebald calls our attention to those photographs that actually constitute the humus from which the novel itself germinated. Following a typically postmodern strategy, the novel stages its birth, the primal scene of creation.

Faithful to its oblique strategy, the volume ends circularly with the narrator who goes back to Belgium, where the story opened. At Breendonk, in the vicinity of the fortress, he takes from his rucksack — an object that underlines the symmetry between Sebald's two main characters, associating them in their destiny as *Wanderers* on a perpetual quest for meaning — the book Austerlitz gave him on their first meeting, *Heshel's Kingdom* (1998). In this book Dan Jacobson recounts his search for the traces of his grandfather, a Rabbi who died in the wake of World War One. Due to this event, in 1920 the wife of the Rabbi abandoned Lithuania to migrate to South Africa, without knowing up to what point this decision would change the destiny of her children. This family memoir pivots on the image of the abandoned diamond mines, huge chasms that visualize the contiguity between ordinary life and the horror, since between firm ground and the abyss "there was no transition, only this dividing line."[63] Those dark chasms become for Jacobson an image of the catastrophe that devoured his family and his people.

In my mind, this image is indelibly associated with another passage in Sebald's novel. During his childhood in Wales, Austerlitz is taken by the minister who adopted him to the shores of an artificial lake, on the bottom of which there is a deserted village called Llanwddyn. We discover

5. W.G. Sebald, Austerlitz (2001)

that the paternal house of the minister is buried under the lake, and the account the minister offers of life in Llanwddyn is so lively as to bring the village back to life in the eyes of the child, who imagines the inhabitants "still down in the depths, sitting in their houses and walking along the road, but unable to speak and with their eyes opened far too wide."[64] This image makes me think of the mute cry and wide-open eyes of the Gorgon, whose severed head Sebald's narrator and his hero carry with them in their rucksacks. Although the writer refused to show us the visage of horror, as a reader I know what is inside those rucksacks and I cannot take my eyes off them.

6

Haruki Murakami, *Kafka on the Shore* (2002)

It is hardly possible to study Haruki Murakami without adopting a comparative perspective. Murakami's characters are so enmeshed in the forms of American culture, as Yoshinobu Hakutani claims, "that they accept these forms as integral to postmodern Japanese life," although "their essential Japaneseness is never truly lost."[1] Thanks to this conflation of cultures in his representation of the world, Murakami has become an author of planetary renown, whose literary identity is elusive — since he can be read as simultaneously familiar and exotic on both sides of the Pacific.[2]

Starting from his first novel — *Hear the Wind Sing* (1979) — Murakami's output has focused on issues such as the quest for identity and the power of the imagination within a global world that is increasingly marked by capitalism. Moreover, there has been a "growing spiritual dimension"[3] in Murakami's recent fiction, as Philip Gabriel points out. The critic identifies the Aum Shinrikyo sect gas attack in the Tokyo underground, in 1995 — and Murakami's treatment of this delicate subject in *Underground* (1997), which collects his interviews with the victims — as the watershed between these two stages in his output.

I will focus my analysis on *Kafka on the Shore* (2002), a novel of fascinating complexity where Murakami — with notable indifference to the restrictive dictates of realism — created parallel inner dimensions to which his characters gain access starting from everyday life. Thus the author has managed to give substance to that unceasing dialogue each of us entertains with his or her inner self, although in a materialist and secularized society we may tend to disregard this inner side of experience to focus on external achievements and on those objects that define our social status. As Matthew Strecher underlines, it is through the fantastic that Murakami pursues his criticism of contemporary society, taking a stance that may remind us of magic realism, although Murakami does not seem interested in a precise political agenda, but rather in investigating the conditions of individuals in contemporary Japanese (and global) mass society.[4]

Rewriting the Enigma of Oedipus

With its eerie correspondences between past and present,[5] *Kafka on the Shore* is an enigmatic and evanescent book, which works at a deep level, and in which it is easy to get lost if one uses only the tools of reason. To experience Murakami's writing, we have to breathe it. Therefore let us linger on the threshold of the novel to inhale the wind that blows through its pages:

> **Sometimes fate is like a small sandstorm that keeps changing directions. You change direction but the sandstorm chases you. You turn again, but the storm adjusts. Over and over you play this out, like some ominous dance with death just before dawn. Why? Because this storm isn't something that blew in from far away, something that has nothing to do with you. This storm is you.**[6]

These are the words the boy named Crow — whose reflections are rendered in bold — addresses to Kafka Tamura, the young protagonist, who is assisted by this inner presence (*Kafka* in Czech means *crow*) at difficult times, when he has to make important decisions. The boy named Crow — whose function is similar to that of the chorus in a Greek tragedy — encourages Kafka to cross that inner sandstorm, although **"there's no sun there, no moon, no direction, no sense of time. Just fine white sand swirling up into the sky like pulverized bones."**[7]

With this message Kafka falls asleep, to wake up the next morning on his 15th birthday, when he flees from home, abandoning his father, who is his only relative, since his mother left Kafka, taking his sister with her, when he was only four. The words of the boy named Crow sound like the prologue to a tragedy. In fact *Kafka on the Shore* is not only pervaded by a sense of fate, but contains an explicit reference to Oedipus, for Kafka's father has prophesied that he will be killed by his son, who will also lie with his mother and sister. Modern science and Greek tragedy — which Freud regarded as an expression of the collective unconscious, since the mechanism of cultural repression was less strong when humanity was in its childhood — combine in this novel where Kafka meditates that there's no way to erase his DNA, describing it as "a mechanism buried inside me."[8]

We accept this novel as we accept our existence, as a matter of fact. Everything here is a mystery, but it tastes like necessity.

Murakami's highly original investigation into the human not only combines Greek tragedy, psychoanalysis and Japanese traditional culture, but also incorporates the icons of our globalized present and the suspenseful plots of crime and science fiction.[9] The odd-numbered chapters tell the story of Kafka, who is traveling from Tokyo to Takamatsu, in the south of Japan, toward a library that inexplicably attracts him. In the Kōmura Library, Kafka meets two characters who will play a major role in his process of development — the androgynous Ōshima, who will turn out to be a young transgender, and the ineffable Miss Saeki, who is the library's director. While the boy is in this city, his father is killed in Tokyo, and the police start looking for him. The police are also chasing an older man — Nakata Satoru, whose childhood was marked by an inexplicable event, as the even-numbered chapters tell us, and who is later suspected to be the actual murderer. Like Kafka, Nakata travels from Tokyo to Takamatsu, pushed by forces that he does not understand, until their paths entwine.

The two characters are complementary in a paradoxical way. While the boy is adroit and determined, the old man is naïve and helpless, but in this novel bodily age does not necessarily coincide with spiritual age. The novel's two plots are also complementary in terms of narrative techniques, since the story of Kafka is told in the present tense and in the first person, as if to emphasize the young hero's agency and the relevance of his current choices, while the story of Nakata is told in the past tense and in the third person, as if to draw our attention to his past and to the forces that inhabit him.

As I was saying, to experience *Kafka on the Shore,* one has to surrender to the logic of tragedy, according to which there are things that must happen.[10] Ōshima himself invites Kafka to read the tragedies of Euripides and Aeschylus, which "show a lot of the essential problems we struggle with even today."[11] Let us remember that oriental thought is based on the concept of karma, which is rooted in our past lives and which influences our present and future, with the result that "even in the smallest events there's no such thing as coincidence."[12] While the Christian doctrine of free will is closely associated with Western individualism, which postulates a separation between the subject and circumambient reality, Eastern thought presents a holistic approach, the "awareness of the unity and mutual interrelation of all things and events,"[13] in Fritjof Capra's words.

Likewise, in Murakami's book individuals are not only acted upon by forces they do not control, but their own actions reverberate well beyond their control. In the novel we witness the turbulence and wandering of those unconscious psychic energies Murasaki Shikibu described around the year 1000 in a classic of Japanese literature — *The Tale of Genji,* where a lady unconsciously metamorphoses every night into an evil spirit with the aim to kill her rival in love, the wife of prince Genji. All the measures the prince takes are to no avail, even his attempt to call in priests to exorcise this spirit. Interestingly, Lady Rokujo has no idea of what is happening although she has terrible nightmares and wakes up to discover that her black hair smells "like smoke."[14] That smell comes from the incense the priests burn during their rituals, and when the lady knows the truth she shaves her hair in a fit of horror and retires from the world.

Due to the multiplicity of cultural referents that Murakami's novel activates, with intertextual voluptuousness, at first reading it is not easy to understand the articulation of this text, which is pervaded by esoteric clues. In *Kafka on the Shore* allusions prevail over explicit comments, while readers are required to make a creative effort to recompose the fragments of this atypical story, a task that can hardly be accomplished within the time of a single reading. As Laura Miller remarks, at the end of the book readers emerge "as if from a trance, convinced they've made contact with something significant, if not entirely sure what that something is."[15] In other words, a form of magic takes place in the novel, although Murakami's detractors would rather label it as illusionism.

Although the writer claims he does not control his creative process in a rational way — "'It's kind of a free improvisation, [...] I never plan. I never know what the next page is going to be. [...] I'm searching for melody after melody'"[16] — *Kafka on the Shore* actually presents a tightly knit symbolic structure. Moreover, the novel simultaneously invites close-reading and resists that strategy, since it teems with clues that do not allow readers to reach a solution, leaving them unable to achieve closure. As we know, at the end of the 19th century Henry James constructed textual engines that both engender interpretations and frustrate them. This narrative strategy — which is based on a principle of structural ambiguity or "openness" — is also at the core of late–20th-century anti-detective novels, the postmodernist subversive revisitation of the detective novel. The readers of Thomas Pynchon's, Umberto Eco's and Paul Auster's texts lose themselves in labyrinths of enigmas which owe much to the genius of Jorge Luis Borges, who taught postmodernists how to deconstruct the traditional concept of plot.[17]

Life on the Shore

While these writers stage the impossibility of knowing, of grasping the essence of reality, to which the subject can relate only in a mediated form, in *Kafka on the Shore* Murakami draws our attention to a different aspect of our existential condition, suspended between reality and the imagination, day life and dreams, or in Freudian terms the conscious and unconscious. Ever since the origin of psychoanalysis, Western literature has explored with various tools and aims that contact zone between ego and id where such an important part of our psychic activity takes place.

Refuting the Freudian attempt to rationalize the psyche, Murakami prefers to locate it within an inter-subjective and trans-temporal field of forces, by drawing both on Greek tragedies and on Japanese literature and myth. The result is a novel that refuses to be caged in by verisimilitude, but which is open to the supernatural and the surreal, also in an attempt to cross the threshold between the consciousness that characterizes life and the unconsciousness that we associate with death. According to Michael Seats, the idea of a threshold is central to the volume right from the title, which evokes the shore as an uncertain border between land and sea, inaugurating a series of shifting oppositions such as "life/death, good/evil, adult/child, consciousness/unconsciousness, god/human."[18]

Kafka on the Shore may well provoke a feeling of estrangement, being oblivious to the materialist view of reality. The novel is inhabited by disembodied entities — similar to the ghosts that in the pre-modern age peopled the imagination of all the planet — who are able to interact with the main characters by borrowing the features of icons of publicity. It is in the shape of Johnnie Walker, with his dog, boots and top hat, that a demonic being appears to poor Nakata, while it is as Colonel Sanders — the logo of Kentucky Fried Chicken — that another supernatural being (a sort of guardian of the threshold) manifests himself to Hoshino, the young truck driver who helps Nakata in his mission, for the old man reminds him of his grandfather. "As I've explained, I don't have any form."— the Colonel claims — "I'm a metaphysical, conceptual object. I can take on any form, but I lack substance. And to perform a real act, I need someone with substance to help out."[19] Hoshino himself will help the Colonel.

In the book, humans and spirits communicate easily — as in a story of distant times or in a David Lynch film (*Mulholland Drive* comes to mind), a director that Murakami loves and has been compared to.[20] While creating these correspondences between the mundane and ultramundane worlds, the novel also foregrounds the fact that humanity has always fashioned the sacred through the imagination:

> "Listen — God only exists in people's minds. Especially in Japan, God's always been kind of a flexible concept. Look at what happened after the war. Douglas MacArthur ordered the divine emperor to quit

being God, and he did, making a speech saying he was just an ordinary person. So after 1946 he wasn't God anymore. [...] A very postmodern kind of thing. If you think God's there, He is. If you don't, He isn't."[21]

Here the author tackles the shadow of World War II and of the traumas it produced within Japanese society. While at the end of the conflict Japan was a discomfited and de-sacralized country — the radio speaker who announced the emperor's renunciation of his divine status committed harakiri — Murakami's characters are in touch with a dimension that is beyond space, time and matter, and in which their lives find their deepest reason of being: "The Earth slowly keeps on turning." — as Murakami writes — "But beyond any of those details of the real, there are dreams. And everyone's living in them."[22]

Studying the cultural development of postwar Japan, Dennis Charles Washburn claims that modernization and the "shattering experience of defeat and guilt"[23] both contributed to an increasing consciousness that values are culturally created and to an ensuing feeling of instability. As a result, culture "emphasised the importance of autonomy, of ethical free will."[24] *Kafka on the Shore* also underlines the unstable condition of the human subject, whose moral responsibility is rooted in an unconscious and oneiric substratum which the individual does not fully control. And yet, only by means of a dialogue with that dimension — only by listening to the wind — can individuals find their path, for without imagination we would be no more than "*hollow men,*"[25] like the ones T.S. Eliot described. The protagonist meditates on the importance of the imagination while he is in the mountain cabin that Ōshima owns on the fringe of a forest. Here Kafka reads a volume that recounts the trial of Adolf Eichmann and comes into contact with the absolute lack of empathy of the Nazi leader, whose only objective was to exterminate the Jews in the most efficient way, without ever questioning the legitimacy of what he was doing. On an otherwise blank page at the end of the book, this sentence has been noted:

> It's all a question of imagination. Our responsibility begins with the power to imagine. It's just like Yeats said: *In dreams begin responsibilities.* Flip this around and you could say that where there's no power to imagine, no responsibility can arise. Just like we see with Eichmann.[26]

Starting from this reflection, Kafka revisits his complex relation with his father. The oedipal impulse to kill him is a component of the malediction from which he was escaping when he fled from home, but miles have little relevance in this novel, where people can meet, love or kill in other dimensions. Fulfilling the prophecy, Kafka actually does kill his father, lie with his mother and also with his sister, but it is difficult to know whether this happens in a trance, in a dream or in reality, since in this book every interpretation of events is only a hypothesis, never an absolute.

Given these premises, let us deal with the complex game of correspondences that Murakami orchestrated to correlate his four main characters. Kafka Tamura embodies the duality that marks the whole book, also because Kafka is not his true name, but the name he chooses when he abandons his family, for he loves the works of the Czech writer, notably "In the Penal Colony." In the eyes of the boy, the machine at the heart of the story is "a sort of substitute for explaining the situation we're in."[27] Through the eyes of a European who is traveling in the tropics, we discover that the previous commander of the penal colony where the story is set has created a perfect machine for executions, which carves the sentence on the body of the condemned using a system of needles. The machine brings actual death only at the end of a slow agony, while the culprit is not even informed of what he has been found guilty of, although everybody else can read this on his body. Kafka regards this apologue as equivalent to the punishment he is destined to suffer due to a guilt he ignores.[28]

To face his destiny, Kafka has reached the Kōmura library, which can be regarded as an inner space associated with consciousness and memory (while the forest surrounding Ōshima's mountain cabin is associated with the unconscious and oblivion). In the elegant head of the library—fifty-year-old Miss Saeki, whose absent gaze is occasionally accompanied by a radiant smile—Kafka recognizes (or believes to recognize) his mother, who left him as a child. According to the oedipal paradigm, Kafka falls in love with the woman, driven by an obscure and powerful current that is rooted in distant events. The past must come full cycle, although at the end of the novel we have not reached the certainty that things happened exactly as we are led to believe, for in this book everything is ambivalent. What follows is therefore the version of facts readers can piece together, although this remains a hypothesis, for in the end we cannot resolutely claim that Miss Saeki is Kafka's mother and Sakura his sister. We have to accept, so to speak, full responsibility for our interpretation.

The Possible Story of Miss Saeki

Little by little, we learn the past of Miss Saeki, since her adolescence, when she reached a perfect physical and spiritual communion with a boy of her age. Due to her fear of losing that condition of bliss—as it soon happened, since the boy died at the age of twenty—a part of her fled from time. The instrument that enabled Miss Saeki to come into contact with another dimension was her song *Kafka on the Shore,* which made her famous in 1970 and also opened the gate leading into another world.[29]

After her soul left the world, Miss Saeki survived like an empty shell, although she pretended to live. If we accept Kafka's hypothesis, she got married to Kafka's father only to leave both her husband and son, and finally became the head of the Kōmura library, which was created by the family of her former boyfriend in the building where he had lived surrounded by books. This would explain not only the orphaned condition of Kafka, but also the hatred of his father — the renowned sculptor Kōichi Tamura, a sort of demiurge, who is endowed with an extraordinary mental strength,[30] and whose thirst for revenge is the prime mover of the story. We may venture to believe that it was he who pushed Kafka towards his mother, in the attempt to achieve through him that deep union that the woman refused him, or perhaps in the attempt to devastate them both.

Although Miss Saeki proved incapable of loving her husband, since her soul was already elsewhere, she is now ready to love her son, in whom — due to another mysterious correspondence — the youth she loved and lost has somehow reincarnated.[31] This explains both the strength that draws Kafka towards the library — where Kafka becomes reunited not only with his mother, but also with his mistress and with home — and the polarity between Kafka and his father, of whom the 15-year-old boy would be at the same time a double and a rival, according to a pattern that echoes the Freudian view of the Oedipus complex.

Fulfilling his destiny, Kafka repeatedly has sex with his presumed mother: first with the spirit of Miss Saeki, who is sleeping at that time, then with the woman as a corporeal entity, but the boy's path is beset with dangerous traps. In his itinerary of self-discovery, Kafka is brought by Ōshima to his cabin at the margins of a forest, where he will have to enter — without the rucksack that contains the few things he carries with him, his few remaining certainties — to find the answers he is looking for. The forest is a metaphor of Kafka's inner labyrinth, and even includes a sort of limbo — a village inhabited by souls that have been caught in between life and death.[32]

In this village Kafka meets Miss Saeki, not in her actual bodily age, but in her spiritual one as a 15-year-old — the age she was when she took the fatal decision of stopping time to keep perfection intact. Kafka risks remaining prisoner in that place, enslaved to the girl who inhabits it, but it is the adult Miss Saeki who rescues him, visiting him in the village and wounding herself to have him suck a drop of her blood. That maternal blood gives the youth the necessary strength to turn his shoulders on the village, overcoming the almost unbearable nostalgia that grips him when it is time to come back to life.

The appearance of Miss Saeki in this village in between life and death can be explained because of what happened in the library while Kafka was in the forest. Miss Saeki has been reached by another individual, who like her has only half a shadow — Nakata Satoru, to whom Miss Saeki had given the notebooks where she collected her memories. By burning those notebooks Nakata has enabled the woman to finally detach herself from her earthly life to resume her journey. Only when Nakata has freed Miss Saeki from her attachment to the past can she in turn free Kafka from the ghost of her former self. The untying of this memorial knot enables Miss Saeki to die and Kafka to live.

Nakata versus Johnnie Walker

Let us now concentrate on Nakata. It is through a document of the American army that we discover what happened in November 1946, when an entire class of children lost consciousness during an outing on the mountains, as in a case of collective hypnosis, while their teacher was unaffected by this. The episode, which reads like a chapter from a science fiction novel, is actually the prelude of a complex existential itinerary. While the other children regained consciousness in the space of two hours, little Nakata was taken to a hospital, where he woke up from that comatose condition only three weeks later, following a banal accident — a drop of his blood that had spilled on the sheets after a blood sample had been drawn. As we have seen, blood is an ambivalent symbol that connects various scenes in the novel, standing for both life and death.

We later discover that the night before the fatal outing, the children's schoolmistress had dreamt of her husband, who was then fighting at the front, and that in the course of the dream she has fused with him with the utmost erotic intensity, although when she woke up she realized that the dream actually forebode death, as facts soon proved. In the course of the mountain walk, the woman — who was still upset because of her physical and spiritual experience — felt her period coming and hid to clean herself, but a little later Nakata approached her with a blood-stained tissue in his hand. It was when the woman started hitting the boy with uncontrollable anger that all her pupils fell into an unconscious state. After the facts, the schoolmistress described Nakata as a particularly sensitive child, who suffered some form of psychological violence at home. This is possibly why Nakata fled from life. When he later came back, he proved unable to read or remember, but he was endowed with the arcane powers of talking with cats, possibly because when he was in a state of lethargy his parents brought him his cat, hoping to wake him up.

Nakata is presented in the novel as "a holy fool"[33] — a pure of heart who is devoid of sexual desires and who is close to the absolute, that "dark abyss"[34] where we find the whole instead of its composite parts. Critics have underlined the Christlike nature of this character, describing the scene where Nakata has mackerels rain from the sky[35] as a parody of the Christian miracle of the multiplication of bread and fish. Murakami may well have chosen to present Nakata as a "fisher of souls," although in this text souls metamorphose into cats, perhaps as an act of homage to Murakami's beloved novel by Natsume Sōseki *I Am a Cat* (1905).

Indeed, to earn some money Nakata looks for lost cats — thanks to the privileged information he obtains from their fellowcats. It is his quest for a lost cat that brings him into contact with Johnnie Walker, whom we recognize as the obscure part of Kafka's father, a creature of evil whose only desire is power. This dark being steals cats to devour their warm heart, and thus their soul, according to a macabre ritual that is aimed to construct a magic flute, by means of which he will collect bigger souls. Johnnie Walker himself induces Nakata to kill him, in an attempt to save a cat, since through this death the man will be able to access a new form of life. Having performed this deed, Nakata loses his senses to wake up in the open air, with no trace of blood on his clothes, but at that time in a distant place Kafka also wakes up in the garden of a Shintoist temple. The boy has on his chest what he at first perceives as a butterfly, but which turns out to be a bloodstain. The prophecy the protagonist was afraid of has therefore come true through Nakata. Following these events, Nakata starts on a journey that will enable him to free Miss Saeki from the burden of her memories and to approach his own death.

No less complex is the itinerary of Johnnie Walker, whom Kafka meets in the village in the middle of the forest. On that occasion, the boy named Crow, who is the spiritual double of Kafka, is provoked by the evil Johnnie Walker and devastates his face with his beak. Once again, this act of aggression has been orchestrated by the victim himself, in order to come back to the earth and pursue his quest for power. To understand this process, we have to keep in mind that in this novel good actions engender further good actions, while evil leads to evil, and every gesture therefore entails a responsibility that goes beyond its immediate mundane effects.

Johnnie Walker is actually using Kafka — who is linked to him by the red thread of heredity — to regain the earth, possibly to relive through him. Johnnie Walker's rebirth actually starts when Kafka rapes a girl in the course of a dream. Kafka met the girl while traveling towards Takamatsu and recognized her — either literally or metaphorically, since these two dimensions are interchangeable in the novel — as his sister. While Kafka is penetrating Sakura without her consent, albeit in a mental space, he feels that a jelly thing is growing inside him.[36] That slimy creature is the same entity that the boy named Crow subsequently tries to kill, with the result of only making it stronger, for it comes out of the disfigured visage of Johnnie Walker in the shape of his tongue. We finally see it again as a giant slug, while it attempts to come back again to the earth through the mouth of Nakata's corpse. It was Nakata himself who offered Johnnie Walker this opportunity to come back from that world in-between life and death, not only by killing him, but also by opening the communication gate between these two dimensions — the gate Miss Saeki discovered years before thanks to the chords of her song.

This time the gate has the shape of a stone placed in the temple garden where Kafka woke up with the bloodstain on his chest. Nakata opens the gate with the help of Hoshino. Although Nakata is often unable to foresee the meaning of the ritual actions he performs, we know that this will enable Kafka to gain access to the limbo and to find his way back from it, but Johnnie Walker uses that channel to regain the earth. In the final section of the novel, after the death of Nakata, it is Hoshino who has the task to kill the slimy creature that has come out of the corpse of his old friend and tries to enter the hole at the center of the stone (yet another penetration). Only now does the transgenerational cycle of events at the core of the novel end. Kafka chooses to come back home to Tokyo and resume his studies, while Hoshino, thanks to his journey to Takamatsu, has discovered classical music, Truffaut's films, a sense of responsibility towards others, and perhaps how to give meaning to his life.

Into the Labyrinth

As we can see, the novel breaks with every model: dialogues of a Jamesian subtlety alternate with erotic scenes of surprising intensity, the sphere of the sacred is the object of both poetic intuitions and irreverent irony, Western music — ranging from Schubert's Sonata in D major to Prince and Duke Ellington — is omnipresent. In an interview Murakami explains the omnivorous character of his cultural imagination by stating that he discovered European writers in opposition to his parents, who were interested mainly in Japanese literature. As a result, he devoured not only classics such as Chekhov, Dostoyevsky, Flaubert and Dickens, but also "hardboiled detective stories. Science fiction. Kurt Vonnegut, Richard Brautigan, Truman Capote," often reading these books in English: "It was like a door was opening to another world. And of course when I was a kid I got a transistor radio. There was music — Elvis, the Beach Boys, the Beatles. That was exciting. And they became a part of my life."[37]

In *Kafka on the Shore* the 45 rpm short song Miss Saeki recorded around 1970 is at the heart of a system of correspondences between past and future that involves other forms of representation, such as the painting that portrays Miss Saeki's boyfriend on a beach and the photograph that shows little Kafka and his sister on another beach. Both these images are labeled as *Kafka on the Shore,* bringing us back to the symbolic core of this novel, teeming with symbols and allusions that turn it into a labyrinth of signs. I have already hinted at the importance the labyrinth has within this story, as is shown by this dialogue between Ōshima and Kafka in the mountain cabin. After claiming that next to the world we inhabit there is another that we can explore up to a point, since it is a labyrinth and we run the risk of losing the path that leads us back, Ōshima goes on to explain that the idea of a labyrinth came from the ancient Mesopotamians, who pulled forth the intestines of animals (and possibly of human beings) to predict the future: "So the prototype for labyrinths is, in a word, guts. Which means that the principle for the labyrinth is inside you."[38]

To complete his itinerary of growth, Kafka has to get lost in the forest, where light is filtered and there is no straight path. Indeed, this book explores the resonance between places and people. While in cities, the heart of civilization, the genius loci is mortified, in forests one can experience solitude and wilderness, establishing contact with unknown inner depths. This journey towards the green core of the planet may thus turn into a backward journey in time. While before the invention of the electric light "the physical darkness outside and the inner darkness of the soul were mixed together, with no boundary separating the two," we have turned the night into an artificial replica of the day, "but the darkness in our hearts remains, virtually unchanged. Just like an iceberg, what we label the ego or consciousness is, for the most part, sunk in a darkness."[39]

After underlining the "complex spiritual environment"[40] (including elements of Shintoism, folk legends, Buddhism, Christianity, Judaism and New Age) in which *Kafka on the Shore* was written, J. Philip Gabriel — who translated it into English — claims that the book echoes "the Jungian idea of the unconscious as the 'source of religious experience,'" and describes it as "Murakami's most extended meditation on the healing found in plumbing the inner self."[41] This idea has been developed by Kanya Wattanagun and Suradech Cotiudompant, who analyze the quest for identity on which Kafka embarks to overcome the childhood trauma of abandonment and reawaken "his suppressed emotions."[42] At the end of his ambivalent itinerary, this solitary and emotionally empty adolescent has reconnected to the body of his "mother" and has reassessed her flight from her point of view, thus achieving the ability to forgive. Drawing a parallel between the inner growth of Kafka and of Ōshima — who is presented at first as an empty man whose identity rests on consumption and whose knowledge of the past is nil — the critics regard the novel as an attempt to alert us to the dangers of capitalist society and to reaffirm the importance of "self-exploration" as a process that enables the subject to approach "the external world in a different manner."[43]

As we can see, in order to appreciate the performative dimension of this novel we need to develop an appropriate interpretative attitude, surrendering to this ambivalent narrative machine, which engenders multiple interpretations, ultimately eschewing closure. Of course one cannot grasp this book by relying exclusively on rationality, for here things do not *simply* make sense. If one adopts this attitude, the result is frustration, as exemplified by a reviewer who laments that Murakami left too many events "hanging," and then concludes: "The potential for this book is overwhelming, but it remains just that, potential."[44]

A very large number of readers and critics, however, have succumbed to the fascination of this novel, which explores cogent psychological issues. *Kafka on the Shore* provides us with a model for self-therapy, that is to say, for sounding our inner self by means of stories, images and symbols that resonate with our unconscious, triggering a response in that deep layer of our inner being that we find virtually impossible to reach by means of logic, since the unconscious refutes the principle of non-contradiction, on which logic is based. Of course our interactions with this deep and dark core of our being can never be straight and simple, but must take the form of negotiations. Self-evolution can be achieved, but the itinerary it involves is often circuitous, and to find our way in the hyper-space of the unconscious we have to abandon our tools and certainties, like Kafka when he enters the forest.

Murakami seduces his readers through mysterious channels. He unsettles them by representing the present with perfect mimicry and by simultaneously staging distortions and transgressions of reality as we know it.

6. *Haruki Murakami,* Kafka on the Shore *(2002)*

One could devote much time to Murakami's gift to render the intangible tangible, to make us touch what has no substance, exploring the flux of energies that individuals — in their complex duality as corporeal beings endowed with consciousness — continuously exchange with fellow human beings and with the environment. The result is a new epic, which forces us to read and think, ultimately leaves us disconcerted and admired, possibly different.

7

Jonathan Safran Foer, *Everything Is Illuminated* (2002)

Discussing the definition of *ontological crime* that Elie Wiesel had coined with reference to the Holocaust, Jeffrey Alexander conversely underlines the *epistemological* character of this event, i.e., the cultural process of universalization through which the Holocaust has taken on the meaning of a collective trauma for the whole of humanity. Alexander draws our attention to the fact that if the allies had not won the war, the extermination of the Jews would have been probably shrouded in silence. Even if the liberation of the prisoners from the camps had been effected by the Soviet troops, the historical account of the Holocaust would have been different:

> It was, in other words, precisely and only because the means of symbolic production were not controlled by a postwar victorious Nazi regime, or even by a triumphant communist one, that the mass killings could be called the Holocaust and coded as evil.[1]

At the end of the 20th century a culture of memory has developed in response to the Nazi attempt to exterminate the Jews and to cancel every trace of the massacre. As Efraim Sicher remarks, "Memory is important to give meaning to the future and to form identity."[2] Yet Sicher himself problematizes this apparently safe assertion by asking: "For what and to whom is memory to be transmitted?"[3] Significantly, the answer the critic offers is shaped as another set of questions:

> Is it to preserve a memory of the dead to accord them a sort of resurrection, to warn the nations of the dangers of fascism so that it will not happen again, or to create a sacred legacy of the Holocaust that consti-

tutes a new Jewish or human identity? Is it a universal property as a metaphor of inhumanity, or is it a historical event central to modern Jewish identity in both Israel and the Diaspora?[4]

This cluster of issues cannot be simplified. Far from being monolithical, cultural memory has various facets and uses. What is certain, the Shoah brings to the fore the dangers inherent in the construction of *otherness* within a society. Only by remembering the death of yesterday's *other* can we safeguard the life of today's *other,* whose identity keeps metamorphosing, since *alterity* is defined in relation to shifting cultural differences.

The awareness that evil can manifest itself in ever-new forms and in ever-new places — and that identifying it as such requires endless vigilance — is an important ethical message. Although the 20th century witnessed first the advent of totalitarianisms — from nazi-fascism to communism — and then the twilight of ideologies, it would nevertheless be illusory to think that evil has been exiled once and for all to other pages of the geographic or historical atlas, since it can resurface at any time — in a casual, isolated way, within our serene and complacent lives, and we risk being unprepared to face it, due to our distraction, indifference, lack of solidarity.

After the fall of the Berlin Wall — an event that has deeply modified the political balance, both in Europe and on a global level — Ian McEwan felt the need to tackle this unceasing resurgence of evil in *Black Dogs* (1992) and captured this phenomenon through the image of the black dogs that a young bride faces in postwar France. The black dogs that assault June in a country lane are associated with a cruel recent past of Nazi abuses and tortures, but they become the emblem of the blind and brutal violence that resurfaced in a late–20th-century Europe defaced by new forms of ethnic hatred, notably in the former Yugoslavia.

Life and death repeatedly cross paths in McEwan's novel. When June confronts the animals, she is pregnant with her daughter Jenny. Some years later, Jenny, who has grown into a young woman, goes to Poland as a member of a cultural delegation which also includes Jeremy. The two exchange a few glances and a kiss, then they run away together, not toward an idyllic place, but to visit the concentration camp of Majdanek, at the periphery of Lublin: "I had not fully understood how close the town was to the camp that had consumed all its Jews, three-quarters of its population. They lay side by side, Lublin and Majdanek, matter and anti-matter."[5] Once they are back at the hotel, Jeremy and Jenny spend three days in their room. This marks the beginning of their common life.

One novel, Two narratives

Like *Black Dogs,* Jonathan Safran Foer's *Everything Is Illuminated* (2005) — which derives from the journey that the Jewish-American writer made to Ukraine in 1999 on the tracks of his ancestors[6] — brings us in touch with death and oblivion to teach us the value of memory and life. In this novel an extraordinary flair for the human combines with a versatile talent, which excels both in the comic and in the pathetic. Moreover, Foer is a master of narrative techniques, for the action of this novel develops by means of two intertwining narrative threads which combine realism with the fantastic. The first voice we hear while reading is that of the Ukrainian Alexander Perchov, called Alex, who studies foreign languages at the university but whose English is studded with hilarious malapropisms and all sorts of creative mistakes. It is he who tells the account of the journey he has made together with the American Jew Jonathan Safran Foer, in search of the village of Trachimbrod. The team that sets out on this expedition, which is financed by Jonathan, also includes Alex's grandfather — who claims he has become blind after the death of his wife, although this does not prevent him from driving his car — and his little dog, Sammy Davis, Junior, Junior, as she is called in homage to the old man's favorite singer. Readers soon discover that the mad dog's favorite hobby is throwing herself against the windows of the car and that poor Jonathan, who is mortally afraid of dogs, will have to share the backseat with her.

The second narrative voice is that of Jonathan himself. After coming back from Ukraine, Jonathan has decided to turn his experience into a novel, which he sends to his friend Alex a little at a time, as soon as he writes each new chapter. This second strand of the book takes us back in time to the end of the 18th century, and it also changes its narrative coordinates from a realism charged with humor to a form of magical realism. In Chapter two we are confronted with a mythical event, the fall of the carriage of Trachim B into the river Brod, from which its contents resurface little by little — at first a variety of objects and then a new-born babe, who is subsequently identified by Jonathan as his great-great-great-great-great-grandmother.[7]

The book has a complex structure, but this interplay of narrative planes enables the author to shift easily between various temporal dimensions. Starting from a present that is marked by the encounter between the Jewish-American culture of Jonathan and the post-Soviet background of Alex, the text proceeds backwards towards the past. The material journey of the main characters towards Trachimbrod is paralleled by the imaginary

7. *Jonathan Safran Foer,* Everything Is Illuminated *(2002)*

journey on which readers embark with the help of Jonathan's narrative, recreating life in the shtetl. To bring that place back to life, to enjoy the flavor of the local festivals, of the mad sex, of the disparate reading and of the endless disputes into which the energies of the Jewish community disperse, we have only words, the bricks of fiction. As Foer tells us, "The origin of a story is always an absence."[8]

The novel is actually structured on as many as three main temporal levels: the present, i.e., the autumn of 1997, when Alex repeatedly writes to his American friend to send him his narrative; the recent past, i.e., the journey they made the previous summer; and finally the remote past, i.e., the wide span of time between 1791, when Trachimbrod was founded, and World War II, when the shtetl was destroyed. Jonathan's grandfather survived the disaster thanks to a Ukrainian family, and the photograph that portrays the man in the company of Augustine, the girl who saved him, acquires the value of a magic object, which brings the characters into contact with the past and exerts a mysterious fascination on Alex's grandfather.

One of the first elements we discover while reading this book is the specularity between Jonathan and Alex, who were both born in 1977, but who are the expression of two distant worlds, although their meeting triggers a current of sympathy. An important motif is associated with these two characters: the idea that each of us is the product of historical events whose development is often unexpected, since good and evil are inextricably entwined. It was the flight of Jonathan's grandfather from Ukraine, due to the persecutions suffered by the Jews, that ultimately made it possible for Jonathan to grow up in the rich United States instead of in the Soviet Union:

> I want to see Trachimbrod," the hero said. "To see what it's like, how my grandfather grew up, where I would be now if it weren't for the war." "You would be Ukrainian." "That's right." "Like me." "I guess." "Only not like me because you would be a farmer in an unimpressive town, and I live in Odessa, which is very much like Miami.[9]

This passage testifies to the difficult narrative choice Foer made when he decided to use a comic tone to convey contents that trigger deep emotions in his readers, according to the strategy Alex describes in a letter: "I know that you asked me not to alter the mistakes because they sound humorous, and humorous is the only truthful way to tell a sad story, but I think I will alter them. Please do not hate me."[10]

It should also be underlined that this novel — like *Atonement*—revolves upon itself, toying with the process of literary creation, as is shown by the letters where Alex discusses Jonathan's comments on the chapters he has written. We know that what we have just read is the spurious original text — before any emendations — and we immediately understand that the alternative versions Jonathan proposes would be impoverished, since it is the blunders and shortcomings and awkward incidents that make us laugh at — and with — the characters, who thus become our friends. Indeed laughing is cathartic in this text, both when it has no second meanings and when conversely it is charged with allusions.

Foer's writing can play with our mood like a juggler. It always knows precisely what it is aiming at. This is shown by the scene where the protagonists finally meet a woman they identify as Augustine. Only a great writer is able to work with two simple elements — a question and an answer in the negative, like an obsessive musical phrase — exploring all the nuances of feeling, from the initial refusal to remember, through the mute prayer and on to the final surrender. Our heroes have long been wandering in the countryside looking for Trachimbrod, and the answer people give to their question is invariably *no* — not an absentminded or indifferent *no*, but rather an enraged *no*, which is accompanied by an obstinate silence. It is a negation that reveals more than it intends to. The same thing happens when the trio arrives at a white wooden house, which in the film version is shown as surrounded by sunflowers (how difficult it is in this epoch of remediation to prevent our imagination from blending the various avatars of a story). A small woman is seated on the steps. Her eyes are blue: her long hair is white. She is dressed in white, and she is peeling the corn. The woman claims she does not know either Trachimbrod or Sofiowka (the old name of the village), but Alex insists, showing her the photo of Augustine and repeating this mantra: "Have you ever witnessed anyone in this photograph?"[11]

Questions and negative answers follow one another with a relentless cruelty which is increasingly tinged with love. Through obsessive repetition, this surreal scene prepares the revelation with a crescendo of suspense, compressing the woman's sentiment within her negation to acknowledge memory until it finally bursts when Alex asks her: "Has anyone in this photograph ever witnessed you?"[12] Instead of soliciting the woman as an agent of testimony, this question paradoxically evokes the dead to testify to her existence, and under this sudden wave of emotions the woman surrenders:

> "I have been waiting for you for so long."
> I pointed to the car. "We are searching for Trachimbrod."
> "Oh," she said, and she released a river of tears. "You are here. I am it."[13]

7. Jonathan Safran Foer, Everything Is Illuminated (2002)

The white-haired woman denies she is Augustine, but after allowing the three men into her home, she shows them the boxes in which she collected the remains of Trachimbrod after its destruction.[14] As Cathy Caruth writes in her seminal study of trauma: "To be traumatized is precisely to be possessed by an image or event."[15] This woman has chosen to surround herself with the relics of Trachimbrod to embody a place which exists only in her memory.

Although she is a non-Jewish witness of the Holocaust, the woman is a figure of mourning. When she accompanies her three guests to the site of Trachimbrod, she repeatedly stops to pick up rocks and move them to the side of the road, with a gesture that ambiguously evokes a Jewish ritual of commemoration. Once the visit to Trachimbrod has been accomplished, she even explains how she reacted to the destruction and pillage of the Shtetl. As Alex explains to Jonathan:

> She discovered the house most proximal to Trachimbrod, all of the ones that weren't destroyed were empty, and she promised herself to live there until she died. She secured all of the things that she had hidden, and she brought them to her house. It was her punishment." "For what?" "For surviving," she said.[16]

Heart of Darkness

In this book on the erasure of collective memory, it is the imagination that occupies its place. Words fill the void, colonizing the blank like a benevolently invasive plant. As Alex writes in a letter to Jonathan: "*We are being very nomadic with the truth, yes?*"[17] Then, Alex wonders, why in the act of reinventing life do we not make it seem more beautiful, instead of rendering it grotesque? Why does Jonathan represent the life of his ancestors as fraught with misadventures and unhappiness and inability to love and qualms concerning the existence of God and sad certainties concerning His inexistence? Why is it that at the end of this journey Jonathan and Alex do not find Augustine? "*We could even find Augustine, Jonathan, and you could thank her, and Grandfather and I could embrace, and it could be perfect and beautiful, and funny, and usefully sad, as you say.*"[18] Conforming to this narrative choice, in the following chapters the white-haired woman we have met in her white wooden house is indeed called simply Augustine, although she subsequently reveals that she is Augustine's sister, Lista.

Instead of focussing on history univocally, as something that has already happened, or deterministically, as the necessary effect that results from a set of causes, this novel on memory and the imagination (re)presents the past as a sum of possible narratives which come to life through the choices and negotiations of the two narrators, Jonathan and Alex. Not only does Alex repeatedly observe that what he is telling does not really correspond to what happened during their journey, but the novel deconstructs the narrative voice itself with a prodigious revelation.

While Alex's grandfather — his eyes "impending tears"[19] — is talking with Augustine, and the two young men are waiting outside, Alex peeks at the journal that Jonathan wrote before leaving for Ukraine, while he was still in Prague, discovering that Jonathan had already hypothesized his existence, albeit without inventing his peculiar language.[20] With a fictional short circuit that breaks the realistic framework of the story and clashes with our *suspension of disbelief,* this character witnesses his own literary genesis.

Moreover, the passage Alex reads on this momentous occasion anticipates the ending of the novel, which is related in a letter Alex's grandfather addresses to Jonathan,[21] although the first germ of the ending and the actual ending do not completely coincide. The author is telling us that a writer reaches the final form of a story by means of a slow process of approximation, by means of stories that resemble it but are not *that* story, and that this process is part of the story itself. Like a genetic critic who studies the various manuscripts of a literary work, comparing its various versions, Foer is a demiurge who traces the history of his own act of creation. At this point readers may well experience a feeling of vertigo, but this is a poetic novel, not a cerebral one, and although sometimes we may fear we are losing our way, we soon find it again thanks to a peal of laughter, which is sooner or later followed by a tear. And we are not able to refrain from sharing either, since Foer is an accomplished magician, an alchemist who transmutes emotions.

Yet, at the core of *Everything Is Illuminated* — an expression Alex repeats over and over again, as if to say "everything is clear" — there is a heart of darkness, as our heroes find out when they follow Augustine/Lista to the site of Trachimbrod, and she suddenly stops in the middle of a field:

> "You are tired?" Grandfather asked her. "You have done a lot of walking." "No," she said, "we are here." "She says we are here," I told the hero. "What?" "I informed you that there would be nothing," she said. "It was all destroyed." "What do you mean we're here?" the hero asked. "Tell him it is because it is so dark," Grandfather said to me," and that we could see more if it was not so dark." "It is so dark," I told him. "No," she said, "this is all that you would see. It is always like this, always dark."[22]

This is the place where everything happened — the Nazi massacre and the Ukrainian pillage, but the darkness of Trachimbrod paradoxically enlightens the conscience of the three characters. According to the complex design Foer is pursuing, the tone of Alex's narrative changes after their visit to Trachimbrod—"I do not want to be disgusting anymore. And I do not want to be funny, either."[23] Alex's letters also show that in that autumn of 1997 something is changing within his family. Alex has distanced himself from his father—who is often drunk and violent—and instead of outwardly conforming to the model of masculinity he imposes, he is becoming true to himself, therefore both vulnerable and responsible. Alex's grandfather is also undergoing an important process of redemption, coming to terms with a guilt that lies buried in time.

In the course of the novel, Alex even stops telling facts in his pidgin English and confides the narration to Jonathan, as if the two halves of the split individual who has written the novel so far could no longer stay apart:

> We are talking now, Jonathan, together, and not apart. We are with each other, working on the same story, and I am certain that you can also feel it. Do you know that I am the Gypsy girl and you are Safran, and that I am Kolker and you are Brod, and that I am your grandmother and you are Grandfather; and that I am Alex and you are you, and that I am you and you are me? Do you not comprehend that we can bring each other safety and peace?[24]

Starting from two boys who belong to distant worlds, but who were born in the same year, the novel recomposes this double into a unity thanks both to friendship[25] and to the labor of memory, which changes the present by delving into the past. *Everything Is Illuminated* explores the many visages of evil and guilt—not only the genocide the Nazi organized with rigorous ferocity, but also the acquiesence of the Ukrainians, and moreover the resurgence of evil in our present, as exemplified by the violent behavior of Alex's father. We discover that Alex's grandfather never told his son about the horrors of war, thus preventing him from acquiring that consciousness of evil that is the only bulwark against it. Foer's novel tells us that in the darkness of silence evil grows undisturbed, while words have the task of illuminating everything so that each human being can recognize him/herself in any other human being, for evil derives from the inability to look beyond the circumference of one's ego.

Beyond the Tragic

The difficulty of representing the Holocaust has been a major concern of cultural theorists in the last few decades, starting from Theodor Adorno's seminal 1949 claim that writing poetry after Auschwitz is barbaric. As

Ronit Lentin meditates, silence is not the appropriate answer to genocide, but we cannot escape "the dilemmas of representation"[26] that this issue involves. *Everything Is Illuminated* is but one of several partly comic — and therefore "unorthodox"— rewritings of the Nazi genocide of Jews. I am thinking of Roberto Benigni's *Life Is Beautiful* (1997) and Radu Mihaileanu's *Train of Life* (1998). In these two films the tragic register that originally marked the cultural treatment of this theme has been superseded by a levity that entails episodes ranging from farce to the fairy tale,[27] where humor and pathos freely mingle. It is against this varied and colorful backdrop that the inhuman attempt to cancel an entire people stands out by contrast. These bravely conceived works have the merit of eschewing a certain rhetoric of memory, the risk of falling into a ritual iteration that is ultimately lacking in genuine emotional involvement. They depict the enormity of horror by way of a representational dynamic that obliges the public to alternate between conflicting moods.

The literature of the Holocaust has deeply changed at the turn of the century, since instead of striving to render the experiences of victims in a realist mode, in order to make them memorable, writers have experimented with a variety of narrative strategies and points of view so as to revitalize the representation of horror. As Raoul Eshelman writes:

> The visual and literary depictions of concentration-camp horrors are so well known that they have either become clichés or diminished greatly in their power to disturb us. In late postmodernism, this exhaustion of original victimary experience has given rise to works whose means of arguing are ultimately more aesthetic than didactic or documentary.[28]

Tracing the evolution of this theme, Eshelman points out two recent trends — on the one hand, the use of an "inappropriate" narrative mode such as the comic, which celebrates life, subverting the centrality of death that pertains to the tragic, and on the other, the new relevance these narratives give to the experiences of the perpetrators. This strategy is apparent in novels such as Bernhard Schlink's *The Reader* (1995) and Jonathan Littel's *The Kindly Ones* (2007), both pivoting on ambiguous figures of Nazis.

Schlink's novel opens in Germany in the aftermath of World War II, exploring the asymmetric relation between a 15-year-old boy, Michael, and a woman who is 36, Hanna. The two are united both by the books he reads aloud for her and by an erotic attraction which alternates with explosions of aggressiveness on her part. The affair lasts through a summer. A few years later, the narrator, who is now a university student in law, observes a trial for war crimes and discovers that Hanna is one of the defen-

7. Jonathan Safran Foer, Everything Is Illuminated (2002) 133

dants. The woman had been an SS guard in a satellite camp of Auschwitz, where the Jewish prisoners, before being gassed, read books aloud for her. Moreover, Hanna is one of the guards who are accused of letting 300 women burn in the fire of a church, and she is actually suspected of directing the operation and writing the report. Although Hanna does not acknowledge it, the narrator understands that she is neither able to write nor read. It is probably not to reveal this shameful reality that Hanna renounces the chance to defend herself and is condemned to life imprisonment.

The novel investigates both the complex relation between perpetrator and victim and the parallel relation between Hanna and the narrator, whose emotional life has been warped by his youthful experience, as is shown by his failure as a husband and father. Michael's feelings towards Hanna are a mixture of oedipal attraction and guilt. Hanna, for her part, is a deeply ambivalent figure, whose role within the concentration camp remains uncertain, although the woman lives her years of imprisonment as a long spiritual retirement. Hanna's relationship with Michael is an uncanny combination of anger and tenderness, and only in his adult age, when he discovers her secret, does he manage to understand, at least in part, her eccentric behavior. Their intimacy is based on the books they share rather than on details about their lives, and the hot bath that marks the transition between reading and lovemaking reminds us of a ritual of purification. The body of the adolescent narrator — who is unsoiled by the war — superimposes on the ill-nourished, ill-treated bodies of the women readers Hanna selected within the camp. Although this is never fully clarified, we are led to regard this practice as a possible act of compassion, for the guard thus managed to employ the weakest prisoners in a less painful job, before sending them to die at Auschwitz when the routine turnover of the camp made this "necessary" — a necessity Hanna never questioned.

This controversial novel has triggered preoccupied reactions on the part of critics who see Hanna as the allegory of an obnubilated but also seductive Nazi Germany, which is contrasted with the victims for whom the text does not invite our full sympathy.[29] *The Reader* oscillates between the *denunciation* of the guilty unawareness that governs Hanna's actions, her mental torpor, her uncritical obedience to perverse rules, and on the other hand *compassion*, since Hanna has been loved by the narrator and has loved him in return. The book addresses delicate subjects such as the search for truth and the possibility of reconciliation, an issue which is suspended in the book. In the penultimate chapter, set in New York, Michael pays a visit to a survivor who testified against Hanna and the other guards.

The lady — who had been interned in the camp as a child, together with her mother, and who had subsequently related her experience in a book — does not accept the small sum of money Hanna saved during her life and bequeathed to her as a naive form of atonement. Yet, with one of those ambiguous gestures that contribute to the depth of this novel, she keeps the old tea caddy where Hanna stored the money. As the survivor explains, this apparently worthless object would take the place of a tea caddy that she had brought to the camp and that somebody had stolen.

The book pivots on the opposition between illiteracy and literacy. The inability to read also stands for a form of autism, for the inability to relate to the *other*, to read the *other*'s heart, to experience empathy. *The Reader* traces the gradual itinerary whereby Hanna — who is at first both illiterate and indifferent — comes into contact with the suffering of the Jews by reading the memoirs of those who were imprisoned in the camps, from Primo Levi to Elie Wiesel, Tadeusz Borowski and Jean Améry.[30] The end of this process of (self-) discovery is Hanna's suicide, on the day before regaining freedom. The narrator plays an essential role in Hanna's progressive opening to awareness and responsibility, since it is he who educates her to reading and to feelings, by means of the classics of literature that he sends to the prison after recording them on tape. This vicarious form of reading then turns into a first-person experience when Hanna herself learns to read. It is ultimately Michael's love that teaches Hanna to read her own and other people's hearts, and this 15-year-old-boy's love that survives time and distance achieves its instinctive goal of redemption by means of books. It is thanks to these uncanny cultural mediators, which enable people to share their experience, that Hanna is able to overcome her identity of horse-woman (an image that is referred to her both by the narrator and by a victim)[31] and to embrace a fuller humanity.

Blindness and Insight

Everything Is Illuminated also explores the perspective of perpetrators, both on a collective level — since it shows the role Ukrainians played in the genocide of the Jews and in the subsequent removal of the event — and on an individual level, through the events Alex's grandfather experienced during the war. Like Augustine/Lista, Alex's grandfather can be regarded as a figure of trauma, whose ambivalent symptom — his supposed blindness — is located in an uncertain zone between the body and the mind. Trauma is characterized by "belatedness," since it manifests itself after a period of latency and therefore may appear as disconnected from the original event that provoked it. Only after the death of his wife, when his affective ties have been broken, does the old man become aware of his blindness, which is rooted however in distant events.

The old man's eyes are involved in his process of self-discovery right from the beginning. When he first sees the photograph of Augustine, "He scrutinized at the photograph [...]. He put it close to his face, like he wanted to smell it, or touch it with his eyes."[32] As we have seen, the journey towards the site of Trachimbrod, the novel's heart of darkness, triggers a painful process of self-inquiry. After talking separately with Augustine, Alex's grandfather is ready to share his moral burden with the two young men who accompany him, acknowledging his unwilling — but all the same guilty — complicity in the death of his best friend Herschel, one of the Jews who lived in the village of Kolki, near Trachimbrod.

Memories are again triggered by mediators. When the three protagonists open a box marked IN CASE that Augustine gave Jonathan, they discover a great number of photographs. One of them features Alex's grandmother, holding his father, together with his grandfather and another man, Herschel. Only now does grandfather confess that he sees ghosts, "on the insides of the lids of my eyes."[33] Like in *Austerlitz*, trauma takes the form of a revenant, which is here associated with (lack of) eyesight. The character's perception of his blindness becomes a trope not only for his unacknowledged guilt, but also for his consequent lack of dreams and of beliefs: "There is no love. Only the end of love."[34] As a civilian who has been forced by the Nazis to choose between his own death and that of his Jewish friend, Alex's grandfather has the ambivalent status of both victim and perpetrator, as is implied in his angry reaction when his nephew urges him to reveal what happened to Herschel: "To him? To him and to me. It happened to everybody, do not make any mistakes. Just because I was not a Jew, it does not mean that it did not happen to me."[35]

At the core of grandfather's guilt, however, we also find a lack of faith in the redemptive power of memory, which translates in his inability to acquaint his own son with the realities of death and shame: "I was the worst father. I desired to remove him from everything that was bad, but instead I gave him badness upon badness. A father is always responsible for how his son is."[36] After his visit to the site of Trachimbrod, however, grandfather's attitude completely changes, and he invests his nephew with the role of witness of his shame, an emotion which implies the full recognition of his responsibility: "I murdered Herschel. Or what I did was as good as murdering him."[37]

Grandfather's heartrending account of being forced by Germans to choose between his own life and Herschel's culminates in the burning of the synagogue where the Jews have been confined. The event is uncannily associated with the central metaphor of the novel, since when a young man — no older than Alex and Jonathan are — lights the first match and flames start spreading, all the witnesses are suddenly "illuminated."[38]

The suicide of grandfather is presented not as an act of desperation, but as the final stage of his itinerary towards illumination, as if this self-sacrifice symbolically cut every link with a violent past, enabling the old man's grandchildren — Alex and Iggy — to live at peace. Foer's novel achieves its conclusion precisely when grandfather is describing the liberating gesture he is about to make:

> Everyone in the house is in bed but me. I am writing this in the luminescence of the television, and I am so sorry if this is now difficult to read, Sasha, but my hand is shaking so much, and it is not out of weakness that I will go to the bath when I am sure that you are asleep, and it is not because I cannot endure. Do you understand? I am complete with happiness, and it is what I must do, and I will do it. Do you understand me? I will walk without noise, and I will open the door in darkness, and I will[39]

Alex's grandfather abandons the world feeling free from the burden of lies and guilt, at the end of a novel where the possibility of reconciliation is associated not with the children of victims and perpetrators but with their grandchildren.

Postmemory Novels

According to Marianne Hirsch, *postmemory* "characterizes the experience of those who grow up dominated by narratives that preceded their birth."[40] Postmemory is not only marked — with comparison to memory — by a larger dose of "imaginative investment and creation,"[41] but it has often to do with the transmission of traumatic memory, notably within a family. In addition, it is often mediated by artifacts such as photographs and other objects, and we have seen how central the role of photographs is in Foer's postmemory novel.

As Hirsch wonders, "Is postmemory limited to victims, or does it include bystanders and perpetrators, or could one argue that it complicates the delineations of these positions which, in Holocaust studies, have come to be taken for granted?"[42] *Everything Is Illuminated* problematizes this issue by juxtaposing a Jewish and a Ukrainian family. While in this novel — which has been written by a third-generation writer — the second generation is prevented from achieving a salvific consciousness of the past, it is the third generation which is able to strive towards reconciliation, thanks to the working of memory. As Alan L. Berger claims, "Seeking to transform trauma into history, third-generation writers simultaneously mourn their loss and work through their legacy in a process which helps them clarify their Jewish identity in the hovering shadows of the Shoah."[43]

Foer, however, achieves an even more ambitious goal in this novel, as Berger himself acknowledges when he writes that "Alex's own unintended pilgrimage of self-discovery in fact eclipses that of the purported hero."[44] Although it is a descendant of the victims who digs into the past, bringing its evils to light, it is a descendant of the perpetrators who learns this lesson in ethics, proving able to respond to present evil — as embodied by Alex's violent father — and taking care of those who need his help, i.e., his mother and younger brother. Foer's choice to intertwine the destinies of his two young protagonists, playing with symmetries and oppositions in their characterization, but ultimately insisting on the mutually enriching value of their relationship, suffices to endow this work of fiction with a message that goes beyond the idea of Holocaust memory as an element of Jewish identity, turning this novel also into a universal parable of guilt and redemption. Of course both these interpretations are possible since this inherently dual novel pivots on the tension between the non–Jewish perspective of Alex and the Jewish perspective of Jonathan, whose trip to Ukraine likewise sheds light where darkness previously was, for he had never asked his grandmother the meaning of the Yiddish words she pronounced, being "just too afraid."[45]

The ultimate message of the novel is therefore the necessity to communicate experience, even when it is painful and/or shameful. As Francisco Collado-Rodriguez asserts, "by employing contrasting perspectives of myth and realism, Foer clearly sides with those who maintain that the Holocaust is not utterly unrepresentable and that keeping silent about it is not the ethical response to the Jew's annihilation."[46] *Everything Is Illuminated* is indeed a moving book on memory and oblivion, on life and death, and also on the power and frailty of language, since Jonathan's exuberant inventiveness is contrasted with the all-too-human imperfection of Alex, who is endowed neither with the linguistic competencies nor with the maturity that he needs to perform his work of mediation between cultures. And yet, the linguistic misunderstandings and the squalor of the Ukrainian hotels and the deadly smell of Sammy Daves, Junior, Junior's farts create a cocktail of humanity that, once we shut the book, makes us long to spend more time within its pages, for its characters have by now become our friends. And when we relive their history in our mind, we strangely feel like crying with them over the destiny of Trachimbrod and the guilts — whatever they are — of our fathers.

8

Azar Nafisi, *Reading Lolita in Tehran* (2003)

Reading Lolita in Tehran: A Memoir in Books is a hybrid text both in terms of genre — for it is suspended between the memoir, the novel and criticism — and because its author, who is of Iranian origin, lives and works in the United States. The volume asserts its transcultural status right from the title, where Nabokov's novel — which has become the emblem of forbidden desire — contrasts with the severity of present-day Tehran. What is difficult to ascertain is whether this ambivalent text is a commercial product, an instrument of political propaganda or the authentic testimony of a woman who has fled from a regime. *Reading Lolita in Tehran* is possibly all these things at once. Indeed, this controversial book has soon become a literary case, since it defies any ideology in the name of an anarchist pleasure of reading, although its detractors remark that the novels Nafisi utilizes to contrast the monological discourse of the Islamic Republic of Iran bring us back to the Anglo-American canon, which is in itself not exempt from ideological elements. We will delve into this debate after discussing the book, where Nafisi invites us to reread Nabokov, Fitzgerald, James and Austen with new eyes, relating them to the social and political reality of a distant country, reassessing our epoch through the literature of the past.

Back to Tehran

Reading Lolita in Tehran burgeons with love for this city, which is portrayed as suffering during the war against Iraq (1980–88). The ingredients of this urban landscape are fear and pain, buildings in ruins, roars and vibrations that wake people up from their sleep, window panes that explode due to the fury of the bombs. Moreover, morality squads patrol the streets in white Toyotas to ensure that women do not transgress the laws that rule their behavior in public by breaking into a run or uncovering their head or shaking hands with a stranger or showing painted nails. Tehran, however, is also a city whose gardens remind us of ancient Persia — a place of long-standing civilization where one can enjoy refined pleasures such as reading poetry with friends.

To enter with our imagination into the Islamic Republic of Iran, where the most banal details of everyday life can trigger the rage of power, we have to overcome a symbolic boundary. Let us accomplish this rite together with Nafisi, who portrays herself as coming back to her native country from the States, where she studied and lived for some years. Only, the country has deeply changed in the intervening period:

> The walls of the airport have dissolved into an alien spectacle, with giant posters of an ayatollah staring down reproachfully. Their mood is echoed in the black and bloodred slogans: DEATH TO AMERICA! DOWN WITH IMPERIALISM & ZIONISM! AMERICA IS OUR NUMBER-ONE ENEMY![1]

Recounting that moment, the author looks at her former self from outside, and even claims she wishes to avoid the young woman, since meeting her involves too much suffering, but "there is no way I can avoid her."[2] This is indeed a book where women's identity is both painful and obliterated. In this scene Nafisi contrasts the festive image of the airport as she remembers it from her childhood with its stern and threatening present appearance, marked by the giant portraits of the ayatollah: "It was as if a bad witch with her broomstick had flown over the building and in one sweep had taken away the restaurants, the children and the women in colorful clothes that I remembered."[3] One of the main coordinates of the book is indeed the contrast between the range of colors that marked Iran before Khomeini — colors that becomes a symbol of pluralism, at least on a personal level, in terms of self-expression — and the omnipresent black that marks the present of the country.

These reflections bring us to the main ambiguity of this book, where Nafisi unhesitatingly criticizes the government of the mullah, but basically suspends her judgments concerning the monarchy of Mohammad Reza Pahlavi, which however degenerated into an absolutist regime founded on torture and on the action of the redoubtable secret police, SAVAK. One should keep in mind that in that period Nafisi's parents were important public figures in the country. Her father was mayor of Tehran, and her mother was one of the six women who were elected as deputies in the

Iranian parliament in 1963, the year Khomeini was exiled for plotting against the Shah. To understand the recent history of the country, which has been marked by the creation of the Islamic Republic, following the exile of the Shah to the U.S. in 1979, it is necessary to remember that in Iran, the mid–20th-century was indeed a time of "modernization," but also of violent political strifes, which culminated in the repression of communist and religious movements by the monarchic government.

Although *Reading Lolita in Tehran* glosses over that period, Nafisi has tried to fill the blanks with *Things I've Been Silent About* (2008), a text which is at the same time more intimate and more political. While in her *Memoir in Books* Nafisi focuses on her role as teacher of literature and devotes much energy to a sociological appraisal of Iran under the ayatollah, her recent book covers a larger time span, telling the story of her family against the background of 20th-century Iranian history. Episodes such as the trial of Mossadegh or the incarceration of Nafisi's father in 1963, when the Shah became increasingly suspicious of the political figures that surrounded him, are presented from a private perspective that does not deprive them of their public dimension. The text — which also draws on Nafisi's father's unpublished and voluminous diaries — abounds in details concerning both the author's family and the historical setting in which they played such a prominent role, coherently with Nafisi's interest for "those fragile intersections — the places where moments in an individual's private life resonate with and reflect a larger, more universal story."[4] The book is definitely a good read, and in its emphasis on the subjectivity of memory it achieves a touching form of truth, but one wonders how many copies such an in-depth investigation would have sold without the immense success of *Reading Lolita in Tehran,* the rhetorical strategies of which I will now explore.

Life in Black

We know that a black object absorbs all the radiations of light, while a white one reflects them all. Black is the *non-color* of conformity, of dictatorship, of slogans — not only anti–American or patriotic slogans, supporting the holy war against Iraq, but those maxims that condition individuals in every aspect of their lives, such as "MY SISTER, GUARD YOUR VEIL. MY BROTHER, GUARD YOUR EYES."[5] While teaching at the university, Nafisi has long conversations with her superiors in the course of which they never look at her directly. Needless to say, this supposed form of respect actually contributes to the erasure of women, undermining their conception of themselves. The veil women are required to wear can likewise be described as a *uniform,* a page covered with black ink, which prevents women from writing themselves by means of signs such as clothes, jewels, makeup, but also their body language. Women are written by the system since their destiny as wives and mothers has already been decided by the religious hierarchies.

While the veil "deprives" women of their body, the repeated searches to which they are subject — for instance when entering the university campus — conversely remind them of their body through humiliation. Women are almost asked to think of their body as dirty and inferior, and only slowly does the protagonist acquire the melancholy freedom to forget her body, to divest herself of it.

Of course, this painful experience of being expropriated of one's body and identity through the veil imposed by the regime is entirely different from the individual experience of religious faith that was previously embodied by the chador. Far from tracing such a simplistic equivalence, the author cherishes her childhood memories of her grandmother's chador, which was "a shelter, a world apart from the rest of the world. I remember the way she wrapped her chador around her body and the way she walked around her yard when the pomegranates were in bloom."[6] While the chador of Nafisi's grandmother is associated with her intimacy and self-respect, the chador of the Islamic republic is an instrument of control and political consensus, and as such is worn by those who support the status quo.

Yet, even in the darkness of a Tehran where fanaticism and militant orthodoxy prevail, colors resurface in the tones of an ice cream or of a rose, but mainly in domestic intimacy. The opposition between private and public takes on various connotations in the book. It translates as the contrast between the university room — a space where the transmission/production of knowledge is subject to censorship — and the drawing room of Nafisi, where in autumn 1995, after the author resigns from her post as professor since the political pressure is too strong, Nafisi and her seven best students meet to discuss literature, but with a proviso: "They were all women — to teach a mixed class in the privacy of my home was too risky, even if we were discussing harmless works of fiction."[7]

The private space enables the girls to manifest their own personality, which has been cancelled in public by the regime. The author conveys the sense of this metamorphosis in a highly symbolic passage where she observes two photographs, both taken immediately before she left Tehran for the U.S.: "In the first there are seven women against a white wall. They are, according to the law of the land, dressed in black robes and head scarves, covered except for the oval of their faces and their hands."[8] The second photograph eloquently portrays the same women without their coverings: "Splashes of color separate one from the next. Each has become distinct through the color and style of her clothes, the color and the length of her hair; not even the two who are still wearing their head scarves look the same."[9] Once the veil has become a personal choice, even those who wear it regain their individuality—the veil is no longer an instrument of erasure but of expression.

The Politics and Poetics of Identity

The author insists on the fact that the impositions women are subject to under the regime are meant to induce conformity, eroding their personality, and she underlines the difficulty her students experience in acknowledging their identity, as is proved by the images the girls choose to represent themselves in the course of a test: "Manna saw herself as a fog, moving over concrete objects, taking on their form but never becoming concrete herself. Yassin described herself as a figment."[10]

Nafisi's female students often feel like the product of an external imposition. To examine the mechanism that turns an individual into an object, Nafisi utilizes a novel that we would hardly associate with the Islamic context—Nabokov's *Lolita*, the story of Humbert Humbert, the nice and persuasive gentleman who falls in love with a 12-year-old girl and manages to keep her prisoner, thanks to her condition as an orphan. Humbert possesses Lolita sexually without possessing her soul, but what Nafisi is mainly interested in is the fact that Humbert, telling Lolita's story in his own voice, manages to conquer the reader's sympathy. Nafisi and her students misread this novel, adapting it to a context that radically differs from that in which it was conceived, and turn Lolita into the emblem of the many children who get married at the age of nine, since this is the age of female consent to marriage in Iran. Thus Humbert comes to embody those tyrants who rewrite the identity of their subjects in their own image, usurping their lives: "To reinvent her, Humbert must take from Lolita her own real history and replace it with his own, turning Lolita into a reincarnation of his lost, unfulfilled young love, Annabel Leigh."[11] Deprived of her past, Lolita "becomes a figment in someone else's dream,"[12] like the girls who meet in Nafisi's drawing room. Possessing the others, depriving them of their dreams to oblige them to inhabit one's own, is regarded by Nafisi as an extreme evil, since the human power to plan one's future ultimately rests on the imagination.

The first text Nafisi and her female students analyze is not a Western novel, but actually a product of the Golden Age of Islam, the *Thousand and One Nights*. Nafisi concentrates on the frame story, famously concerning a Persian king whose wife is unfaithful and is therefore executed. The king's hatred of women, however, is not sated. Thus he marries a long series of virgins only to have them killed the morning after, until Scheherazade escapes this fate by telling him a story that she promises to end the following night. While the virgins passively accept the arbitrary dictate of the king, Scheherazade "fashions her universe [...] through imagination and reflection."[13]

This brings us back to Nafisi's view of literature as a decisive instrument in the formation of identity and in our lifelong exploration of the human. The author believes that energies continually overflow from the imaginative dimension to reality, and it is this faith in our ability to conceive alternative worlds that reinforces her opposition to the ayatollah's regime. Those who embrace orthodoxy are interested only in verifying the morality of a literary work, but Nafisi fights against this narrow-minded attitude, which reduces novels to their ideological dimension. Nafisi conversely shows her students the beauty and complexity of writing, which often prevents us from formulating facile moral judgments, since a novel "can be called moral when it shakes us out of our stupor and makes us confront the absolutes we believe in."[14]

For Nafisi, who conceives reading and criticism as tools of resistance against a totalitarian society, novels constitute a space of freedom, a room of one's own in an inner space that is increasingly invaded by political slogans. The writer repeatedly underlines the necessity for individuals to maintain control of their private space, refuting those external influences that would deprive them of a fundamental right. While a left-wing slogan of years ago, maintains that the private is political, Nafisi resolutely denies this.

> At the core of the fight for political rights is the desire to protect ourselves, to prevent the political from intruding on our individual lives. Personal and political are interdependent but not one and the same thing. The realm of the imagination is a bridge between them, constantly refashioning one in terms of the other.[15]

In passages such as this Nafisi takes a political stance that is opposed both to communism and Islamic fundamentalism. According to Nafisi, after the banishment of the Shah and the first attempts to establish a democratic government, the country's future was jeopardized by two opposite forms of extremism: left-wing and religious radicalism. Both these systems of thought deny individuals their space, depriving them of the right to nourish their dreams, but literature is the best antidote against any pervasive and totalizing ideology: "A good novel is one that shows the complexity of individuals, and creates enough space for all these characters to have a voice; in this way a novel is called democratic."[16]

When she discusses Fitzgerald's *Great Gatsby*—which is denounced by orthodox students as a decadent text, a product of the ailing culture of the United States — Nafisi remarks that the novel, contrary to their assertions, does not deal with adultery at all, but with "the loss of dreams," and adds: "A great novel heightens your senses and sensitivity to the complexities of life and of individuals, and prevents you from the self-righteousness that sees morality in fixed formulas about good and evil...."[17] Novels educate to subjectivity and difference, to pluralism and democracy — all values which are founded on the respect of the other. Needless to say, the regime of Tehran follows another course, preferring the monologue of divine revelation to the polyphony of the novel.

What is the strongest temptation Nafisi and her female students experience in late–20th-century Iran? It is a yearning for escape, the desire to disappear. Nafisi falls into a state of deep alienation, a condition of solitude and suspect from which she recovers thanks to her books and her students. Her room thus becomes "a place of transgression," "a wonderland"[18] where they move in and out of the novels they read. Nafisi is rescued from hostile everyday life by books, which engender knowledge, complicity, affection, laughter, tears, happiness, according to dynamics which are sometimes contradictory. As Mitra meditates:

> Why is it that stories like *Lolita* and *Madame Bovary*—stories that are so sad, so tragic — make us happy? Is it not sinful to feel pleasure when reading about something so terrible? Would we feel this way if we were to read about it in the newspapers or if it happened to us? If we were to write about our lives here in the Islamic Republic of Iran, should we make our readers happy?[19]

This is one of those self-reflexive passages that typify contemporary literature. We should thank Mitra for the question she poses since she is giving voice to a deep truth — books have this mysterious power to make us happy by telling sad stories, but happy is probably not the right word. Books have rather the paradoxical power to make us feel more alive precisely when we forget real life to immerse ourselves in reading.

This power of books is explored in the chapter Nafisi devotes to the humanitarian engagement of Henry James during World War I. This is the climax of a letter James wrote to a female friend whose husband had died in battle:

"I am incapable of telling you not to repine and rebel," he wrote, "because I have so, to my cost, the imagination of all things, and because I am incapable of telling you not to feel. Feel, feel, I say — feel for all you're worth, and even if it kills you, for that is the only way to live."[20]

Like James, Nafisi invites her readers to feel, suffer and laugh, and her ability to use different registers to communicate at an emotional level has definitely contributed to the great success of this book, which has acquired an important — albeit controversial — role within the cultural debates of our present.

Narratives of the Iranian Diaspora

Before delving into the reception of *Reading Lolita in Tehran*, I wish to contextualize the volume within the subgenre of the autobiographical narratives that have resulted from the Iranian diaspora, such as Marjane Satrapi's graphic novel *Persepolis* (2000–2003), which has appeared in Paris, where Satrapi lives and works,[21] or Azadeh Moaveni's *Lipstick Jihad* (2006) and *Honeymoon in Tehran* (2009). Moaveni — an American journalist of Iranian origin — is also co-author of Shirin Ebadi's *Iran Awakening* (2006).[22] Ebadi embodies a particular aspect of this phenomenon, since although her books were published in Western countries, the author has continued to live in Iran, fighting against totalitarianism from the inside. Ebadi — who became a judge in 1969, under the Shah regime, and was dismissed from her post after the Revolution of 1979 — managed to set up her own practice as a lawyer in 1992, helping dissidents, supporting the freedom of the press, advocating women's and children's rights. Both *Iran Awakening* and *The Golden Cage* (2008) were published after Ebadi obtained the Nobel Prize for Peace in 2003,[23] thus achieving planetary recognition.

The Golden Cage — which has appeared in various languages, but not yet in English[24] — is another hybrid narrative, part memoir and part novel, providing an extensive historical commentary on the transition between the Shah regime and the Islamic Republic of Iran, which the narrator describes mainly through the tormented story of a female friend whose family progressively falls apart, like the country itself. Each of the girl's three brothers responds to the ideological calling which is closest to his personality, and they respectively become a general of the Shah, a Marxist and a follower of the mullahs, while their sister is rather sensitive to the hedonist calling of the West, but also fights to keep the family together, to prevent ideological closure from prevailing over affection. The great evil that Ebadi's characters have to fight is ideology itself—the golden cage which is mentioned in the title. In her book Ebadi renders the mechanism of progressive detachment that transforms a community—be it a family or a country—into a battlefield, in which contrasting ideologies take on an absolute value, leaving no space for mediation and dialogue. Despite her tragic analysis, however, Ebadi takes a clear stance against expatriation. While the narrator's friend, after witnessing the disruption of her family, migrates to Great Britain, the narrator reasserts the necessity to be rooted in one's own country and fight for a better future.

We can read Ebadi's book as a response to that of Nafisi. It is undoubtedly an attempt to render—through the vicissitudes of a family—the complex field of forces that clashed in Iran in the second half of the 20th century, relating the tormented history of the Islamic Republic and the events that led to its formation. In this respect, Ebadi's criticism is leveled at the notorious CIA-backed Operation Ajax, which in August 1953 resulted in a coup that overthrew the prime minister, Mohammad Mosaddegh, who was responsible for the nationalization of the Iranian oil industry, which had previously been under foreign control. The return of the Shah from exile marked the beginning of the absolutist and repressive phase of Reza Pahlavi's government, which led to the 1979 revolution.

What these narratives of the Iranian diaspora have in common is their cross-cultural status, insofar as they depict the Iranian situation but are addressed to a mainly Western public, and moreover describe the identity negotiations their protagonists have gone through to adapt to different cultural contexts. Azadeh Moaveni's *Lipstick Jihad* is eloquently subtitled: *A Memoir of Growing Up Iranian in America and American in Iran*. Likewise, as Gillian Whitlock writes, in Nafisi's and Satrapi's texts "loss of the self and its place in the world engenders a resurrection through memoir as a Western metropolitan intellectual and a diasporic subject with a troubled and ambivalent relation to a lost homeland."[25]

As a result, Nafisi—who abandoned Iran at 13 to study in the West, returned to post–Revolution Iran only to find the country deeply changed, and moved back to the U.S. as an exile in 1997—has developed the ability to associate the feeling of home to an inner space she can inhabit at any time, regardless of external circumstances. As she claims, this inner space harbors not only those personal memories on which the core of her self rests, but also those books which have helped her bridge the gap between the East and the West. Starting from this diasporic conception of identity, Nafisi comes to argue in favor of an identification of the individual with the planetary: "The real home we have transcends ethnicity and nationality, gender, sex, and religion. It is a universal space where we can all live in."[26]

Ebadi's and Nafisi's books also need to be contextualized within a larger body of cultural works authored by women from Arab countries and that have obtained worldwide renown. I am thinking of books such as *Beyond the Veil* (1975), *Dreams of Trespass* (1994) and *Scheherazade Goes West* (2000), which were originally published in the United States by the Moroccan feminist and sociologist Fatema Mernissi.[27] The documentary *Beneath the Veil* (2001) by the British-Afghan filmmaker Saira Shah is another case in point. Reading Nafisi's text against this production reveals the contradiction at the core of *Reading Lolita in Tehran,* for on the one hand Nafisi proclaims the independence of literature from politics (its kinship to a private space that must be protected from state control) while on the other she offers full proof of the subversive power of literature as a weapon against totalitarianism.

A Heated Critical Debate

These reflections help us understand why the reception of this novel has been so controversial. While Michiko Kakutani describes it as "an eloquent brief on the transformative powers of fiction,"[28] the book's detractors have underlined Nafisi's complacent attitude towards the Shah and the proximity of her family to this regime.[29] Various essays have been written to demonstrate that Nafisi's text artfully conceals a precise political strategy, starting from the violent attack Hamid Dabashi — who teaches Iranian studies and comparative literature in the U.S.— published in 2006 in the Egyptian newspaper *Al Ahram.* The attack is fully fledged: on a political level the author is accused of conniving with the imperialism of the Bush administration, while the cover of the book — featuring two veiled teenagers whose downcast eyes seem to point towards the title, and thus creating a cross-cultural short circuit with Lolita as a sexual stereotype — "insidiously unleashes a phantasmagoric Oriental fantasy."[30]

This cover, which was chosen by the publisher, has indeed triggered a polemic. While the portrait of two veiled girls seemingly evokes a remissive attitude, hinting at the subordinate condition of women in Iran, it is actually a detail taken from a photograph in which the two girls are reading a newspaper concerning the election of President Khatami. Dabashi and other critics regard this cover as the symbol of the biased perspective that marks the book, which reflects only part of the reality of Iran.[31]

The list of protesters — often Americans of Iranian origin — includes the feminist Mitra Rastegar, who unequivocally associates the "recent proliferation of memoirs by Iranian and Iranian American women" with "an increased U.S. focus on Iran as part of the Bush administration-dubbed 'axis of evil.'"[32] She also notices that the book was launched in the States in late March 2003, while Iraq was being invaded by a coalition led by the U.S. According to Rastegar, *Reading Lolita in Tehran* actually revives the orientalist tradition, reinforcing the perception of a modern and rational West versus an anti-modern and irrational East, and thus consolidating the prejudices of Western readers. Rastegar also focuses on the ambivalent transcultural status of the author, who is regarded by her Western public as an "insider," and therefore a reliable witness, but whose life experiences and worldviews are actually cosmopolitan, marking her point of view on Iran as exceptional, as is proved also by her biased account of 20th-century Iranian history.

Following in Rastegar's footsteps, Fatemeh Keshavarz — whose volume *Jasmine and Stars: Reading More than "Lolita" in Tehran* appeared in 2007 — accuses Nafisi of offering a false perspective on the role of women in Iranian society: "Like many works contributing to the New Orientalist narrative, *RLT* contains a few patches of truth. In its entirety, however, it is a tapestry with many holes, a mosaic that has every other piece missing."[33] According to Keshavarz, instead of enhancing transcultural understanding, this New Orientalist attitude emphasizes opposition, exciting to clash. While Keshavarz's book is characterized by a poetic tone — in an attempt to give voice to Iranian culture, which has been passed over in silence by Nafisi — rather than by a convincing argumentative structure, other recent essays pursue more complex and effective strategies.

Simon Hay, for instance, discusses *Reading Lolita in Tehran* starting from the fact that at Connecticut College in summer 2004 the book was part of the summer reading list for incoming first-year students. Exploring the implications of this choice, Hay claims that in the context of American universities Nafisi's book does not support critical thinking, but rather consolidates values which have been abundantly institutionalized. Hay also accuses Nafisi of titillating her readers, drawing on the lure of oriental women. In particular, he points to a scene where the protagonist portrays herself while meditating in the shower, thus calling the attention of readers on her own naked body: "Part of Nafisi's project is to insist on her — and her students' — *right* to disrobe, their right to be naked, and a refusal of a politics that understands the naked female body as inherently sinful."[34] Although the critic acknowledges that this project is important, he also reminds us that "the covering and uncovering of Eastern women's bodies for the benefit of Western audiences [...] has a long history. A long colonial, orientalist history."[35]

These words foreground the ambivalence of a text whose political message is conveyed by strategies of representation that are meant to please the Western public. While great literature provokes a state of crisis, this book is far too reassuring for Western readers, whose worldviews are not questioned by Nafisi: "Rather than encouraging an engaged understanding of [Islam], the book encourages sympathy *at the individual level* with these women while insistently asserting the superiority of Western culture."[36]

Another article — which was published by John Carlos Rowe in 2007 — highlights the danger that *Reading Lolita in Tehran* may be instrumentalized by neoconservatives — with Nafisi's implicit approval — to justify at a cultural level the imperialistic politics of the United States in the Middle East. Rowe supports his hypothesis by means of various arguments. Not only does Nafisi teach at the School for Advanced International Studies of the Johns Hopkins University, where she directs a project on the development of democracy and human rights in the Muslim world, but the book was also partly funded by the Smith Richardson Foundation, of conservative orientation.

While offering this — and other — "circumstantial evidence,"[37] Rowe himself does not hesitate to claim that *Reading Lolita in Tehran* has become "a classic"[38] with the consensus of writers and intellectuals of the most diverse political provenance, although he is concerned about the basic assumption that he believes underlies the volume, that is to say, the idea that the Anglo-American texts Nafisi utilized are beyond ideology, while they actually express a liberal ideology. According to Rowe, Nafisi has not simply fallen into a trap, but "she actively participates in the agenda of an overtly 'depoliticized' cultural study that is in fact profoundly *political.*"[39] The critic concludes by alerting his readers to the very real danger that the United States may fall prey to forms of totalitarianism "equivalent to what Nafisi finds in the Islamic Republic of Tehran."[40] This risk has, however, been acknowledged by Nafisi herself, as is proved by a 2004 interview where she claims: "Fundamentalism in [the] U.S. is also very strong. Whenever religion, no matter where it comes from, when it claims to spread the word of God through [the] State it becomes dangerous."[41]

Amy DePaul, however, reacts to the tendency to present Nafisi as a pawn in the hands of neoconservatives, since this attitude not only fails to acknowledge her literary talent, but "negates the truth of what she and other women who opposed Islamism suffered during the revolution."[42] After extensively analyzing the critical debate on the book, DePaul comes to the conclusion that "Nafisi's more severe critics unwittingly demonstrate one of the main themes of the book, which is that ideological extremism can lead to irrational accusations and sometimes simplistic conclusions."[43]

Another element critics have interestingly taken into account is the role book clubs have played in the reception of *Reading Lolita in Tehran*, the kind of public the publisher deliberately geared the book towards, also because Nafisi and her seven female students constitute — again in DePaul's words — "a subversive book club."[44] Catherine Burwell has also delved into this aspect of reception, underlining the political dimension of the book-club reading practice, focussing on "the ways in which women living in Canada and the United States think, read and talk about the texts of women living in the Third World."[45]

As further proof of the importance *Reading Lolita in Tehran* has assumed as a catalyst of the political and cultural discourses on Iran, we should also note that its central metaphor reappears at the core of the volume journalist Danny Postel devoted to the Iranian situation in 2006: *Reading Legitimation Crisis in Tehran: Iran and the Future of Liberalism*. The same metaphor recurs in "Reading Machiavelli in Tehran," where the Iranian philosopher Ramin Jahanbegloo — who was imprisoned in his country and subsequently moved to Canada — studies the Italian thinker as "the first political theorist of a disenchanted world in which the individual stands alone without God, with no motives and purposes except those supplied by his own subjectivity."[46] In an interview where they are confronted, Postel and Jahanbegloo underline the Iranians' thirst for knowledge concerning Western thought, from Kant and Hegel to Arendt and Habermas. In present-day Iran — which is marked, according to the two thinkers, by lively cultural ferment — a particular form of contact between Western and Eastern cultures is taking place.[47] As Postel remarks elsewhere, Nafisi has been able to grasp the character of this contact zone, where Western texts are rewritten — so to speak — by the context of reception.[48]

Language and Democracy

Although many of the essays that have been written on *Reading Lolita in Tehran* criticize its ambivalences, I find it wrong to delegitimize a volume that tells us important things concerning the relation between literature and politics. Suffice it to compare *Reading Lolita in Tehran* with Shirin Ebadi's *The Golden Cage* or Magda Szabó's *The Door* to realize up to what point those writers who fight against a totalitarian regime are afraid of written words as the vehicle of pre-confectioned ideologies that prevent open forms of debate ultimately resulting in forms of intellectual stunting. Although it is undesirable and unrealistic to reduce writing to its aesthetic dimension, regarding it as foreign to politics, the converse choice of politicizing the act of reading by means of predetermined categories that reduce the range of interpretations, caging the text, is no less dangerous. The relationship between author and reader is open and partakes of anarchism. Moreover, the best novels are often architectures of complexity, which intentionally stage aporia, double binds, the difficulty or impossibility of choosing between belongings and loyalties that have become incompatible.

I believe that *Reading Lolita in Tehran*, despite the limits of its historical perspective on the Shah regime or the risk of a Neo-Orientalist complacency in the description of female intimacy, contains important reflections on reading intended as an endless quest for meaning — which lies suspended halfway between the individual and the collective, creativity and conventions — and on the novel as a polyphonic literary form. Due to their inherent ambivalence, polyphonic texts — including not only novels, but of course Greek tragedies and Shakespeare's plays, to name but two examples — dramatize both the diversity of human beings and their necessity to establish interpersonal links. The result of these negotiations is a public space that provides us with a model for those other public spaces we enclose under the label of democracy.

In one of her first classes, Nafisi asks her students to explain the meaning of the word *Upsilamba*, which was actually created by Nabokov. Nafisi and her students come to regard that fanciful term, whose meaning is open to endless personal interpretations, as an emblem of the freedom that is inherent in language — "a symbol, a sign of that vague sense of joy, the tingle in the spine, Nabokov expected his readers to feel in the act of reading fiction."[49] As Nafisi claims in an essay on "The Republic of the Imagination," the *fatwa* that was launched against Salman Rushdie "was precisely aimed against the dangers of the imagination," or in other words "against the democratic form of the novel, which frames a multiplicity of voices, opposing perspectives, active dialogue. What more dangerous subversion can there be than this democracy of voices?"[50]

If we take time to think about it, we realize that not only novels, but words themselves teach us democracy, insofar as the meaning of words — as Ferdinand De Saussure explained in his lectures on general linguistics at the beginning of the 20th century — actually results from a social pact: "A language [...] is something in which everyone participates all the time and that is why it is constantly open to the influence of all."[51] This accounts for both the inertia of language — since a sudden linguistic revolution is unthinkable — and for its variability. Words have no fixed meaning apart from the slowly ever-changing meanings a community of speakers projects on them. As Virginia Woolf famously wrote:

> [Words] are the wildest, freest, most irresponsible, most un-teachable of all things. Of course, you can catch them and sort them and place them in alphabetical order in dictionaries. But words do not live in dictionaries; they live in the mind. [...] They hate being useful; they hate making money; they hate being lectured about in public. In short, they hate anything that stamps them with one meaning or confines them to one attitude, for it is their nature to change.[52]

Being mediated by language, even religious revelation — whose meaning is regarded as monumentally stable by fundamentalists — rests on a sea of words, which constantly shifts according to the individual and collective experiences of a community. Of course fundamentalists — a term that can be applied to any religious belief, as Edna Ullmann-Margalit clarifies — harbor a static view of the world, or better of the "lost paradise" they are attempting to regain, as an entity that is "fossilized, frozen in time, closed, awe-inspiring."[53] As we can see, words can teach us much in terms of political thought, since in order to adapt to the ever-changing needs of a biological community, which is itself marked by unceasing change, rules — like words — must be flexible, and public spaces must result from an endless mechanism of negotiation.

Conclusion

Traveling with Mr. Bean

Mr. Bean is a paragon of childish impishness and curiosity rather than a figure we would associate with responsibility, and *Mr. Bean's Holiday* (2007) seems to reassert this image. The protagonist has won the first prize in a parish raffle — a holiday in Cannes in the days of the film festival and a brand new video camera. At first the film looks like a satire of contemporary traveling, and the camera Bean uses to portray himself against the places he visits symbolizes the duplication of the real that marks our epoch. When he begins his journey, Bean is just an egoistic and lonely man, but everything changes when he finds himself on a train bound to Cannes, together with a Russian child whose father has been left behind at the station. This mishap was due to Bean himself, who now begins to feel responsible and discovers the importance of human relations thanks both to his young Russian friend and to Sabine, the beautiful actress who will eventually drive Bean and the child to Cannes.

The contrast between narcissism and altruism eventually explodes in one of the final scenes set at the film festival. The police are pursuing Bean, for they believe he has kidnapped the child, when the main characters enter the Palais des Festivals, where a film is being shown in which Sabine also played. *Playback Time* is a scathing parody of self-referentiality — the same person is credited as screenwriter, director, producer and main actor, and the camera is always pointed at him. Even the short sequence in which Sabine appears has been further cut down to give him more space. In the cinema the audience is dozing, but Bean enters the projection cabin and connects his camera to the screen, giving the film an unforeseen ending, in which friendship, irony and the joy of life triumph. The desolate spectators wake up, and applause is raging. The child finds his father. Sabine will possibly become a famous actress. The self-conceited screenwriter/director/actor masks his irritation with a smile. Bean, however, is interested only in the beach of Cannes, where the story ends on the notes of Charles Trenet's *La Mer.*

Mr. Bean's Holiday underlines the importance of *encounter,* which is here contrasted with both the initial indifference of Bean and the narcissism of the filmmaker. The video camera and the cinema screen are only mirrors for these two characters, who are both incapable of looking beyond themselves, but destiny opens a door for Bean to enter. Reading may elicit the same phenomenon. A good narrative opens a door for us, makes an encounter possible, ultimately changes us, for behind a good narrative there is life, and when we read we establish affective bonds. The threads that unite imagination to experience are thin but strong, and we find it difficult to understand up to what point they give our life direction.

As *Mr. Bean's Holiday* shows, the self-referential dimension of postmodernism appears by now outdated — a condition of cultural crisis that various critics denounced in the 1990s. Writing in 1993, Heide Ziegler claimed that metafiction had degenerated into "playfulness and narcissism," which stood out "in the eye of the general public as the distinctive features of postmodernism."[1] In 1995 David Foster Wallace argued that metafictional techniques had been appropriated and emptied by the media, which had turned the rebellious and idealistic irony of early postmodernism into a debased cultural norm, lulling viewers into a condition of passive entertainment, to the point that programs started "to resemble commercials."[2] Against this stultifying trend, Wallace advocated the rise of a new generation of literary rebels who would be brave enough to "treat old untrendy human troubles and emotions in U.S. life with reverence and conviction,"[3] eschewing self-consciousness and even risking accusations of sentimentality and melodrama.

Robert L. McLaughlin's account of what he terms "Post-Postmodern Discontent" (2004) is no less harsh, since he claims that "many of the fiction writers who have come on the scene since the late 1980s seem to be responding to the perceived dead end of postmodernism" due to postmodernism's "immersion in a world of nonreferential language."[4] In the critic's eyes, this "aesthetic change" is "inspired by a desire to reconnect language to the social sphere or, to put it another way, to reenergize literature's social mission, its ability to intervene in the social world."[5]

We have seemingly entered a time when writing is motivated by a desire to produce an action, *to write the world while writing of the world*. This propensity to tackle problematic issues, both on a personal and on a collective plane, characterizes the most interesting narratives of the turn of the millennium. While mainstream postmodernist culture emphasizes the barrier between language (or thought) and reality, many writers today aim to exert an action. According to Raoul Eshelman, this *performative* view of literature contrasts with "postmodernism's modes of dispersal, deconstruction and proliferation," creating a refuge "in which all those things are brought together that postmodernism and poststructuralism thought definitively dissolved: the *telos,* the author, belief, love, dogma and much, much more."[6]

Of course I am not implying that the literary value of a text should be assessed in terms of its engagement. What I am interested in is the interplay between the aesthetic and the ethical value of a work of literature. Literature cannot be reduced to a political arena. Yet, it provides responsibility, notably within our present transcultural societies, where morality is no longer regarded as the prerogative of religious authorities or as coinciding with traditional common sense, but is being refounded in a secular perspective, in an attempt to create a container that embraces a mosaic of ethnic, religious and cultural affiliations.

As Edward Said — an intellectual who described himself as "amphibious or bicultural"[7] — claimed in his famous essay on *Humanism and Democratic Criticism* (2004): "The core of humanism is the secular notion that the historical world is made by men and women, and not by God, and that it can be understood rationally."[8] In the same essay, Said defined human history as "a continuous process of self-understanding and self-realization."[9] Against the anesthetizing character of mass culture, where violence is a form of entertainment — as is shown by videogames, horror films and the torture images that are available on the Internet — novels are maps that *orient,* giving a sense to reality, reestablishing a network of relations and contrasting the syndrome of passive spectatorship, which is marked by detachment, fragmentation, transitoriness.

Yet, to rediscover the social function of humanism — a word that encompasses creative and critical writing and reading — one has to acknowledge, as Said did, "the subjective element in humanistic knowledge and practice [...] since there is no use in trying to make a neutral, mathematical science out of it."[10] Humanism is a product of the human in all its complexity, as a rational and emotional creature. The novels and memoirs we have read make something happen also by appealing to the readers' emotions, but in their effort to legitimate their discipline as a "science," late–20th-century literary critics have often been wary of emotions, which they associate with the traditional impressionistic attitude they are striving to avoid.

Things are changing, however, due to the interdisciplinary development of new theoretical tools and critical approaches. At the beginning of the 1990s, the concept of *emotional intelligence* was proposed by psychologists John Mayer and Peter Salovey, and then disseminated by scientific reporter Daniel Goleman with his best-selling *Emotional Intelligence* (1995). This concept is part of a wider effort to reappraise not only the connection between thoughts and emotions (or cognition and affect), but also to study their culturally determined dimension, and conversely their role in shaping human relationships, social behavior, empathy and compassion.[11] Partly as a result of this renewed scientific interest in the cognitive import of emotions, various scholars — notably in the fields of trauma and Holocaust studies — advocate a form of criticism that takes the readers' emotional response into account, also following the lesson Martha Nussbaum has offered in *Upheavals of Thought* (2001), where the scholar claims that the rediscovery of the cognitive and evaluative power of emotions implies a redefinition of the relation between emotions and ethics.

In his study of testimony as a genre, Robert Eaglestone highlights an interesting paradox when he reminds us that the process of reading often pivots on identification while "much of the teaching of literature is — perhaps rightly — aimed at destroying precisely that comfortable sense of identification."[12] Yet, many contemporary life narratives engender forms of identification that are far from reassuringly "comfortable" and that may rather remind us of *catharsis,* the phenomenon Aristotle described in his *Poetics.* As Laurie Vickroy claims, trauma fiction employs narratives "to make readers experience emotional intimacy and immediacy,"[13] positioning them "in ethical dilemmas analogous to those of trauma survivors."[14] Although Plato was afraid of the formative power of art and excluded poets from his ideal Republic, poetics can be subservient to ethics, as the best contemporary literature shows.

Bearing Witness

At the turn of the millennium, writers have increasingly felt the need to use narratives to preserve the collective memory and investigate the psychological consequences of genocide, colonization, racism, totalitarianism and other forms of oppression. Rediscovering language as an assumption of responsibility, novels have become closer to the act of bearing witness,[15] which generates emotional solidarity through the sharing of one's personal experience. Individual and collective trauma is a revenant that keeps reemerging from the past, incapable of finding rest, and the only way to exorcise it is to reconnect it to the present by turning it into a symbol (the Greek verb *symballein* means "to put together"), by joining what had been previously separated — a survivor and its community or even, paradoxically, victim and perpetrator. Owing to their power to provoke catharsis, narratives — which are figurations of reality — can engender a process of purification.

The act of narrating is central to most of the novels I have analyzed, where it is often related to memory and trauma, both personal and collective, and presented as a process that involves fashioning and refashioning painful stories in order to fill gaps and overcome personal defenses. At the end of *Flaubert's Parrot* we discover that the narrator's quest is but a means to come to terms with his own grief for his wife's infidelity and death. *The Door* circularly ends with the same nightmare the narrator related at the beginning of the volume, putting us in touch with the impossibility to overcome the trauma of individual betrayal. In *Atonement* the travail of rememoration accompanies Briony throughout her adult life, although this incessant reshaping of the past remains implicit until the last chapter, when readers finally become aware of the confessional and compensatory character of Briony's novel. While the previous versions of Cecilia and Robbie's story that Briony had written all ended on a tragic note, reflecting the inner tumult of her guilt, the last version — which abandons the realm of reality to stage the two lovers' reunion — testifies to Briony's pacification.

In *Austerlitz*, too, writing takes on the role of an investigation into the mnestic processes of the main character, who first removes his past as a victim of Nazism and then remembers it. The individual memories Austerlitz loses and retrieves stand for the collective memory of the Holocaust, which was initially removed by the Germans and has been subsequently elaborated, also thanks to writers such as Sebald, whose revision of his nation's past and whose redefinition of his own identity were significantly preceded by his choice to expatriate.

The theme of memory — in its relation with the Holocaust — is likewise at the heart of *Everything Is Illuminated*, where the novel Jonathan writes recreates imaginatively a past that cannot be otherwise attained due to the cancellation of the Jewish Shtetl, Trachimbrod. It is precisely the act of confronting that *nothing* that triggers a process of self-inquiry in the

Ukrainian characters, therefore setting the ground for reconciliation between victims and perpetrators.

As we can see, memory and trauma recur as major concerns in these contemporary novels, whose substance is tragic since here the postwar generations come to terms with the sins of their fathers and grandfathers. This dynamic also marks *Kafka on the Shore*, which indirectly deals with the violent core of Japanese nationalism and imperialism. This is how Murakami recounts his contact with the ghost of the war through the experience of his father, a "retired teacher and a part-time Buddhist priest" who died at the age of 90:

> As a child born after the war, I used to see him every morning before breakfast offering up long, deeply felt prayers at the Buddhist altar in our house. One time I asked him why he did this, and he told me he was praying for the people who had died in the battlefield. He was praying for all the people who died, he said, both ally and enemy alike.[16]

As a literary genre, the novel complements other forms of investigation into the past — such as those of history and sociology — and is therefore a hermeneutic tool of primary importance due to its power to condense history into stories, offering us the opportunity to confront past events with all the ambiguity they had for those who lived them in the first person, i.e., rendering the disquieting ambivalence of the present, with its difficult choices to be made. In this respect, the novel has not only the function of *orienting* us, but also that of *disorienting* us, unsettling the certainties of those who relate to a phenomenon a posteriori, as spectators — rather than actors — of history.

It is in *Black Dogs* (1992) that McEwan renders the fragility of a present that is unconscious of its future, a condition that we share with the generations that came before us. This fragility emerges fully when the protagonist — Jeremy — observes, in the hospital room where his mother-in-law is about to die, a photograph that portrays her as a young woman together with her husband, in the aftermath of the second world conflict:

> It was the innocence that was so appealing, not only of the girl, or the couple, but of the time itself [...]. The innocent time! Tens of millions dead, Europe in ruins, the extermination camps still a news story, not yet our universal reference point of human depravity. It is photography itself that creates the illusion of innocence. Its ironies of frozen narrative lend to its subjects an apparent unawareness that they will change or die. Fifty years on we look at them with the godly knowledge of how they turned out after all — who they married, the date of their death — with no thoughts for who will one day be holding photographs of us.[17]

The novel ends with the painful but not nihilistic awareness that evil cannot be extirpated once and for all. Of course, this does not mean that we should not fight against it, but rather that this fight is endless. As we can see, in recent years novels have played a major role as mediators of the cultural memories concerning World War II, in an attempt to relate past conflicts to our present and to pursue a project of reconciliation that is grounded on awareness.

What is more, novels prove capable of redefining our notion of truth. While meditating on the task of the novelist, Murakami wrote:

> By telling skillful lies — which is to say, by making up fictions that appear to be true — the novelist can bring a truth out to a new location and shine a new light on it. In most cases, it is virtually impossible to grasp a truth in its original form and depict it accurately. This is why we try to grab its tail by luring the truth from its hiding place, transferring it to a fictional location, and replacing it with a fictional form. In order to accomplish this, however, we first have to clarify where the truth lies within us.[18]

The problem of truth, in its relation to human subjectivity, notably to memory and trauma, remains central for today's novelists, as is shown by Bernard Schlink's *The Reader*. At the end of the story, the narrator meditates on the importance of writing as an instrument to come to terms with the most painful aspects of one's past:

> Soon after her death, I decided to write the story of me and Hanna. Since then I've done it many times in my head [...]. Thus there are many different stories in addition to the one I have written. The guarantee that the written one is the right one lies in the fact that I wrote it and not the other versions. The written version wanted to be written, the many others did not.[19]

These words resonate with the ending of *Atonement*. Alongside the factual truth concerning the past, there is always a subjective truth, a moment when one's inner tumult calms down and a vision takes shape. As Schlink's narrator reflects:

> At first I wanted to write our story in order to be free of it. But the memories wouldn't come back for that. Then I realized our story was slipping away from me and I wanted to recapture it by writing, but that didn't coax up the memories either. For the last few years I've left our story alone. I've made peace with it. And it came back, detail by detail and in such a fully rounded fashion, with its own direction and its own sense of completion, that it no longer makes me sad.[20]

Yet, memory is subject to unceasing emotional oscillations, and it is impossible to freeze one's own relation with the past within a reassuring mental framework. One never stops coming to terms with the past. Old wounds may reopen at any time, and our new feelings reflect those we have already lived. As Schlink's narrator meditates, "We always come up against earlier events in later ones, not as matter that has been fully formed and pushed aside, but absolutely present and alive."[21]

Exploring the complex relation between history and trauma, Cathy Caruth asserts that "what trauma has to tell us — the historical and personal truth it transmits — is intricately bound up with its refusal of historical boundaries; [...] its truth is bound up with its crisis of truth."[22] The same issue has been tackled by Shoshana Felman, who claims that psychoanalysis has radically renewed "the very concept of the testimony," recognizing for the first time in the history of culture "that one does not have to *possess,* or *own* the truth, in order to effectively bear witness to it."[23]

When dealing with memory and trauma we inevitably enter not only the dimension of subjectivity, but also that of the unconscious. The act of testimony calls into question the relation between historical truth (as resulting from the pursuit of scientific objectivity) and personal truth (as grounded on experience and tinged with emotions). As Sarah R. Horowitz remarks, Holocaust fiction poses even greater problems in terms of truth value, and is "seen by many readers as — at best — a weaker, softer kind of testimony"; yet her study is aimed precisely to show that fiction is "a serious vehicle for thinking about the Holocaust."[24]

The key to understanding this renewed interest of writers and critics for the investigative and memorial potential of the novel is related to the development of scientific approaches to the past that are alternative to traditional historical inquiry. Vickroy puts the matter in a nutshell when she comments that "discoveries about the nature of traumatic experience as overwhelming, alien, amnesiac, and often incomprehensible have necessitated new historiographic, testimonial and representational approaches."[25] Writers have therefore internalized "the rhythms, processes and uncertainties of trauma" within the "sensibilities and structures"[26] of their works.

As a result, trauma fiction is marked by elements such as a disruption of chronology, sites of memory which trigger revelation, and also the inner dissociation of characters who are haunted by the past and yet deny it, finding it painful to communicate their experience to others. Authors not only aim to represent this paradoxical condition, but also find themselves in a similar position, as Horowitz clarifies when she underlines the contradiction at the heart of Holocaust narratives: "an impossibility to express the experience, coupled with a psychological and moral obligation to do so."[27] The position of readers is no less paradoxical since "the suspension of disbelief integral to the reading of fiction runs counter to the exacting demands one places upon testimony."[28]

As we can see, we are in the realm of complexity, but the novelists who courageously engage in the representation of atrocity are far from oblivious to these issues, which they incorporate into their metafictional narratives,[29] and they have also developed strategies to render the post-traumatic condition of loss, silence and absence. The South-African mine that is evoked at the end of *Austerlitz*—a big hole with no premonitory signs—and the empty field on the site of Trachimbrod in *Everything Is Illuminated* are tropes that stand for what is no more, and the same could be said for the metaphor on which Art Spiegelman's representation of the 9/11 trauma pivots—the shadow of towers that no longer exist.

Inner Frontiers

Contemporary life narratives not only cross the historical and psychological boundaries between present and past, enabling us to meditate on atrocities, conflicts and traumas, but they also dramatize the hybrid identities that all over the world characterize the individual experience of many. As Amin Maalouf—a Lebanese author whose native language is Arabic, who was brought up as a Christian and who now lives in France—writes: "Every individual is a meeting ground for many different allegiances, and sometimes these loyalties conflict with one another," confronting the person with "difficult choices."[30] This is the stuff tragedies are made of, and Maalouf underlines the specificity of those people who, due to their complex identity, live in a sort of inner "frontier zone criss-crossed by ethnic, religious and other fault lines."[31] These people have an important function to fulfill, since they can act "as bridges, go-betweens, mediators," but if they are "continually being pressed to take sides" they can also be turned into elements of disruption. Maalouf warns us to refrain from the "narrow, exclusive, bigoted, simplistic attitude that reduces identity in all its many aspects to one single affiliation, and one that is proclaimed in anger."[32]

Maalouf has chosen to be a builder of bridges, like many other writers that I have not been able to include in my critical itinerary. I am thinking, for example, of Orhan Pamuk, whose *Snow* (2002) takes us to an obscure Turkish town on which the snow falls incessantly. We thus discover, together with the poet Ka, a provincial society that is lacerated by the conflict between central power, whose secular character has the aftertaste of arrogance, and a religious experience that borders on fanaticism. The protagonist himself, who spent many years in Germany before returning to his home country, embodies the conflict between contrasting allegiances Maalouf described in his essay.

I am also thinking of *Gate of the Sun* (1998), where Elias Khuri shows the Israel-Palestinian conflict from the point of view of the Palestinians who live in the Lebanese refugee camps. The novel is written in the form of a long dialogue — which is actually a monologue — between the narrator and a friend who lies in a coma in a camp hospital. Khuri is capable of highly poetical writing, such as the scene that depicts the visit of a Palestinian lady to her former house in the occupied territories. The building is now inhabited by a Jewish settler, but while the Palestinian woman contemplates that place with a desperate feeling of homesickness, the Jewish woman, who grew up in Lebanon and was uprooted from that place, longs to be back in Beirut. The episode stages an absurd mutual displacement of which both Palestinians and Jews are victims insofar as the logic of segregation prevails over that of coexistence.

Narratives and Remediation

There is another element of our present I wish to hint at before concluding this volume — the re-modulation that the system of arts and literary genres went through in the course of the 20th century and whose consequences are now apparent in all their amplitude. The position of the novel within the galaxy of arts and genres changed in the first half of the century due to the advent of the cinema, and the process increased in the following decades in relation to the phenomenon Jay David Bolter and Richard Grusin define as *remediation*,[33] that is to say, the tendency of cultural products to metamorphose, translating from one medium into another.

Cinema and television adaptations of novels come to mind, but the relation between graphic novels and animation cinema is also part of the phenomenon of remediation, which is of course far from new, as the theatrical adaptations of 18th- and 19th- century novels show.[34] Remediation, however, has reached unprecedented proportions today, intensifying that exchange between arts and genres that has always marked the evolution of culture. The interaction between cinema and the novel, for instance, has helped to modify the narrative syntax of written texts in the direction of montage, and also to favor a closer relation between iconic and verbal language.

The term *multimodal novel* has recently been coined to define those texts which do not rely solely on written words, but which communicate also by means of mainly nonverbal components such as photographs, paintings, sketches and handwriting. Of course, far from being simply decorative, these elements are an integral part of the text, and readers are expected "to incorporate them in their cognitive construction of the narrated world and narrative meaning,"[35] as Wolfgang Hallet writes. Sebald's *Austerlitz*—with its apparatus of images and documents — is a perfect example of this new narrative trend.

Another phenomenon that testifies to the novel's evolution in the direction of the visual is the development of the graphic novel. Emphasizing its descendance from the novel, this hybrid form has overcome its initially marginal status, which was disreputably associated with escapism, seriality and paraliterature.[36] Will Eisner's *Contract with God, and Other Tenement Stories* (1978), which deals with the poor life of Jewish immigrants in a Bronx building, is commonly regarded as the founding text of this new genre, since its practitioners and fans wish to underline the aptness of this expressive medium to deal with grave subjects, offering the kind of meditation on the tragic side of life that cartoons had previously never aimed at. Significantly, the last graphic novel Eisner completed before dying is *The Plot: The Secret Story of the Protocols of the Elders of Zion* (2005).

The subjects that are at the heart of this critical volume have been recently addressed in a particularly effective way by a related subgenre of graphic novels, that is to say graphic memoirs. Art Spiegelman's *Maus* (1972–91) tells the story of his father Vladek, a Polish Jew who survived the camps, and also delves into his own inherited trauma. Marjane Satrapi's *Persepolis* (2000–03), describing her life under the Iranian regime, was turned into an animated film in 2007. In terms of remediation, *Waltz with Bashir* had an opposite destiny, since it was originally conceived in 2008 as a cartoon film, thanks to the cooperation between the Israeli director and screenwriter Ari Folman and the Israeli cartoonist David Polonski, and one year later became a graphic novel.

Waltz with Bashir tackles the delicate subjects of post-conflict memory and war trauma, through the story of an Israeli soldier who shares the author's name, Ari. Several years have elapsed since the 1982 Lebanon war when Ari — due to a friend's recurring nightmare, the vision of dogs running through nocturnal streets — is struck by his own surprising lack of memories concerning those events. Only after Ari has confronted his friend's inner ghosts does his own past start resurfacing, at first in the form of an enigmatic vision. This marks the beginning of an itinerary of self-discovery that is both individual and collective, since it is by talking with his fellow soldiers that Ari pieces together his own memories, until we are brought in touch with the ground-zero of this memorial journey — the massacres in the refugee camps of Sabra and Shatila, where Israeli-allied Christian militias slay a large number of civilians. Ari witnessed this event as a powerless spectator and feels responsible for his own inability to act.

Other titles could be mentioned. Joe Sacco's *Palestine* (1993–2001) deals with the author's own experience in the West Bank and Gaza Strip at the beginning of the 1990s, while *In the Shadow of No Towers* (2004) has enabled Art Spiegelman to analyze the trauma of 9/11. As we can see, these graphic narratives tackle important issues in a documentary attempt to combine history and memoir. Gillian Whitlock has coined the term *autographics* to define these texts, which testify to "the extraordinary potential of the comics in autobiographical narratives of trauma."[37]

This potential partly rests on the fact that these narratives utilize non-mimetic or partly-mimetic visual codes. Compared with photographs (such as the ones we see at the end of *Waltz with Bashir*), drawings "de-realize" the narrated reality. In *Maus* this happens through the allegorical mode of the animal fable, whereby Jews are portrayed as mice, Germans as cats, Poles as pigs, etc. In *Persepolis* the extreme simplification of the highly-stylized black- and-white drawings likewise produces an effect of de-realization. *Waltz with Bashir* is characterized by subjective or oneiric frames that intensify the emotional dimension of the story, rendering the protagonist's perception of events rather than external reality.

Grasping Complexity

As this critical itinerary has shown, life narratives are an extremely vital component of contemporary literature. Thanks to their power to cross boundaries, life narratives offer a transcultural arena for discussing not only issues concerning conflict, reconciliation, identity, memory and trauma, but also the relation between the private and the public spheres, imagination and power. Moreover, life narratives ultimately foreground a basic dimension of the human experience — our quest for meaning.

My contention is that life narratives — including novels, memoirs and their hybrid offspring — are contributing to the metamorphosis of postmodernism into a new stage of our cultural evolution. The human is back, right at centre stage.

In a recent interview, McEwan has declared that he considers novels as "forms of investigation, at its broadest and best, into human nature."[38] In their pursuit of that investigation, contemporary narratives are not only thematically versatile and technically sophisticated, but also conjugate social and political engagement with freedom of thought. Today's best literature bravely attempts to understand the multiple facets of reality as seen from different points of view. Instead of transmitting a predefined set of values, it invites us to look for them, without selling ourselves to easy certainties — be they ideological or religious — or to the illusions of consumerism. For our inner life is a delicate entity, a part of us that we need to cultivate in its uniqueness and in the encounter with the other(s), without whom we are no one.

Notes

Introduction

1. Edward Said, *Humanism and Democratic Criticism* (New York: Columbia University Press, 2004), 125.

2. Leo Spitzer's and Erich Auerbach's major contributions to comparatism are also significantly linked to War World II since these two scholars developed their philological studies while in exile from Nazi Germany, first in Istanbul and then in the United States. It was in Istanbul that Auerbach's *Mimesis* was written, as the critic famously acknowledged in his postscript.

3. T.S. Eliot, *What Is a Classic?* (London: Faber & Faber, 1945), 26.

4. Ibid., 31.

5. The scope of *new cosmopolitanism* — so-called by Robert Fine in contrast with the cosmopolitanism of the ancient Greeks and of philosophers such as Kant, Hegel and Marx — is analyzed by Robert Fine in *Cosmopolitanism* (Abingdon, UK: Routledge, 2007).

6. Sheldon Pollock, Homi K. Bhabha, Carol A. Breckenridge and Dipesh Chakrabarty, "Cosmopolitanisms," in *Cosmopolitanism*, eds. Sheldon Pollock, Homi K. Bhabha, Carol A. Breckenridge and Dipesh Chakrabarty (Durham, NC: Duke University Press, 2002), 1.

7. Kwame Anthony Appiah, *Cosmopolitanism: Ethics in a World of Strangers* (New York: W.W. Norton, 2006), xvi.

8. Ibid., xxi.

9. John Pizer, *The Idea of World Literature: History and Pedagogical Practice* (Baton Rouge: Louisiana State University Press, 2006), 4.

10. Wolfgang Welsch, "Transculturality — The Puzzling Form of Cultures Today," in *Spaces of Culture: City, Nation, World*, eds. Mike Featherstone and Scott Lash (London: Sage, 1999), 196.

11. Ibid., 197.

12. Ibid.

13. Virginia H. Milhouse, Molefi Kete Asante, and Peter O. Nwosu, *Transcultural Realities: Interdisciplinary Perspectives on Cross-Cultural Relations* (Thousand Oaks, CA: Sage, 2001), ix.

14. David Damrosch, *What Is World Literature?* (Princeton, NJ: Princeton University Press, 2003), 5.

15. Stephen Greenblatt and Giles Gunn, eds., introduction to *Redrawing the Boundaries: The Transformation of English and American Literary Studies* (New York: The Modern Language Association of America, 1992), 2.

16. Roland Robertson, *Globalization, Social Theory and Global Culture* (London: Sage, 1992), 8.

17. See Malcolm Waters, *Globalization* (London: Routledge, 1995, 2001), 184–87.

18. Ulf Hannerz, *Cultural Complexity: Studies in the Social Organization of Meaning* (New York: Columbia University Press, 1992), 218.

19. See Alastair Fowler, *Kinds of Literature: An Introduction to the Theory of Genres and Modes* (Cambridge, MA: Harvard University Press, 1982); Claudio Guillén, *Literature as System: Essays Toward the Theory of Literary History* (Princeton, NJ: Princeton University Press, 1971); Claudio Guillén, *The Challenge of Comparative Literature*, trans. Cola Franzen (Cambridge, MA: Harvard University Press, 1993).

20. This idea is actually older, as John Pizer remarks in *The Idea of World Literature: History*

and Pedagogical Practice (Baton Rouge: Louisiana State University Press, 2006). The concepts of European identity and of World Literature have been explored by the Hermes group in *World Literature: World Culture: History, Theory, Analysis*, eds. Karen-Margrethe Simonsen and Jacob Stougaard-Nielsen (Aarhus, DK: Aarhus University Press, 2008); *Re-Thinking Europe: Literature and (Trans)National Identity*, eds. Nele Bemong, Mirjam Truwant and Pieter Vermeulen (Amsterdam: Rodopi, 2008).

21. Franco Moretti, "Conjectures on World Literature." *New Left Review* 1 (January-February 2000): 54.

22. George Steiner, *What Is Comparative Literature?* (Oxford: Clarendon Press, 1995), 6.

23. See Gayatri Chakravorty Spivak, "Perché il pianeta? Un'[Al]autobiografia intellettuale," in Sergia Adamo, ed., *Culture planetarie? Prospettive e limiti della teoria e della critica culturale* (Rome: Meltemi, 2007), 42. See also her book, *Death of a Discipline* (New York: Columbia University Press, 2003).

24. As Rebecca Suter argued in her seminal study of Haruki Murakami, the debate on modernity, modernism and postmodernism has been ultimately characterized by a West-centered perspective that has made it difficult "to apply such concepts to non-Western cultures." Rebecca Suter, *The Japanization of Modernity: Murakami Haruki between Japan and the United States* [A2] (Cambridge, MA: Harvard University Press, 2008), 2.

25. Moretti, "Conjectures on World Literature," 66.

26. Ibid., 57.

27. Greenblatt and Gunn, introduction to *Redrawing the Boundaries*, 6.

28. Harold Bloom, *The Western Canon: The Books and School of the Ages* (New York: Riverhead Books, 1995), 492.

29. Edward Said, *Humanism and Democratic Criticism*, 27.

30. See Suter, *The Japanization of Modernity*, 1.

31. Julian Barnes, *Something to Declare: Essays on France* (New York: Alfred A. Knopf, 2002), xiv.

32. See Homi K. Bhabha, *The Location of Culture* (London: Routledge, 1994).

33. Maya Jaggi, "The Last Word," interview with W.G. Sebald, *The Guardian*, December 21, 2001. <http://www.guardian.co.uk/education/2001/dec/21/artsandhumanities.highereducation>.

34. Agota Kristof, *L'analphabète: récit autobiographique* (Geneva: Zoé, 2004).

35. See Zygmunt Bauman, *Liquid Modernity* (Cambridge: Polity Press, 2000); Richard Sennett, *The Corrosion of Character: The Personal Consequences of Work in the New Capitalism* (New York: Norton, 1999). The experience of expatriation already pervasively characterized Anglo-American modernism. Suffice it to think of the cosmopolitanism of writers such as Henry James, Ford Madox Ford, Katherine Mansfield, D.H. Lawrence, James Joyce, T.S. Eliot, Samuel Beckett, Gertrude Stein and Jean Rhys. This phenomenon, however, has taken on very different proportions in recent decades.

36. Arjun Appadurai, *Modernity at Large: Cultural Dimensions of Globalisation* (Minneapolis: University of Minnesota Press, 1996), 7.

37. Sven Boedecker, "Menschen auf der anderen Seite," interview with W.G. Sebald, *Rheinische Post*, Oct. 9, 1993, quoted in Amir Eshel, "Against the Power of Time: The Poetics of Suspension in W.G. Sebald's *Austerlitz*," *New German Critique* 88 (2003): 76.

38. See Dominique Moïsi, *La Géopolitique de l'émotion* (Paris: Flammarion, 2008), 18.

39. Daniel Goleman, *Destructive Emotions and How We Can Overcome Them: A Dialogue with the Dalai Lama* (London: Bloomsbury, 2003), xix.

40. Martha Craven Nussbaum, *Hiding from Humanity: Disgust, Shame and the Law* (Princeton, NJ: Princeton University Press, 2004), 5.

41. Ibid., 6.

42. See *The Anthropology of Ethnicity: Beyond Ethnic Groups and Boundaries*, eds. H. Vermeulen and C. Govers (Amsterdam: Het Spinhuis, 1994); *Beyond Boundaries*, ed. Gìsli Pàlsson (London: Berg, 1993); *Ethnic Groups and Boundaries: The Social Organization of Culture Difference*, ed. Frederick Barth (Oslo: Univ. Forlaget; London: George Allen & Unwin, 1969); Ulf Hannerz, "Flows, Boundaries and Hybrids: Keywords in Transnational Anthropology." <http://www.transcomm.ox.ac.uk/working%20papers/hannerz.pdf>; Mary Louise Pratt, "Arts of the Contact Zone." *Profession* 91 (1991): 33–40; Mary Louise Pratt, *Imperial Eyes: Travel Writing and Transculturation* (London: Routledge, 1992); *Signifying Identities: Anthropological Perspectives on Boundaries and Contested Values*, ed. Anthony P. Cohen (London: Routledge, 2000); *Symbolising Boundaries*, ed. Anthony P. Cohen (Manchester, UK: Manchester University Press, 1986).

43. See Stephanos Stephanides, ed., *Cultures of Memory/Memories of Culture* (Nicosia, CY: University of Nicosia Press, 2007).

44. "LEADALL: Pope Visit to Bethlehem Sets Stage for Political Speeches," *EarthTimes*, May 13, 2009. <http://www.earthtimes.org/articles/show/268700.leadall-pope-visit-to-

bethlehem-sets-stage-for-political-speeches.html>.

45. "The Nobel Peace Prize for 2009," October 9, 2009. <http://nobelprize.org/nobel_prizes/peace/laureates/2009/press.html>.

46. Hoda Barakat, *The Tiller of Waters* (*Hàrith al-miyàh*, 1998; Cairo: The American University of Cairo Press, 2001), 24–25.

47. Haruki Murakami, "The Novelist in Wartime," February 20, 2009. <http://www.salon.com/books/feature/2009/02/20/haruki_murakami/>.

48. Ibid.

49. Sidonie Smith and Julia Watson have defined life writing "as a general term for writing that takes a life, one's own or another's, as its subject. Such writing can be biographical, novelistic, historical, or explicitly self-referential and therefore autobiographical." Sidonie Smith and Julia Watson, *Reading Autobiography: A guide for interpreting life narratives* (2001; Minneapolis, MN: University of Minnesota Press, 2010).

50. See Hillary L. Chute and Marianne DeKoven. "Introduction: Graphic Narratives," *Modern Fiction Studies* 52.4 (Winter 2006): 767–82.

51. The term was coined by the French novelist and critic Serge Doubrovsky.

52. See Chloë Taylor, *The Culture of Confession from Augustine to Foucault: A Genealogy of the "Confessing Animal"* (New York: Routledge, 2009).

53. Ian McEwan, *"Jerusalem Prize Acceptance Speech,"* February 20, 2011. <http://www.ianmcewan.com/bib/articles/jerusalemprize.html>.

54. See Emmanuel Levinas, *Totality and Infinity: An Essay on Exteriority*, trans. Alphonso Lingis (*Totalité et infini*, 1961; Pittsburgh: Duquesne University Press, 1969).

55. Linda Hutcheon, *The Politics of Postmodernism*, 1.

56. Lawrence Cahoone, ed., *From Modernism to Postmodernism: An Anthology* (Malden, MA: Blackwell, 2003), 3.

57. Ibid., 4.

58. See Bran Nicol, *The Cambridge Introduction to Postmodern Fiction* (Cambridge: Cambridge University Press, 2009), 9–12.

59. Ibid., xv.

60. Suffice it to think of the latest generation of the casinos that have been built along the *strip* in Las Vegas, from the Venice to the Bellagio, and also of the centrality of theme parks to the postmodern imagination. See Robert Venturi, Denise Scott Brown and Steven Izenour, *Learning from Las Vegas* (1972); new edition, eds. Kester Rattenbury and Samantha Hardingham (Abingdon, UK: Routledge, 2007). A theme park is at the core of one of Julian Barnes's most interesting novels, *England, England* (1998).

61. In Wolf's text the heroine becomes a scapegoat, a foreigner who is the victim of the Corinthians' hatred, who is destined to witness the death of her children and even to be remembered as their murderer. Drawing on the earliest versions of the myth, which antedate Euripides's tragedy, Wolf not only deconstructs the political practice of the scapegoat that characterized the DDR, but also meditates on the passage from matriarchy to patriarchy, putting into question the gender myth of male rationality and describing it as grounded in violence.

62. See Gerard Delanty, "Peripheries and Borders in a Post-western Europe," *Eurozine* (August 29, 2007). <http://www.eurozine.com/articles/2007-08-29-delanty-en.html>.

63. See J.-F. Lyotard, *Le Postmoderne expliqué aux enfants: correspondance 1982–1985* (Paris: Galilée, 1986).

64. Samuel Huntington, "The Clash of Civilizations?," *Foreign Affairs* (Summer 1993). <http://history.club.fatih.edu.tr/103%20Huntington%20Clash%20of%20Civilizations%20full%20text.htm>.

65. Akbar S. Ahmed, "Postmodernism and Islam: After 9/11," *Daily Times*, January 10, 2004. <http://www.dailytimes.com.pk/default.asp?page=story_9-1-2004_pg3_5>.

66. See Edward Said, *Orientalism. Western Conceptions of the Orient* (Harmondsworth, UK: Penguin, 1978, 2003).

67. See Ian Buruma and Avishai Margalit, *Occidentalism: The West in the Eyes of Its Enemies* (New York: Penguin, 2004).

68. It suffices to compare Dennett's own definition of religion with William James's (which Dennett quotes) to realize how the debate on the sacred has changed in the course of a century. See Daniel C. Dennett, *Breaking the Spell: Religion as a Natural Phenomenon* (London: Penguin, 2006), 9–11.

69. Michiko Kakutani, "A Hero with 9/11 Peripheral Vision," *The New York Times*, March 18, 2005. <http://query.nytimes.com/gst/fullpage.html?res=9E01E0DD103CF93BA25750C0A9639C8B63>.

70. Mohsin Hamid, "The Pathos of Exile," *Time Magazine*, Special Issue: *The Asian Journey Home*, 162.7, August 18, 2003. <http://www.time.com/time/asia/2003/journey/pakistan_lahore.html>.

71. See James Lasdun, "The Empire Strikes Back," review of *The Reluctant Fundamentalist*, *The Guardian*, March 3, 2007. <http://www.guardian.co.uk/books/2007/mar/03/featuresreviews.guardianreview20>.

72. Chris Cleave, "Too Soon to Write the Post-9/11 Novel?," *The New York Times*, September 12, 2005. <http://www.nytimes.com/2005/09/12/opinion/12iht-edcleave.html>.

73. Eric W. Rothenbuhler, "Ground Zero, the Firemen and the Symbolics of Touch on 9/11 and After," in *Media Anthropology*, eds. Eric W. Rothenbuhler and Mihai Coman (Thousand Oaks, CA: Sage, 2005), 176.

74. See Linda Hutcheon, *A Poetics of Postmodernism: History, Theory, Fiction* (New York: Routledge, 1988).

75. See Salman Rushdie, "The Empire Writes Back with a Vengeance," *Times*, July 3, 1982, 8.

76. See Bill Ashcroft, Gareth Griffiths and Helen Tiffin, *The Empire Writes Back: Theory and Practice in Post-Colonial Literatures* (London: Routledge, 1989).

77. See Fredric Jameson, "Postmodernism, Or, The Cultural Logic of Late Capitalism," *New Left Review* 146 (July–August 1984), 59–62. The essay was subsequently included in this volume: *Postmodernism, Or, The Cultural Logic of Late Capitalism* (Durham, NC: Duke University Press, 1991).

78. Jameson, *Postmodernism*, 19.

79. Ibid., 5.

80. I am thinking of the subversive feminist subtext of the postmodernist fairy tales Angela Carter collected in *The Bloody Chamber* (1978) or more generally of the cultural and political awareness of many postmodernist rewritings.

81. Linda Hutcheon, "Irony, Nostalgia, and the Postmodern," University of Toronto English Language Main Collection, 1998. <http://www.library.utoronto.ca/utel/criticism/hutchinp.html>.

82. See Marcos Piason Natali, "History and the Politics of Nostalgia," *Iowa Journal of Cultural Studies* 5 (Fall 2004): 10–25. <http://www.uiowa.edu/~ijcs/nostalgia/nostfel.htm>.

83. See Walter Busch, "Testimonianza, trauma e memoria," in *Memoria e saperi: percorsi transdisciplinari*, eds. Elena Agazzi and Vita Fortunati (Rome: Meltemi, 2007), 547–64.

84. Andreas Huyssen, "Present Pasts: Media, Politics, Amnesia," *Public Culture*, 12.1 (2000), 22.

85. Ibid., 23.

86. Aleida Assmann, *Erinnerungsräume. Formen und Wandlungen des kulturellen Gedächtnisses*, 1999; *Ricordare: Forme e mutamenti della memoria culturale*, trans. Simona Paparelli (Bologna: il Mulino, 2002), 14. See also David Bidussa, *Dopo l'ultimo testimone* (Turin: Einaudi, 2009).

87. See Remo Ceserani, *Raccontare il postmoderno* (Turin: Bollati Boringhieri, 1997), 67–101.

88. See David Harvey, *The Condition of Postmodernity* (Oxford: Basil Blackwell, 1989); David Harvey, *The New Imperialism* (Oxford: Oxford University Press, 2003); Linda Hutcheon, *The Politics of Postmodernism*.

89. Antonio Negri and Michael Hardt, *Empire* (Cambridge, MA: Harvard University Press, 2000), 150.

90. See Zygmunt Bauman, *Liquid Modernity*, 8.

91. Alan Kirby, "The Death of Postmodernism and Beyond," 2006. <http://www.philosophynow.org/issue58/58kirby.htm>. The nexus between 9/11 and the end of postmodernism recurs also in Samuel R. Smith, "Distributed Culture and the Rise of the Network Age." <http://www.intelligentagent.com/archive/Vol3_No1_polisci_smith.html>.

92. Josh Toth and Neil Brooks, introduction to *The Mourning After: Attending the Wake of Postmodernism*, eds. Neil Edward Brooks and Josh Toth (Amsterdam: Rodopi, 2007), 3.

93. Ibid.

94. Herbert W. Simons and Michael Billig, eds., *After Postmodernism: Reconstructing Ideology Critique* (1994); José López and Garry Potter, eds., *After Postmodernism: An Introduction to Critical Realism* (1995); Mark America and Lance Olsen, eds., *In Memoriam to Postmodernism: Essays on the Avant-Pop* (1995); Klaus Stierstorfer, ed., *Beyond Postmodernism: Reassessments in Literature, Theory and Culture* (2003); Raoul Eshelman, *Performatism, or the End of Postmodernism* (2008).

95. Stephen J. Burn, *Jonathan Franzen and the End of Postmodernism* (London: Continuum, 2008), 10.

96. Ibid., 3.

97. Ibid., 4.

98. Ibid., 11.

99. Matthew Beaumont, "Baudrillard and the End of Postmodernism: What Next?," March 9, 2007. <http://www.guardian.co.uk/books/booksblog/2007/mar/09/baudrillardandtheendofpos>.

100. See Carolyn Hudson and Pamela Smiley, "Obama's Election and the End of Postmodernism," *International Journal of the Humanities* 7.2: 35–46[A3].

101. André Glucksmann, "The Postmodern Financial Crisis," *City Journal* 19.1 (Winter 2009). <http://www.cityjournal.org/2009/19_1_snd-postmodern-financial-crisis.html>.

102. Ibid.

103. Bhabha, *The Location of Culture*, 2.

104. Oscar Wilde, *The Picture of Dorian Gray*, in *The Complete Works*, with an intro-

duction by Vyvyan Holland (London: Collins, 1966), 17.
105. See Umberto Eco, *The Role of the Reader: Explorations in the Semiotics of Texts* (Bloomington: Indiana University Press, 1979).
106. See David Gascoigne, *The Games of Fiction: George Perec and Modern French Ludic Narrative* (Bern: Peter Lang, 2006), 150.
107. Burn, *Jonathan Franzen and the End of Postmodernism*, 4.
108. Barack Obama, "Inaugural Address," January 20, 2009. <http://www.nytimes.com/2009/01/20/us/politics/20textobama.html?_r=1&pagewanted=print>.
109. For a reflection on the concept of moral witness, see Avishai Margalit, *The Ethics of Memory* (Cambridge, MA: Harvard University Press, 2002), 147–82.
110. Magda Szabó, *The Door*, trans. Len Rix (*Az ajtó*, 1987; London: Vintage Books, 2005), 2.
111. Marianne Hirsch, "The Generation of Postmemory," *Poetics Today* 29.1 (Spring 2008): 103.
112. Ibid., 104.
113. Laurie Vickroy, *Trauma and Survival in Contemporary Fiction* (Charlottesville: University of Virginia Press, 2002), ix.
114. Ibid.
115. Ibid., xiv.
116. Kalí Tal, *Worlds of Hurt: Reading the Literatures of Trauma* (Cambridge: Cambridge University Press, 1996), 5.
117. This category has been famously deconstructed by Catherine Belsey in *Critical Practice* (London: Routledge, 1980), 1–36.
118. Abraham B. Yehoshua, *The Terrible Power of a Minor Guilt: Literary Essays*, trans. Ora Cumming (*Koḥah ha-nora shel ashmah ketanah: ha-heksher ha-musari shel ha-tekst ha-sifruti*, 1998; Syracuse, NY: Syracuse University Press, 2000), vii.
119. Ibid., xviii.
120. Stephen K. George, ed., *Ethics, Literature, Theory: An Introductory Reader* (Lanham, MD: Rowman & Littlefield, 2005), xi.
121. Jane Adamson, Richard Freadman, and David Parker, eds., *Renegotiating Ethics in Literature, Philosophy, and Theory* (Cambridge: Cambridge University Press, 1998), 1.
122. Umberto Galimberti, *La casa di Psiche: Dalla psicoanalisi alla pratica filosofica* (Milan: Feltrinelli, 2005), 426. My translation.
123. Ibid., 439. My translation.
124. Zygmunt Bauman, *Modernity and the Holocaust* (Cambridge: Polity Press, 1989), 163.
125. Zygmunt Bauman and Keith Tester, *Conversations with Zygmunt Bauman* (Cambridge: Polity Press, 2001), 53.
126. See Raoul Eshelman, "Performatism, or the End of Postmodernism," *Anthropoetics* 6.2 (Fall 2000 / Winter 2001). <www.anthropoetics.ucla.edu/ap0602/perform.htm>.
127. Terry Eagleton, *After Theory* (New York: Basic Books, 2003), 144.
128. Ibid., 143.
129. See Tina Beattie, "The End of Postmodernism: The New Atheists and Democracy," 2007. <http://www.opendemocracy.net/article/faith_ideas/the_new_atheists>.

Chapter 1

1. As Merritt Moseley wrote, though this text raises many "epistemological questions," the central one is "reference." Merritt Moseley, *Understanding Julian Barnes* (Columbia: University of South Carolina Press, 1997), 84.
2. Julian Barnes, *Flaubert's Parrot* (1984; London: Jonathan Cape, 1992), 153.
3. Ibid., 1.
4. Vanessa Guignery, "Julian Barnes in Conversation," interview with Julian Barnes, November 2001, *Cercles* 4 (2002): 259. <http://www.cercles.com/n4/barnes>.
5. Ibid.
6. Ibid., 259–60.
7. Barnes, *Flaubert's Parrot*, 3.
8. Ibid.
9. Ibid., 7.
10. See Hayden White, *Metahistory: The Historical Imagination in Nineteenth-Century Europe* (Baltimore: The Johns Hopkins University Press, 1973).
11. See Eric J. Hobsbawm and Terence Ranger, eds., *The Invention of Tradition* (Cambridge: Cambridge University Press, 1983).
12. See Dominick LaCapra, *History and Criticism* (Ithaca, NY: Cornell University Press, 1985).
13. Hutcheon, *A Poetics of Postmodernism*, 106.
14. Ibid.
15. See Ronald H. McKinney, "The Greening of Postmodernism: Graham Swift's *Waterland*," *New Literary History* 28.4 (1997): 821–32.
16. Barnes, *Flaubert's Parrot*, 137.[A4]
17. Umberto Eco, "Postille a *Il nome della Rosa*" (*Alfabeta* 49, June 1983), rept.[A5] as a Postscript to *Il nome della Rosa* (Milan: Bompiani, 1984), 38–39. My translation.
18. See Virginia Woolf, "The New Biography" (1927), in *Selected Essays*, ed. David Bradshaw with a biographical preface by Frank

Kermode (Oxford: Oxford University Press, 2008), 95–100.

19. Laura Giovannelli, "I codici infranti: inclusività, riscrittura e metanarratività in 'Flaubert's Parrot' di Julian Barnes," *Strumenti Critici* 2 (May 1995): 273. My translation.

20. Barnes, *Flaubert's Parrot*, 134.

21. See Roland Barthes, "The Death of the Author" (1968), trans. Richard Howard. <http://evans-experientialism.freewebspace.com/barthes06.htm>. On the relation between Flaubert, Barthes and Barnes, see William Bell, "Not Altogether a Tomb. Julian Barnes: *Flaubert's Parrot*," in *Imitating Art: Essays in Biography*, ed. David Ellis (London: Pluto Press, 1993), 156–59; Peter Brooks, "Obsessed with the Hermit of Croisset," review of Julian Barnes's *Flaubert's Parrot*, *The New York Times*, March 10, 1985. <http://www.nytimes.com/books/01/02/25/specials/barnes-parrot.html>.

22. See Guignery, "Julian Barnes in Conversation," 263.

23. Ibid., 257.

24. Barnes, *Flaubert's Parrot*, 9.

25. Ibid., 10.

26. Ibid., 12.

27. Gustave Flaubert, *Madame Bovary*, trans. Raymond N. Mackenzie (Indianapolis, IN: Hackett, 2009), 3.

28. Alison Lee, *Realism and Power: Postmodern British Fiction* (London: Routledge, 1990), 39.

29. Barnes, *Flaubert's Parrot*, 46.

30. Ibid.

31. Ibid., 167.

32. Barnes celebrated the 150th anniversary of the publication of *Madame Bovary* with a short story entitled "The Rebuke," *The Guardian*, September 30, 2006. <http://www.guardian.co.uk/books/2006/sep/30/fiction.julianbarnes>.

33. See Julian Barnes, "When Flaubert Took Wing," *The Guardian*, March 5, 2005. <http://www.guardian.co.uk/books/2005mar/05/fiction.julianbarnes>.

34. Barnes, *Flaubert's Parrot*, 267.

35. Ibid., 271.

Chapter 2

1. In the course of an interview the author reasserted that the novel is rooted in fact — although the name of her real housekeeper was Juliska. See Csaba Károly, "Putting the Manuscript in the Lap of God," interview with Magda Szabó, *The Hungarian Quarterly* 190 (2008): 98–102. <http://www.ceeol.com>.

2. A few years later, Bernard Schlink would utilize a dream to open his novel *The Reader* (1995), to introduce us to the inner life of his narrator, that intimate dimension where tormented and tormenting memories keep boiling throughout the years.

3. Magda Szabó, *The Door*, trans. Len Rix (*Az ajtó*, 1987; London: Vintage Books, 2005), 1–2.

4. Ibid., 3.

5. Ibid., 114.

6. Ibid., 132.

7. Martha C. Nussbaum, *Upheavals of Thought: The Intelligence of Emotions* (Cambridge: Cambridge University Press, 2001), 1.

8. Ibid., 90.

9. Ibid., 93.

10. Szabó, *The Door*, 69. Later in the novel, the dog actually becomes a figuration for the unconditional love Emerence bestows on her mistress. See Szabó, *The Door*, 73.

11. Nussbaum, *Upheavals of Thought*, 91.

12. Szabó, *The Door*, 70.

13. Ibid., 65.

14. Ibid.

15. Ibid., 71.

16. Ibid., 67.

17. Ibid., 106.

18. Ibid., 110

19. Ibid., 24.

20. Ibid., 151.

21. Ibid., 39.

22. *New American Standard Bible*. <http://www.biblegateway.com/>.

23. Szabó, *The Door*, 104.

24. Ibid., 105.

25. Ibid., 80.

26. Ibid., 84.

27. Ibid., 133.

28. Ibid., 100–101.

29. Ibid., 113.

30. Dóra Elekes, "A Passion for Hungarian Fiction: An interview with translator Len Rix," *Hungarian Literature Online*. <http://www.hlo.hu/object.2A8D3A10-53C3-4B7E-83131836F447119C.ivy>.

31. Ibid.

32. Szabó, *The Door*, 165.

Chapter 3

1. See Nancy E. Berg, "The Politics of Paternity and Patrimony," *Shofar: An Interdisciplinary Journal of Jewish Studies* 24.3 (2006): 100–114.

2. Bernard Horn and Abraham B. Yehoshua, *Facing the Fires: Conversations with A.B. Yehoshua* (Syracuse, NY: Syracuse University Press, 1997), 2.

3. Adam Katz, "The Originary Scene, Sacrifice, and the Politics of Normalization in A.B. Yehoshua's *Mr. Mani*," *Anthropoetics* 7.2 (Fall 2001/Winter 2002): 2. <http://www.anthropoetics.ucla.edu/ap0702/sacrifice.htm>.

4. See Arnold J. Band, "'Mar Mani': The Archeology of Self-Deception," *Prooftexts* 12.3 (September 1992): 231–44.

5. *New American Standard Bible*. <http://www.biblegateway.com/>.

6. See Maya Jaggi, "Power and Pity," an interview with Abraham B. Yehoshua, *The Guardian*, June 24, 2006. <http://www.guardian.co.uk/books/2006/jun/24/featuresreviews.guardianreview11>.

7. Abraham B. Yehoshua, *Mr. Mani*, trans. Hillel Halkin (*Mar Mani*, 1990; London: Halban, 2002), 256.

8. Ibid., 190–91.

9. Arthur James Balfour, "The Balfour Declaration," November 2, 1917. <http://www.mfa.gov.il/MFA/Peace+Process/Guide+to+the+Peace+Process/The+Balfour+Declaration.htm>.

10. The triangle between Abraham, Sarah and Hagar is at the heart of Margaret Atwood's *The Handmaid's Tale* (1985).

11. *The Holy Qur'an*, Sahih International. <http://quran.com/>.

12. Yehoshua explores the relevance of incest in contemporary Israeli literature in *The Terrible Power of a Minor Guilt*, 108.

13. Guido Fink, "Il calendario impazzito di Yeoshua," *L'indice* 5 (May 1995): 17.

14. See Louis Jacobs, "The *Akedah*: Binding Isaac," in *The Jewish Religion: A Companion* (Oxford: Oxford University Press, 1995), 18–19.

15. Yehoshua, *Mr. Mani*, 321.

16. Ibid., 318.

17. Ibid.

18. See Arnold J. Band, "'Mar Mani': The Archeology of Self-Deception": 239–40.

19. See Abraham B. Yehoshua, "*Mr. Mani* and the *Akedah*," *Judaism* (Winter 2001): 61–65. <http://findarticles.com/p/articles/mi_m0411/is_5_49/ai_73180736>.

20. Ibid.

21. Ibid.

22. Adam Katz, "The Originary Scene, Sacrifice, and the Politics of Normalization in A.B. Yehoshua's *Mr. Mani*": 1.

23. For an interesting discussion of Jewish identity—which argues in favor of a condition of diaspora, arguing for a renunciation of territorial sovereignty, against the basic assumption of Zionism—see Daniel Boyarin and Jonathan Boyarin, "Diaspora: Generation and the Ground of Jewish Identity," *Critical Inquiry* 19.4 (Summer, 1993): 693–725.

24. See Abraham B. Yehoshua, *Antisemitismo e sionismo: una discussione*, trans. Glauco Felici (Turin: Einaudi, 2004), 16. My translation. Parts of this text have been published in English, respectively as "An Attempt to Identify the Root Cause of Antisemitism," *Azure* 32 (Spring 2008). <http://www.azure.org.il/article.php?id=18>; and as "The Zionist Revolution: Is It Continuing?," *CCAR Journal* 54.2 (2007): 123–45.

25. Yehoshua, *Antisemitismo e sionismo*, 38.

26. See Jaggi, "Power and Pity."

27. See Dino Messina, "Abraham Yehoshua, perché Israele rimuove la storia," July 1, 2008. <http://lanostrastoria.corriere.it/2008/07/abraham-yehoshua-rimuovere-la.html>.

28. The contrast between these two forms of Zionism is apparent in an article Martin Buber published on May 14, 1948, less than two weeks after the Israeli proclamation of independence. See Martin Buber, "Zionism and 'Zionism,'" in *A Land of Two Peoples: Martin Buber on Jews and Arabs*, ed. Paul Mendes Flohr (Chicago: The University of Chicago Press, 1983, 2005), 220–23.

29. Yehoshua, "*Mr. Mani* and the *Akedah*."

30. Ibid.

31. See Jaggi, "Power and Pity."

32. Gilead Morahg, "Borderline Cases: National Identity and Territorial Affinity in A.B. Yehoshua's Mr. Mani," *AJS Review* 30.1 (2006): 169.

33. Yehoshua, *Mr. Mani*, 32.

34. Ibid., 87.

35. Ibid., 91.

36. Ibid., 93.

37. Ibid., 103.

38. Ibid., 107.

39. Ibid., 108.

40. Ibid., 120.

41. Ibid., 123.

42. Ibid., 124.

43. Ibid., 125.

44. Ibid., 127.

45. Ibid., 137.

46. Morahg, "Borderline Cases: National Identity and Territorial Affinity in A.B. Yehoshua's Mr. Mani": 171.

47. Ibid., 171–72.

48. Ibid., 170.

49. Ibid., 179.

50. Laura Guglielmi, "Yehoshua: noi ebrei col divieto di sbagliare," an interview with Abraham B. Yehoshua, *Il secolo XIX*, November 7, 2002. <http://www.ilportoritrovato.net/html/biblioyehoshua.html>. My translation.

51. Band, "'Mar Mani': The Archeology of Self-Deception," 237.

52. Gilead Morahg, "The Heritage of

the Akedah in A.B. Yehoshua's *Mr. Mani*," in *Unbinding the Binding of Isaac*, eds. Mishael Caspi and John T. Greene (Lanham, MD: University Press of America, 2007), 188.

53. See Fredric Jameson, *The Political Unconscious* (1981; London: Routledge, 2002).

Chapter 4

1. John Fowles, *The French Lieutenant's Woman* (1969; New York: Signet, 1970), 266.
2. Ibid., 317.
3. See Geoff Dyer, "Who's Afraid of Influence?," *The Guardian*, September 22, 2001. <http://books.guardian.co.uk/reviews/general fiction/0,,555614,00.html>.
4. Ibid.
5. Daniel Mendelsohn, "Unforgiven," review of *Atonement*, Books, *New York*, March 11, 2002. <http://nymag.com/nymetro/arts/books/reviews/5776/>.
6. The vase — which was given to uncle Clem by the inhabitants of a French village that he saved, and which is destined to be destroyed in the course of the novel — has been considered by critics as an important symbol. According to Maria Margaronis, the vase, which is linked to the memory of war, is "a reification of history," and the damage it suffers marks "the end of many kinds of innocence: sexual, literary, moral." Maria Margaronis, "The Anxiety of Authenticity: Writing Historical Fiction at the End of the Twentieth Century," *History Workshop Journal* 65 (Spring 2008): 144–45. Likewise, according to Frank Kermode, the breaking of the vase "echoes what happens to other fragile objects highly valued but easily ruined, such as Cecilia's virginity, and indeed life itself." Frank Kermode, "Point of View," review of *Atonement*, *London Review of Books*, October 4, 2001. <http://www.lrb.co.uk/v23/n19/kerm01_.html>.
7. Ian McEwan, *Atonement* (London: Jonathan Cape, 2001), 38.
8. Ibid., 39.
9. While here the theme of water and drowning is associated with sexual attraction, in the chapter on war the lack of water Robbie suffers indicates his erotic and emotional deprivation.
10. McEwan, *Atonement*, 56.
11. Ibid., 60.
12. Ibid.
13. Ibid., 60–61.
14. Ibid., 62.
15. Ibid., 85–86.
16. Ibid., 119.
17. Ibid., 166.
18. Michiko Kakutani, "And When She Was Bad She Was...," review of *Atonement*, *The New York Times*, March 7, 2002. <http://query.nytimes.com/gst/fullpage.html?res=9E04E1DD1530F934A35750C0A9649C8B63>.
19. McEwan, *Atonement*, 166.
20. Ibid., 217.
21. Ian McEwan, "An Inspiration, Yes. Did I Copy from Another Author? No," *The Guardian*, November 27, 2006. <http://www.guardian.co.uk/uk/2006/nov/27/books comment.topstories3>.
22. Ibid.
23. McEwan, *Atonement*, 349.
24. Ibid., 357–58.
25. Ibid., 369.
26. Ibid., 370.
27. Ibid., 370–71.
28. Kermode, "Point of View."
29. See Laura Miller, "'Atonement' by Ian McEwan," Salon.com. <http://dir.salon.com/story/books/review/2002/03/21/mcewan/index.html>.
30. See Omer Ali, "The Ages of Sin," review of *Atonement*, *Time Out*, September 26, 2001, 59. Cited in Brian Finney, "Briony's Stand Against Oblivion: The Making of Fiction in Ian McEwan's *Atonement*," *Journal of Modern Literature* 27.3 (2004): 72.
31. For an analysis of this intertextual connection see Earl G. Ingersoll, "Intertextuality in L.P. Hartley's *The Go-Between* and Ian McEwan's *Atonement*," *Forum for Modern Language Studies* 40.3 (July 2004): 241–58.
32. L.P. Hartley, *The Go-Between* (1953; Harmondsworth, UK: Penguin, 1958), 279.
33. See Finney, "Briony's Stand Against Oblivion: The Making of Fiction in Ian McEwan's *Atonement*," 68–82.
34. Ibid., 72.
35. See Geoff Dyer, "Who's Afraid of Influence?"; Hermione Lee, "If Your Memories Serve You Well," review of *Atonement*, *The Observer*, September 23, 2001. <http://www.guardian.co.uk/books/2001/sep/23/fiction.booker prize2001>.
36. See Finney, "Briony's Stand Against Oblivion: The Making of Fiction in Ian McEwan's *Atonement*": 71–72; Margaronis, "The Anxiety of Authenticity: Writing Historical Fiction at the End of the Twentieth Century": 142; Peter Kemp, "*Atonement* by Ian McEwan," *The Sunday Times*, September 16, 2001. <http://entertainment.timesonline.co.uk/tol/arts_and_entertainment/books/fiction/article2379965.ece>.
37. Armelle Parey's reading of *Atonement* is focused on the opposition between the chaos of the real and the order of narration, which is

characterized by causality and finality. See Armelle Parey, "Ordre et chaos dans Atonement d'Ian McEwan," *Cercles*, Occasional Paper Series (2007): 93–102. <http://www.cercles.com/occasional.html>.

38. On the creative power of lying, see Oscar Wilde, "The Decay of Lying," in *The Complete Works*, with an introduction by Vyvyan Holland (London: Collins, 1966): 970–72; George Steiner, *After Babel: Aspects of Language and Translation* (New York: Oxford University Press, 1975).

Chapter 5

1. Mel Gussow, "W.G. Sebald, Elegiac German Novelist, Is Dead at 57," December 15, 2001. <http://query.nytimes.com/gst/fullpage.html?res=9505E7D61E3FF936A25751C1A9679C8B63>.

2. See Joyce Carol Oates, "Lest We Forget," review of *Austerlitz*, *The New York Review of Books* 54.12 (July 19, 2007). <http://www.nybooks.com/articles/20399>; Carol Bere, "The Book of Memory: W.G. Sebald's *The Emigrants* and *Austerlitz*," *Literary Review* (Fall 2002). <http://findarticles.com/p/articles/mi_m2078/is_1_46/ai_94983806/pg_2?tag=artBody;col1>.

3. Jens Brockmeier, "Austerlitz's Memory," *Partial Answers: Journal of Literature and the History of Ideas* 6.2 (June 2008): 347.

4. Arthur Lublow, "Arts Abroad; Preoccupied with Death, but Still Funny," *The New York Times*, December 11, 2001. <http://query.nytimes.com/gst/fullpage.html?res=9E05EEDC163FF932A25751C1A9679C8B63>.

5. Maya Jaggi, "Recovered Memories," interview with W.G. Sebald, *The Guardian*, September 22, 2001. <http://www.guardian.co.uk/books/2001/sep/22/artsandhumanities.highereducation>.

6. W.G. Sebald and Gordon Turner, "Introduction and Transcript of an Interview given by Max Sebald" (interviewer Michaël Zeeman), In Scott Denham and Mark McCulloh, eds., *W.G. Sebald. History—Memory—Trauma* (Berlin: de Gruyter, 2006), 23.

7. Sebald and Turner, "Introduction and Transcript of an Interview Given by Max Sebald," 23.

8. Efraim Sicher, introduction to *Breaking Crystal: Writing and Memory after Auschwitz*, ed. Efraim Sicher (Urbana: University of Illinois Press, 1998), 2.

9. The travelogue is also associated with the sense of an ethnographic research, both into individual life stories and into the European heritage of modernity, which helps us understand the national history of Germany. See Philip Schlesinger, "W.G. Sebald and the Condition of Exile," *Theory, Culture & Society* 21.2 (April 2004): 49–51.

10. For a study of the role photographs play in *Austerlitz*, see Carolin Duttlinger, "Traumatic Photographs: Remembrance and the Technical Media in W.G. Sebald's *Austerlitz*," in J.J. Long and Anne Whitehead, eds., *W.G. Sebald: A Critical Companion* (Seattle: University of Washington Press, 2004), 155–71. See also Dora Osborne, "Blind Spots: Viewing Trauma in W.G. Sebald's *Austerlitz*," *seminar* 43.4 (November 2007): 517–33; Hirsch, "The Generation of Postmemory": 115–25.

11. This transcultural dimension is partly lost in translation. See Noam M. Elcott, "Tattered Snapshots and Castaway Tongues: An Essay at Layout and Translation with W.G. Sebald," *The Germanic Review* 79.3 (Summer 2004): 209.

12. Amir Eshel, "Against the Power of Time: The Poetics of Suspension in W.G. Sebald's *Austerlitz*": 77.

13. Maya Jaggi, "The Last Word," interview with W.G. Sebald, *The Guardian*, December 21, 2001. <http://www.guardian.co.uk/education/2001/dec/21/artsandhumanities.highereducation>.

14. Ibid.
15. Ibid.

16. Richard Eder, "Excavating a Life," review of *Austerlitz*, *The New York Times*, October 28, 2001. <http://query.nytimes.com/gst/fullpage.html?res=9B0CE2D9153EF93BA1575 3C1A9679C8B63>.

17. W.G. Sebald, *Austerlitz*, trans. Anthea Bell (*Austerlitz: Bericht*, 2001[A6]; London: Penguin, 2002), 1.

18. Ibid., 2.
19. Ibid.
20. Maya Jaggi, "Recovered Memories."

21. See Adriana Cavarero, *Horrorism: Naming Contemporary Violence* (*Orrorismo: ovvero della violenza sull'inerme*, 2007; New York: Columbia University Press, 2009), 17–18.

22. Ibid., 34.
23. Sebald, *Austerlitz*, 6.
24. Ibid.
25. Ibid.
26. Ibid., 13.

27. See James Chandler, "About Loss: W.G. Sebald's Romantic Art of Memory," *The South Atlantic Quarterly* 102.1 (Winter 2003): 253.

28. Sebald, *Austerlitz*, 13.
29. Ibid., 13–14.

30. See Christopher C. Gregory-Guider, "The 'Sixth Emigrant': Traveling Places in the Works of W.G. Sebald," *Contemporary Literature* 46.3 (Fall 2005): 429.

31. Sebald, *Austerlitz*, 16.
32. Ibid., 16–17.
33. Elsewhere Sebald underlined that Nazi architecture "was prefigured by the bombast of the 19th-century bourgeois style" and that in both cases these immense buildings "depended on slave labour." Maya Jaggi, "Recovered Memories."
34. Ibid., 26
35. Ibid., 33.
36. Ibid., 37.
37. Ibid., 38.
38. Bauman, *Modernity and the Holocaust*, 93.
39. As a critic reminds us, in Sebald's works *coincidence* is "a loaded term," since it suggests "a random event that, upon reflection, exhibits a predetermined, fated quality." Gregory-Guider, "The 'Sixth Emigrant': Traveling Places in the Works of W.G. Sebald": 438.
40. John Zilcosky contrasts the authorial presence in *Vertigo* or *The Rings of Saturn*—which border on autobiography, featuring photographs of Sebald himself—with the more fictional character of *Austerlitz*, in which photographs are part of a fictional strategy. See John Zilcosky, "Lost and Found: Disorientation, Nostalgia, and Holocaust Melodrama in Sebald's *Austerlitz*," *Modern Language Notes* 121.3 (April 2006): 684–87.
41. Sebald, *Austerlitz*, 44.
42. Ibid., 143.
43. Ibid., 144.
44. Ibid., 174.
45. Ibid.
46. E.A. Poe, "The Man of the Crowd," in *Tales of Mystery and Imagination*, ed. Graham Clarke (London: Dent, 1984), 107.
47. See Marie Bonaparte, *The Life and Works of Edgar Allen Poe: A Psychoanalytic Interpretation*, foreword by Sigmund Freud, trans. John Rodker (London: Imago, 1949).
48. Sebald, *Austerlitz*, 180.
49. Anne Whitehead, *Trauma Fiction* (Edinburgh: Edinburgh University Press, 2004), 6.
50. Ibid., 12.
51. John Wylie, "The Spectral Geographies of W.G. Sebald," *cultural geographies* 14 (2007): 172.
52. Sebald, *Austerlitz*, 189.
53. Ibid., 192.
54. Ibid., 192–93.
55. Ibid., 193.
56. Ibid., 55.
57. Sebald utilized the rucksack to draw a parallel between his character and the philosopher Ludwig Wittgenstein, who came from a wealthy family of Austrian Jews. See Sebald, *Austerlitz*, 55–56.
58. See Maya Jaggi, "Recovered Memories."
59. Stuart Taberner, "German Nostalgia? Remembering German-Jewish Life in W.G. Sebald's *Die Ausgewanderten* and *Austerlitz*," *The Germanic Review* 79.3 (Summer 2004): 186.
60. Sebald, *Austerlitz*, 215–16.
61. Ibid., 407.
62. Ibid., 408.
63. Ibid., 414.
64. Ibid., 72.

Chapter 6

1. Yoshinobu Hakutani, "No Place I Was Meant to Be: Postmodern Japan in Haruki Murakami's Fiction," in *Postmodernity and Cross-Culturalism*, ed. Yoshinobu Hakutani (Madison, NJ: Fairleigh Dickinson University Press; London: Associated University Press, 2002), 17.
2. According to Matthew Richard Chozick, Murakami's "new cultural plurality" defies "common historical conceptions of national identity or literary canons." Matthew Richard Chozick, "De-Exoticising Haruki Murakami's Reception," *Comparative Literature Studies* 45.1 (2008): 65.
3. J. Philip Gabriel, *Spirit Matters: The Transcendent in Modern Japanese Literature* (Honolulu: University of Hawai'i Press, 2006), 106.
4. See Matthew Strecher, "Magical Realism and the Search for Identity in the Fiction of Haruki Murakami," *Journal of Japanese Studies* 25.2 (Summer 1999): 263–98. The Japanese approach to the fantastic has also been explored by Susan Jolliffe Napier in *The Fantastic in Modern Japanese Literature: The Subversion of Modernity* (London: Routledge, 1996).
5. This novel has similarities with Carlos Ruiz Zafón's *The Shadow of the Wind* (2001), an apology of reading as an experience that is capable to influence reality, changing the course of events due to a mysterious exchange of energies. Both these Bildungsromane pivot on a library which triggers the main character's process of development, through his contact with a past that must be exorcised in the present.
6. Haruki Murakami, *Kafka on the Shore*, trans. Philip Gabriel (*Umibe no Kafuka*, 2002; New York: Vintage Books, 2005), 5.
7. Ibid.
8. Ibid., 11.
9. See Steffen Hantke, "Postmodernism and Genre Fiction as Deferred Action: Haruki Murakami and the Noir Tradition," *Critique* 49.1 (Fall 2007): 3–23.

10. See Murakami, *Kafka on the Shore*, 257.
11. Ibid., 163.
12. Ibid., 35.
13. Fritjof Capra, *The Tao of Physics* (Boston: Shambhala, 1975), 130.
14. Murakami, *Kafka on the Shore*, 235.
15. Laura Miller, "Crossing Over," review of *Kafka on the Shore*, *The New York Times*, February 6, 2005. <http://query.nytimes.com/gst/fullpage.html?res=9A02E5DC173BF935A35751C0A9639C8B63>.
16. Richard Williams, "Marathon Man," *The Guardian*, May 17, 2003. <http://www.guardian.co.uk/books/2003/may/17/fiction.harukimurakami>.
17. See Stefano Tani, *The Doomed Detective: The Contribution of the Detective Novel to Postmodern American and Italian Fiction* (Carbondale: Southern Illinois University Press, 1984); Elizabeth Dipple, *The Unresolvable Plot: Reading Contemporary Fiction* (New York: Routledge, 1988).
18. Michael Seats, *Murakami Haruki[A7]: The Simulacrum in Contemporary Japanese Culture* (Lanham, MD: Lexington Books, 2006), 337.
19. Murakami, *Kafka on the Shore*, 297.
20. See Laura Miller, "Crossing Over," and Laura Miller, "Haruki Murakami on the Darkness of the Subconscious, the Aum Cult, Subway Gas Attack and Being an Individualist in Japan." <http://www.salon.com/books/int/1997/12/cov_si_16int.html>. The mackerels and leeches that rain from the sky in the novel remind one of the rain of frogs in the Paul Thomas Anderson film *Magnolia* (2000).
21. Murakami, *Kafka on the Shore*, 299.
22. Ibid., 312.
23. Dennis Charles Washburn, *Translating Mount Fuji: Japanese Fiction and the Ethics of Identity* (New York: Columbia University Press, 2007), 2.
24. Ibid., 4.
25. Murakami, *Kafka on the Shore*, 191.
26. Ibid., 139. "In Dreams Begin Responsibilities" is also the title of a short story Delmore Schwartz published in the *Partisan Review* in 1937.
27. Ibid., 61. In the novel there is no reference to the famous "Letter to his father" where Kafka explores his difficult relation with the paternal figure.
28. Laura Miller relates this negative message to the sense of guilt postwar Japanese youth felt due to the involvement of their fathers in Nazi-Fascism. See Miller, "Crossing Over."
29. See Murakami, *Kafka on the Shore*, 307.
30. Miss Saeki seems to have been attracted by this man because he too had half a shadow, having been struck by lightning. See Murakami, *Kafka on the Shore*, 331.
31. When at the end of the novel Miss Saeki gives Kafka her beloved painting featuring her adolescent boyfriend, she actually tells him: "After all, the painting is originally *yours*.... You were there. And I was there beside you, watching you." Murakami, *Kafka on the Shore*, 460.
32. The people who inhabit this timeless place have lost their memories, which are collected in a library. See Murakami, *Kafka on the Shore*, 458.
33. See Janet Maslin, "Adrift in a Universe in Flux Like Some FedEx Box," review of *Kafka on the Shore*, *The New York Times*, January 31, 2005. <http://query.nytimes.com/gst/fullpage.html?res=940CE1D8153BF932A05752C0A9639C8B63>.
34. See Murakami, *Kafka on the Shore*, 90.
35. See Amy Ty Lai, "Memory, Hybridity, and Creative Alliance in Haruki Murakami's Fiction," *Mosaic: a Journal for the Interdisciplinary Study of Literature* 40.1 (March 2007): 173.
36. See Murakami, *Kafka on the Shore*, 384–85.
37. Williams, "Marathon Man."
38. Murakami, *Kafka on the Shore*, 366.
39. Ibid., 236.
40. Gabriel, *Spirit Matters*, 2.
41. Ibid., 8–9. For a Jungian reading of this novel, see also Inez Martinez, "Haruki Murakami reimagining of Sophocles's Oedipus," in *Psyche and the Arts: Jungian Approaches to Music, Architecture, Literature*, ed. Susan Rowland (Hove, UK: Routledge, 2008), 56–65.
42. Kanya Wattanagun and Suradech Chotiudompant, "The Quest and Reconstruction of Identity in Haruki Murakami's *Kafka on the Shore*," *Manusya Journal of Humanities*, 12:1 (2009): 31. <http://www.manusya.journals.chula.ac.th/files/essay/Kanya_26-39.pdf>.
43. Ibid., 39.
44. Erik Chalhoub, "Tight Potential, Loose Ends," review of *Kafka on the Shore*, *Porter Gulch Review* (2007), 26. <http://www.cabrillo.edu/publications/portergulch/2007/PGR%20Book%20reviews.pdf>.

Chapter 7

1. Jeffrey Alexander, *The Meanings of Social Life: A Cultural Sociology* (Oxford: Oxford University Press, 2003), 32–33.
2. Efraim Sicher, "The Burden of Memory: The Writing of the Post-Holocaust Generation," in *Breaking Crystal*, ed. Efraim Sicher (Urbana: University of Illinois Press, 1998), 19.

3. Ibid., 20.
4. Ibid.
5. Ian McEwan, *Black Dogs* (1992; London: Picador, 1993), 109.
6. This text has even helped engender what is now called a *tourism of memory* whose focus is the Galicia region. (See Gad Lerner, "Sulle tracce degli scomparsi: viaggio nelle terre della Shoah," *Repubblica*, August 12, 2008, 45.) This memorial itinerary is also at the heart of more recent literary works, such as Daniel Mendelsohn, *The Lost: A Search for Six of Six Million* (New York: HarperCollins, 2006).
7. See Jonathan Safran Foer, *Everything Is Illuminated* (2002; London: Penguin, 2003), 16.
8. Ibid., 230.
9. Ibid., 59.
10. Ibid., 53.
11. Ibid., 117–18.
12. Ibid., 118.
13. Ibid.
14. Ibid., 150.
15. Cathy Caruth, introduction to *Trauma: Explorations in Memory*, ed. Cathy Caruth, (Baltimore: The Johns Hopkins University Press, 1995), 4–5.
16. Foer, *Everything Is Illuminated*, 189.
17. Ibid., 179.
18. Ibid., 179–80.
19. Ibid., 156.
20. Ibid., 160.
21. Ibid., 274.
22. Ibid., 184.
23. Ibid., 219.
24. Ibid., 214.
25. Menachem Feuer actually believes that Alex's thirst for friendship contrasts with Jonathan's detachment. According to the critic, the tension between comic and tragic is left unresolved in the book, where the possibility of a reconciliation between the descendants of perpetrators and those of the survivors is suspended. See Menachem Feuer, "Almost Friends: Post-Holocaust Comedy, Tragedy, and Friendship in Jonathan Safran Foer's *Everything Is Illuminated*," *Shofar: An Interdisciplinary Journal of Jewish Studies* 25.2 (Winter 2007): 24–48.
26. Ronit Lentin, "Postmemory, Received History and the Return of the Auschwitz Code," *Eurozine*, 36.4 (2002): 2. <http://www.eurozine.com/articles/2002-09-06-lentin-en.html>.
27. The use of the fantastic, folklore and magic realism in recent literary representations of the Holocaust has been explored by Lee Behlman, "The Escapist: Fantasy, Folklore, and the Pleasures of the Comic Book in Recent Jewish American Holocaust Fiction," *Shofar: An Interdisciplinary Journal of Jewish Studies* 22.3 (2004): 56–71.
28. Raoul Eshelman, "After Postmodernism: Performatism in Literature," *Anthropoetics*, 11.2 (Fall 2005 / Winter 2006). <http://www.anthropoetics.ucla.edu/ap1102/perform05.htm>.
29. See Jane Alison, "The Third Victim in Bernhard Schlink's *Der Vorleser*," *The Germanic Review* 81.2 (Spring 2006): 163–78; Joseph Metz, "'Truth Is a Woman': Post-Holocaust Narrative, Postmodernism, and the Gender of Fascism in Bernhard Schlink's *Der Vorleser*," *German Quarterly* 77.3 (Summer 2004): 300–323; John E. MacKinnon, "Crime, Compassion, and *The Reader*," *Philosophy and Literature*, 27.1 (2003): 1–20.
30. See Bernhard Schlink, *The Reader* (*Der Vorleser*, 1995; London: Phoenix, 2008), 203.
31. Foer, *Everything Is Illuminated*, 118–19.
32. Ibid., 62.
33. Ibid., 246.
34. Ibid., 245.
35. Ibid., 245–46.
36. Ibid., 247.
37. Ibid.
38. Ibid., 251.
39. Ibid., 276.
40. Marianne Hirsch, *Family Frames: Photography, Narrative and Postmemory* (Cambridge, MA: Harvard University Press, 1997), 22.
41. Ibid.
42. Hirsch, "The Generation of Postmemory," 107.
43. Alan L. Berger, "Unclaimed Experience: Trauma and Identity in Third Generaton Writing about the Holocaust," *Shofar* 28.3 (Spring 2010): 151.
44. Ibid., 155.
45. Foer, *Everything Is Illuminated*, 159.
46. Francisco Collado-Rodriguez, "Ethics in the Second Degree: Trauma and Dual Narratives in Jonathan Safran Foer's *Everything Is Illuminated*," *Journal of Modern Literature* 32.1 (Fall 2008): 61.

Chapter 8

1. Azar Nafisi, *Reading Lolita in Tehran: A Memoir in Books* (2003; London: Harper, 2008), 81.
2. Ibid.
3. Ibid., 82.
4. Azar Nafisi, *Things I've Been Silent About: Memories of a Prodigal Daughter* (London: Windmill Books, 2010), xx.
5. Nafisi, *Reading Lolita in Tehran*, 27.

6. Ibid., 192.
7. Ibid., 3. The only man who is allowed to participate in this private seminar has to do so at a distance, since Nafisi gives him the necessary materials and then discusses them with him separately.
8. Ibid., 4.
9. Ibid.
10. Ibid., 75.
11. Ibid., 36.
12. Ibid., 37.
13. Ibid., 19.
14. Ibid., 129.
15. Ibid., 273.
16. Ibid., 132.
17. Ibid., 133.
18. Ibid., 8.
19. Ibid., 44.
20. Ibid., 215.
21. See Marjane Satrapi, *Persepolis*, Vols. 1–4 (Paris: L'Association, 2000–2003).
22. Although the book originally appeared as Shirin Ebadi, *Iran Awakening: A Memoir of Revolution and Hope* (New York: Random House, 2006), Moavenis's name features as co-author in subsequent publi-cations, such as Shirin Ebadi with Azadeh Moaveni, *Iran Awakening: One Woman's Journey to Reclaim Her Life and Country* (New York: Random House, 2007).
23. Ebadi's political agenda emerges from the lecture she gave when she accepted the Nobel Prize, on December 10, 2003. <http://nobelprize.org/nobel_prizes/peace/laureates/2003/ebadi-lecture-e.html>.
24. I have read the Italian edition: Shirin Ebadi, *La gabbia d'oro: Tre fratelli nell'incubo della rivoluzione iraniana*, trans. Ella Mohammadi (Milan: Rizzoli, 2008).
25. Gillian Whitlock, "Autographics: The Seeing 'I' of the Comics," *Modern Fiction Studies* 52.4 (Winter 2006): 972.
26. "A Conversation with Azar Nafisi," in appendix to Azar Nafisi, *Reading Lolita in Tehran*, 5.
27. See Fatema Mernissi, *Beyond The Veil: Male-Female Dynamics in Modern Muslim Society* (Cambridge, MA: Schenkmann, 1975); *Dreams of Trespass: Tales of a Harem Girlhood* (Reading, MA: Addison-Wesley, 1994); *Scheherazade Goes West: Different Cultures, Different Harems* (New York: Washington Square Press, 2001).
28. Michiko Kakutani, "Book Study as Insubordination under the Mullahs," review of *Reading Lolita in Tehran, The New York Times*, April 15, 2003. <http://query.nytimes.com/gst/fullpage.html?res=9C04E7DC103BF936A25757C0A9659C8B63>.

29. See John Carlos Rowe, "Reading *Reading Lolita in Tehran* in Idaho," *American Quarterly* 59.2 (2007): 258.
30. See Hamid Dabashi, "Native Informers and the Making of the American Empire," *Al-Ahram Weekly Online* 797 (June 1–7, 2006). <http://weekly.ahram.org.eg/2006/797/special.htm>.
31. See "Reading More Than *Lolita* in Tehran: An Interview with Fatemeh Keshavarz," *Monthly Review*, March 12, 2007. <http://www.monthlyreview.org/mrzine/keshavarz120307.html>.
32. Mitra Rastegar, "Reading Nafisi in the West: Authenticity, Orientalism, and 'Liberating' Iranian Women," *Women's Studies Quarterly* 34.1/2 (2006): 108.
33. See Fatemeh Keshavarz, *Jasmine and Stars: Reading More Than* Lolita *in Tehran* (Chapel Hill: University of North Carolina Press, 2007), 18.
34. Simon Hay, "Why Read *Reading Lolita*? Teaching Critical Thinking in a Culture of Choice," *Pedagogy: Critical Approaches to Teaching Literature, Language, Composition, and Culture* 8.1 (Winter 2008): 12.
35. Ibid.
36. Ibid., 16.
37. Rowe, "Reading *Reading Lolita in Tehran* in Idaho," 255.
38. Ibid., 257.
39. Ibid., 271.
40. Ibid., 272.
41. Robert Birnbaum, "Azar Nafisi, Author of *Reading Lolita in Tehran*, converses with Robert Birnbaum," February 5, 2004. <http://www.identitytheory.com/interviews/birnbaum139.php>.
42. Amy DePaul, "Fighting Words: Reading Lolita in Tehran," July 31, 2008. <http://www.popmatters.com/pm/feature/58030/fightingwords/>.
43. Amy DePaul, "Re-Reading *Reading Lolita in Tehran*," *MELUS* 33.2 (Summer 2008): 90.
44. Ibid., 74.
45. Catherine Burwell, "Reading Lolita in Times of War: Women's Book Clubs and the Politics of Reception," *Intercultural Education* 18.4 (October 2007): 282.
46. Ramin Jahanbegloo, "Reading Machiavelli in Tehran: Beyond the Theological-Political." <http://jahanbegloo.com/articles/Machiavelli.html>.
47. See Danny Postel, "Ideas Whose Time Has Come: A Conversation with Iranian Philosopher Ramin Jahanbegloo." <http://www.logosjournal.com/issue_5.2/jahanbegloo_interview.htm>.

48. See Danny Postel, "A Fighting Faith," in *The Liberal*, 2008. <http://www.theliberal.co.uk/issue_12/politics/iran_postel.1_12.html>.
49. Nafisi, *Reading Lolita in Tehran*, 21.
50. Azar Nafisi, "The Republic of the Imagination," *Washington Post*, December 5, 2004. <http://www.washingtonpost.com/wp-dyn/articles/A30117-2004Dec2.html>.
51. Ferdinand de Saussure, *Course in General Linguistics*, trans. Roy Harris (*Cours de linguistique générale*, 1916; Peru, IL: Open Court, 1986), 74.
52. Virginia Woolf, "Craftsmanship," in *The Death of the Moth and Other Essays*. <http://ebooks.adelaide.edu.au/w/woolf/virginia/w91d/chapter24.html>.
53. Edna Ullmann-Margalit, "Between Basis and Roots: Religious Fundamentalism, Radicalism, and {PRIVATE} Women," *Dones Mediterrànies*. <http://www.mediterraneas.org/article.php3?id_article=387>.

Conclusion

1. Heide Ziegler, introduction to *The End of Postmodernism: New Directions Proceedings of the First Stuttgart Seminar in Cultural Studies, 04.08.-18.08.1991*, ed. Heide Ziegler (Stuttgart: M & P Verlag fur Wissenschaft und Forschung, 1993), 7.
2. David Foster Wallace, "E Unibus Pluram: Television and U.S. Fiction," *Review of Contemporary Fiction* 13.2 (Summer 1993): 177.
3. Ibid., 192–93.
4. Robert McLaughlin, "Post-Postmodern Discontent: Contemporary Fiction and the Social World," *symploke* 12.1–2 (2004): 55.
5. Ibid.
6. Raoul Eshelman, "Performatism, or the End of Postmodernism," *Anthropoetics* 6.2 (Fall 2000 / Winter 2001). <www.anthropoetics.ucla.edu/ap0602/perform.htm>.
7. Said, *Humanism and Democratic Criticism*, 1.
8. Ibid., 11.
9. Ibid., 26.
10. Ibid., 12.
11. See Joseph Ciarrochi, Joseph P. Forgas, and John D. Mayer, eds, *Emotional Intelligence in Everyday Life: A Scientific Enquiry* (New York: Psychology Press, 2001); Robert J. Emmerling, Vinod K. Shanwal, and Manas K. Mandal, eds., *Emotional Intelligence: Theoretical and Cultural Perspectives* (New York: Nova Science Publishers, 2008).
12. Robert Eaglestone, *The Holocaust and the Postmodern* (Oxford: Oxford University Press, 2004), 24.
13. Vickroy, *Trauma and Survival in Contemporary Fiction*, xvi.
14. Ibid., 1.
15. See Shoshana Felman and Dori Laub, *Testimony: Crises of Witnessing in Literature, Psychoanalysis, and History* (London: Routledge, 1992).
16. Murakami, "The Novelist in Wartime."
17. McEwan, *Black Dogs*, 37.
18. Murakami, "The Novelist in Wartime."
19. Schlink, *The Reader*, 214–15.
20. Ibid., 215.
21. Ibid., 215–16.
22. Caruth, introduction to *Trauma: Explorations in Memory*, 8.
23. Shoshana Felman, "Education and Crisis, or the Vicissitudes of Teaching," in *Trauma: Explorations in Memory*, ed. Cathy Caruth, 24.
24. Sarah R. Horowitz, *Voicing the Void: Muteness and Memory in Holocaust Fiction* (Albany: State University of New York Press, 1997), 1.
25. Vickroy, *Trauma and Survival in Contemporary Fiction*, 1.
26. Ibid., 3.
27. Horowitz, *Voicing the Void*, 16.
28. Ibid., 20.
29. Ibid., 39.
30. Amin Maalouf, *In the Name of Identity: Violence and the Need to Belong*, trans. Barbara Bray (*Identités meutrières*, 1996; New York: Arcade Publishing, 2001), 4.
31. Ibid.
32. Ibid., 5.
33. See Jay David Bolter and Richard Grusin, *Remediation: Understanding New Media* (Cambridge, MA: MIT Press, 1998).
34. See Linda Hutcheon, *A Theory of Adaptation* (New York: Routledge, 2006).
35. Wolfgang Hallet, "The Multimodal Novel: The Integration of Modes and Media in Novelistic Narration," in *Narratology in the Age of Cross-Disciplinary Narrative Research*, eds. Sandra Heinen and Roy Sommer (Berlin: Walter de Gruyter, 2009), 131.
36. Neither should we forget the contribution of the cinema to the birth of the graphic novel, since the realization of a film also involves the creation of a *storyboard*, therefore of a sequence of cartoons that anticipate its articulation into scenes.
37. Whitlock, "Autographics: The Seeing 'I' of the Comics": 966.
38. Dan Cryer, "A Novelist on the Edge," interview with Ian McEwan, *Newsday*, April 24, 2002, B6. Quoted in Finney, "Briony's Stand Against Oblivion: The Making of Fiction in Ian McEwan's *Atonement*": 76.

Bibliography

Primary Sources

Amis, Martin. *The Second Plane: September 11: Terror and Boredom*. New York: Alfred A. Knopf, 2008.
Atwood, Margaret. *The Handmaid's Tale*. 1985; London: Virago, 1987.
Barakat, Hoda. *The Tiller of Waters* [*Hàrith al-miyàh*, 1998]. Cairo: The American University of Cairo Press, 2001.
Barnes, Julian. *Cross Channel*. London: Jonathan Cape, 1996.
_____. *England, England*. 1998; New York: Random House, 1999.
_____. *Flaubert's Parrot*. 1984; London: Jonathan Cape, 1992.
_____. "The Rebuke." *The Guardian*, September 30, 2006. <http://www.guardian.co.uk/books/2006/sep/30/fiction.julianbarnes>.
_____. *Something to Declare: Essays on France*. New York: Alfred A. Knopf, 2002.
_____. "When Flaubert Took Wing." *The Guardian*, March 5, 2005. <http://www.guardian.co.uk/books/2005/mar/05/fiction.julianbarnes>.
Calvino, Italo. *Se una notte d'inverno un viaggiatore*. Turin: Einaudi, 1979.
Carter, Angela. *The Bloody Chamber and Other Stories*. 1978; London: Victor Gollancz, 1989.
Coetzee, J.M. *Foe*. Harmondsworth, UK: Penguin, 1986.
DeLillo, Don. *Falling Man*. New York: Scribner, 2007.
Ebadi, Shirin. *Iran Awakening: A Memoir of Revolution and Hope*. New York: Random House, 2006.
_____. *La gabbia d'oro. Tre fratelli nell'incubo della rivoluzione iraniana*. Translated by Ella Mohammadi. Milan: Rizzoli, 2008.
_____. "Nobel Lecture," December 10, 2003. <http://nobelprize.org/nobel_prizes/peace/laureates/2003/ebadi-lecture-e.html>.
_____ with Azadeh Moaveni. *Iran Awakening: One Woman's Journey to Reclaim Her Life and Country*. New York: Random House, 2007.
Flaubert, Gustave. *Madame Bovary*. Translated by Raymond N. Mackenzie. 1857; Indianapolis, IN: Hackett, 2009.
Foer, Jonathan Safran. *Everything Is Illuminated*. 2002; London: Penguin, 2003.
_____. *Extremely Loud and Incredibly Close*. 2005; London: Penguin, 2006.
Folman, Ari, and David Polonski. *Waltz with Bashir: A Lebanon War Story*. London: Atlantic, 2009.
Fowles, John. *The French Lieutenant's Woman*. 1969; New York: Signet, 1970.
Guibert, Emmanuel, Didier Lefèvre, and Frédéric Lemercier. *Le Photographe* (Marcinelle, BE: Dupuis, 2003–2006), 3 vols.
Hamid, Mohsin. *The Reluctant Fundamentalist*. Orlando, FL: Harcourt, 2007.
Hartley, L.P. *The Go-Between*. 1953; Harmondsworth, UK: Penguin, 1958.
The Holy Qur'an. Sahih International. <http://quran.com/>.

Hosseini, Khaled. *The Kite Runner*. London: Bloomsbury, 2003.
_____. *A Thousand Splendid Suns*. New York: Riverhead Books, 2007.
Ishiguro, Kazuo. *Never Let Me Go*. London: Faber & Faber, 2005.
James, Henry. "The Birthplace," in *The Better Sort*. London: 1903[A1].
Keshavarz, Fatemeh. *Jasmine and Stars: Reading More Than* Lolita *in Tehran*. Chapel Hill: University of North Carolina Press, 2007.
Khuri, Elias. Translated by Humphrey Davies [A2] [*Bab al-Shams*, 1998]. London: Harvill Secker, 2005.
Kristof, Agota. *L'analphabète: récit autobiographique*. Geneva: Zoe_, 2004.
McEwan, Ian. *Atonement*. London: Jonathan Cape, 2001.
_____. *Black Dogs*. 1992; London: Picador, 1993.
_____. "An inspiration, yes. Did I copy from another author? No." *The Guardian*, November 27, 2006. <http://www.guardian.co.uk/uk/2006/nov/27/bookscomment.topstories3>.
McInerney, Jay. *The Good Life*. New York: Alfred A. Knopf, 2006.
Mendelsohn, Daniel. *The Lost: A Search for Six of Six Million*. New York: HarperCollins, 2006.
Michaels, Anne. *Fugitive Pieces*. 1996; London: Bloomsbury, 2009.
Murakami, Haruki. *Kafka on the Shore*. Translated by Philip Gabriel [*Umibe no Kafuka*, 2002]. New York: Vintage Books, 2005.
Nafisi, Azar. *Reading Lolita in Tehran: A Memoir in Books*. 2003; London: Harper, 2008.
_____. "The Republic of the Imagination." *Washington Post*, December 5, 2004. <http://www.washingtonpost.com/wp-dyn/articles/A30117-2004Dec2.html>.
_____. *Things I've Been Silent About: Memories of a Prodigal Daughter*. London: Windmill Books, 2010.
New American Standard Bible. <http://www.biblegateway.com/>.
Pamuk, Orhan. *Snow* [*Kar*, 2002]. London: Faber & Faber, 2004.
Pynchon, Thomas. *The Crying of Lot 49*. 1966; London: Picador, 1979.
Ramini, Atiq (Atiqolla). *Earth and Ashes*. Translated by Erdağ M. Göknar [*Khakestar-o-khak*, 2000]. London: Chatto & Windus, 2002.
_____. *Le Retour imaginaire*. Translated by Sabrina Nouri. Paris: POL, 2005.
_____. *A Thousand Rooms of Dreams and Fear*. Translated by Sarah Maguire and Yama Yari [*Hazār khañah-'i khab va ikhtināq*, 2002]. London: Chatto & Windus, 2006.
Rushdie, Salman. *Midnight's Children*. London: Picador, 1981.
Satrapi, Marjane. *Persepolis*. Vols. 1–4. Paris: L'Association, 2000–2003.
Schlink, Bernhard. *The Reader* [*Der Vorleser*, 1995]. London: Phoenix, 2008.
Sebald, W.G. *Austerlitz*. Translated by Anthea Bell [*Austerlitz: Bericht*, 2001[A6]]. London: Penguin, 2002.
_____. *The Emigrants*. Translated by Michael Hulse [*Die Ausgewanderten*, 1992]. New York: New Directions, 1996.
Spiegelman, Art. *In the Shadow of No Towers*. New York: Pantheon; Toronto: Random House, 2004.
_____. *Maus: A Survivor's Tale* [*My Father Bleeds History*, 1986; *And Here My Troubles Began*, 1991]. New York: Pantheon Books, 1992.
Swift, Graham. *Waterland*. London: Heinemann, 1983.
Szabó, Magda. *The Door*. Translated by Len Rix [*Az ajtó*, 1987]. London: Vintage Books, 2005.
Updike, John. *Terrorist*. New York: Alfred A. Knopf, 2006.
Wilde, Oscar. *The Complete Works*, with an introduction by Vyvyan Holland. London: Collins, 1966.
Wolf, Christa. *Medea: A Modern Retelling*. Translated by John Cullen [*Medea: Stimmen*, 1996[A7]]. London: Virago, 1998.
Yehoshua, Abraham B. *Mr. Mani*. Translated by Hillel Halkin [*Mar Mani*, 1990]. London: Halban, 2002.
Zafón, Carlos Ruiz. *The Shadow of the Wind*. Translated by Lucia Graves [*La sombra del viento*, 2001]. London: Weidenfeld & Nicolson, 2004.

Films

11'09"01— September 11, directed by Alain Brigand.
Everything Is Illuminated, 2005, directed by Liev Schreiber.
Life Is Beautiful (*La vita è bella*), 1997, directed by Roberto Benigni.

Magnolia, 2000, directed by Paul Thomas Anderson.
Mr. Bean's Holiday, 2007, directed by Steve Bendelack.
Persepolis, 2007, directed by Marjane Satrapi and Vincent Paronnaud.
The Reader, 2008, directed by Stephen Daldry.
Train of Life (*Train de vie*), 1998, directed by Radu Mihaileanu.
Waltz with Bashir, 2008, directed by Ari Folman.

Critical Works

Adamo, Sergia. *Culture planetarie? Prospettive e limiti della teoria e della critica culturale*. Rome: Meltemi, 2007.
Adams, Tim. "How to Have Sex with a Ghost." Review of *Kafka on the Shore*, *The Observer*, January 2, 2005. <http://books.guardian.co.uk/print/0,3858,5094656-99930,00.html>.
Adamson, Jane, Richard Freadman, and David Parker, eds. *Renegotiating Ethics in Literature, Philosophy, and Theory*. Cambridge: Cambridge University Press, 1998.
Agazzi, Elena, and Vita Fortunati, eds. *Memoria e saperi: percorsi transdisciplinari*. Rome: Meltemi, 2007.
Ahmed, Akbar S. "Postmodernism and Islam: After 9/11?" *Daily Times*, January 10, 2004. <http://www.dailytimes.com.pk/default.asp?page=story_9-1-2004_pg3_5>.
———. *Postmodernism and Islam: Predicament and Promise*. London: Routledge, 1992.
Albertazzi, Silvia. "'Madame Bovary, c'est lui!' Gustave Flaubert, Julian Barnes e l'eterna monotonia della passione." *Francofonia* 54 (Spring 2008): 127–39.
Alexander, Jeffrey. *The Meanings of Social Life: A Cultural Sociology*. Oxford: Oxford University Press, 2003.
Ali, Omer. "The Ages of Sin." Review of *Atonement*, *Time Out*, September 26, 2001: 59.
Alison, Jane. "The Third Victim in Bernhard Schlink's *Der Vorleser*." *The Germanic Review* 81.2 (Spring 2006): 163–78.
Allen, Paul. "Through the Veil." Review of *Reading Lolita in Tehran*, *The Guardian*, September 13, 2003. <http://www.guardian.co.uk/books/2003/sep/13/featuresreviews.guardianreview1>.
America, Mark, and Lance Olsen, eds. *In Memoriam to Postmodernism: Essays on the Avant-pop*. San Diego: San Diego State University Press, 1995.
Anderson, Mark M. "Documents, Photography, Postmemory: Alexander Kluge, W.G. Sebald, and the German Family" *Poetics Today* 29.1 (2008): 129–53.
Annesley, James. *Fictions of Globalization*. London: Continuum, 2006.
Appadurai, Arjun. *Modernity at Large: Cultural Dimensions of Globalization*. Minneapolis: University of Minnesota Press, 1996.
Appiah, Kwame Anthony. *Cosmopolitanism: Ethics in a World of Strangers*. New York: W.W. Norton, 2006.
Arendt, Hannah. *The Origins of Totalitarianism*, ed. Samantha Power. 1951; New York: Schocken Books, 2004.
Ashcroft, Bill, Gareth Griffiths and Helen Tiffin. *The Empire Writes Back: Theory and Practice in Post-Colonial Literatures*. London: Routledge, 1989.
Assmann, Aleida. *Erinnerungsräume. Formen und Wandlungen des kulturellen Gedächtnisses*, 1999; *Ricordare: Forme e mutamenti della memoria culturale*. Translated by Simona Paparelli. Bologna: il Mulino, 2002.
Atilla, Aylin. "Reinterpreting History: Julian Barnes' *A History of the World in 10 1/2 Chapters* and *Flaubert's Parrot*." *Interactions: Aegean Journal of English and American Studies* 13 (Fall 2003): 1–11.
Bahramitash, Roksana. "The War on Terror, Feminist Orientalism and Orientalist Feminism: Case Studies of Two North American Bestsellers." *Critique: Critical Middle Eastern Studies* 14.2 (Summer 2005): 221–35.
Balfour, Arthur James. "The Balfour Declaration." November 2, 1917. <http://www.mfa.gov.il/MFA/Peace+Process/Guide+to+the+Peace+Process/The+Balfour+Declaration.htm>.
Band, Arnold J. "'Mar Mani': The Archeology of Self-Deception." *Prooftexts* 12.3 (September 1992): 231–44.
Banerjee, Mita. "Roots Trips and Virtual Ethnicity: *Jonathan Safran Foer's Everything Is Illuminated*," in *Transnational American Memories*, ed. Udo J. Hebel. Berlin: Walter de Gruyter, 2009: 145–70.
Barth, Frederick, ed. *Ethnic Groups and Boundaries: The Social Organization of Culture Difference*. Oslo: Univ. Forlaget; London: George Allen & Unwin, 1969.

Barthes, Roland. *Camera Lucida: Reflections on Photography*. Translated by Richard Howard [*La Chambre claire: Note sur la photographie*, 1980]. London: Vintage, 2000.
_____. "The Death of the Author." Translated by Richard Howard ["La Mort de l'auteur," 1968]. <http://evans-experientialism.freewebspace.com/barthes06.htm>.
_____. *The Rustle of Language*. Translated by Richard Howard [*Le Bruissement de la langue: Essais critiques IV*, 1984]. Oxford: Basil Blackwell, 1986.
Bauman, Zygmunt. [A9]*Liquid Life*. Cambridge: Polity Press, 2005.
_____. *Liquid Modernity*. Cambridge: Polity Press; Oxford: Blackwell, 2000.
_____. *Modernity and the Holocaust*. Cambridge: Polity Press, 1989.
_____. *Postmodern Ethics*. Oxford: Blackwell, 1993.
_____ and Keith Tester. *Conversations with Zygmunt Bauman*. Cambridge: Polity Press, 2001.
Beattie, Tina. "The End of Postmodernism: The New Atheists and Democracy." 2007. <http://www.opendemocracy.net/article/faith_ideas/the_new_atheists>.
Beaumont, Matthew. "Baudrillard and the End of Postmodernism: What Next?" March 9, 2007. <http://www.guardian.co.uk/books/booksblog/2007/mar/09/baudrillardandtheendofpos>.
Behlman, Lee. "The Escapist: Fantasy, Folklore, and the Pleasures of the Comic Book in Recent Jewish American Holocaust Fiction." *Shofar: An Interdisciplinary Journal of Jewish Studies* 22.3 (2004): 56–71.
Beck, Ulrich. *The Cosmopolitan Vision*. Translated by Ciaran Cronin [*Der kosmopolitische Blick oder: Krieg ist Frieden*, 2004]. Cambridge: Polity, 2006.
Bell, William. "Not Altogether a Tomb. Julian Barnes: *Flaubert's Parrot*," in *Imitating Art: Essays in Biography*, ed. David Ellis. London: Pluto Press, 1993: 149–73.
Belsey, Catherine. *Critical Practice*. London: Routledge, 1980.
Bemong, Nele, Mirjam Truwant, and Pieter Vermeulen, eds. *Re-Thinking Europe: Literature and (Trans)National Identity*. Amsterdam: Rodopi, 2008.
Bere, Carol. "The Book of Memory: W.G. Sebald's *The Emigrants* and *Austerlitz*." *Literary Review* 46.1 (Fall 2002): 184–92.
Berg, Nancy E. "The Politics of Paternity and Patrimony." *Shofar: An Interdisciplinary Journal of Jewish Studies* 24.3 (2006): 100–114.
Berger, Alan L. "Unclaimed Experience: Trauma and Identity in Third Generaton Writing about the Holocaust." *Shofar: An Interdisciplinary Journal of Jewish Studies* 28.3 (Spring 2010): 149–58.
Bernard, Catherine. "*Flaubert's Parrot*: le reliquaire mélancolique." *Etudes anglaises* 54.4 (2001): 453–64.
Bhabha, Homi K. *The Location of Culture*. London: Routledge, 1994.
Bidussa, David. *Dopo l'ultimo testimone*. Turin: Einaudi, 2009.
Birnbaum, Robert. "Azar Nafisi, Author of *Reading Lolita in Tehran*, converses with Robert Birnbaum." February 5, 2004. <http://www.identitytheory.com/interviews/birnbaum139.php>.
Blackler, Deane. *Reading W.G. Sebald: Adventure and Disobedience*. Rochester, NY: Camden House, 2007.
Bloom, Harold. *The Western Canon: The Books and School of the Ages*. New York: Riverhead Books, 1995.
Boccardi, Mariadele. "Biography, the Postmodern Last Frontier: Banville, Barnes, Byatt, and Unsworth." *Q/W/E/R/T/Y* 11 (Oct. 2001): 149–57.
Bolter, Jay David, and Richard Grusin. *Remediation: Understanding New Media*. Cambridge, MA: MIT Press, 1998.
Bonaparte, Marie. *The Life and Works of Edgar Allen Poe: A Psychoanalytic Interpretation*. Foreword by Sigmund Freud. Translated by John Rodker. London: Imago, 1949.
Boyarin, Daniel, and Jonathan Boyarin. "Diaspora: Generation and the Ground of Jewish Identity." *Critical Inquiry* 19.4 (Summer, 1993): 693–725.
Brockmeier, Jens. "Austerlitz's Memory." *Partial Answers: Journal of Literature and the History of Ideas* 6.2 (June 2008): 347–67.
Brooks, Neil. "Interred Textuality: *The Good Soldier* and *Flaubert's Parrot*." *Critique: Studies in Contemporary Fiction* 41.1 (Fall 1999): 45–51.
_____. "The Silence of the Parrots: Repetition and Interpretation in Flaubert's Parrot." *Q/W/E/R/T/Y* 11 (Oct. 2001): 159–66.
Brooks, Neil Edward, and Josh Toth, eds. *The Mourning After: Attending the Wake of Postmodernism*. Amsterdam: Rodopi, 2007.
Brooks, Peter. "Obsessed with the Hermit of Croisset." Review of *Flaubert's Parrot*, *The New York Times*, March 10, 1985. <http://www.nytimes.com/books/01/02/25/specials/barnes-parrot.html>.

Buber, Martin. *A Land of Two Peoples: Martin Buber on Jews and Arabs*, ed. Paul Mendes Flohr. 1983; Chicago: The University of Chicago Press, 2005.
Burn, Stephen J. *Jonathan Franzen and the End of Postmodernism*. London: Continuum, 2008.
Buruma, Ian, and Avishai Margalit. *Occidentalism: The West in the Eyes of Its Enemies*. New York: Penguin, 2004.
Burwell, Catherine. "Reading Lolita in Times of War: Women's Book Clubs and the Politics of Reception." *Intercultural Education* 18.4 (October 2007).
Burwell, Catherine, Hilary E. Davis, and Lisa K. Taylor. "Reading Nafisi in the West: Feminist Reading Practices and Ethical Concerns." *TOPIA: Canadian Journal of Cultural Studies* 19 (Spring 2008): 63–84.
Cahoone, Lawrence, ed. *From Modernism to Postmodernism: An Anthology*. Malden, MA: Blackwell, 2003.
Caldwell, Roger. "How to Get Real." 2003. <http://www.philosophynow.org/issue42/42caldwell1.htm>.
Calvino, Italo. *Six Memos for the Next Millennium*. Translated by Patrick Creagh [*Lezioni americane: sei proposte per il prossimo millennio*, 1988]. London: Jonathan Cape, 1992.
Capra, Fritjof. *The Tao of Physics*. Boston: Shambhala, 1975.
Caruth, Cathy, ed. *Trauma: Explorations in Memory*. Baltimore: The Johns Hopkins University Press, 1995.
Cavarero, Adriana. *Horrorism: Naming Contemporary Violence* [*Orrorismo: ovvero della violenza sull'inerme*, 2007]. New York: Columbia University Press, 2009.
Ceserani, Remo. *Raccontare il postmoderno*. Turin: Bollati Boringhieri, 1997.
Chalhoub, Erik. "Tight Potential, Loose Ends." Review of *Kafka on the Shore*, *Porter Gulch Review* (2007), 26. <http://www.cabrillo.edu/publications/portergulch/2007/PGR%20Book%20reviews.pdf>.
Chandler, James. "About Loss: W.G. Sebald's Romantic Art of Memory." *The South Atlantic Quarterly* 102.1 (Winter 2003): 235–62.
Chozick, Matthew Richard. "De-Exoticising Haruki Murakami's Reception." *Comparative Literature Studies* 45.1 (2008): 62–73.
Chute, Hillary L., and Marianne DeKoven. "Introduction: Graphic Narratives," *Modern Fiction Studies* 52.4 (Winter 2006): 767–82.
Ciarrochi, Joseph, Joseph P. Forgas, and John D. Mayer, eds. *Emotional Intelligence in Everyday Life: A Scientific Enquiry*. New York: Psychology Press, 2001.
Cleave, Chris. "Too Soon to Write the Post-9/11 Novel?" *The New York Times*, September 12, 2005. <http://www.nytimes.com/2005/09/12/opinion/12iht-edcleave.html>.
Cohen, Anthony P., ed. *Signifying Identities: Anthropological Perspectives on Boundaries and Contested Values*. London: Routledge, 2000.
———, ed., *Symbolising Boundaries*. Manchester, UK: Manchester University Press, 1986.
Cohen, Simona. "The Early Renaissance Personifications of Time and Changing Concepts of Temporality." *Renaissance Studies* 14.3 (2000): 301–28.
Collado-Rodriguez, Francisco. "Ethics in the Second Degree: Trauma and Dual Narratives in Jonathan Safran Foer's *Everything Is Illuminated*." *Journal of Modern Literature* 32.1 (Fall 2008): 54–68.
Corbella, Walter. "Strategies of Resistance and the Problem of Ambiguity in Azar Nafisi's *Reading Lolita in Tehran*." *Mosaic: A Journal for the Interdisciplinary Study of Literature* 39.2 (June 2006): 107 23.
Cox, Emma. "'Abstain, and Hide Your Life': The Hidden Narrator of Flaubert's Parrot." *Critique: Studies in Contemporary Fiction* 46.1 (Fall 2004): 53–62.
Crosthwaite, Paul. "Speed, War, and Traumatic Affect: Reading Ian McEwan's *Atonement*." *Cultural Politics* 3.1 (March 2007): 51–70.
Cryer, Dan. "A Novelist on the Edge." Interview with Ian McEwan, *Newsday*, April 24, 2002, B6.
Dabashi, Hamid. "Native Informers and the Making of the American Empire," *Al-Ahram Weekly Online* 797 (June 1–7, 2006). <http://weekly.ahram.org.eg/2006/797/special.htm>.
Damrosch, David. *What Is World Literature?* Princeton, NJ: Princeton University Press, 2003.
Delanty, Gerard. "Peripheries and Borders in a Post-western Europe." *Eurozine* (August 29, 2007). <http://www.eurozine.com/articles/2007-08-29-delanty-en.html>.
Dennett, Daniel C. *Breaking the Spell: Religion as a Natural Phenomenon*. London: Penguin, 2006.

DePaul, Amy. "Fighting Words: Reading Lolita in Tehran." July 31, 2008. <http://www.popmatters.com/pm/feature/58030/fighting-words/>.
―――. "Re-Reading *Reading Lolita in Tehran*." *MELUS* 33.2 (Summer 2008): 73–92.
Denham, Scott, and Mark McCulloh, eds. *W.G. Sebald. History—Memory—Trauma*. Berlin: de Gruyter, 2006.
Dipple, Elizabeth. *The Unresolvable Plot: Reading Contemporary Fiction*. New York: Routledge, 1988.
Donadio, Rachel. "Revisiting the Canon Wars." *The New York Times*, September 16, 2007. <http://www.nytimes.com/2007/09/16/books/review/Donadio-t.html?pagewanted=1&_r=1>.
Duffy, Martha. "Pleasures of Merely Circulating Flaubert's Parrot." April 8, 1985. <http://www.time.com/time/magazine/article/0,9171,965521,00.html>.
Duttlinger, Carolin. "Traumatic Photographs: Remembrance and the Technical Media in W.G. Sebald's *Austerlitz*," in *W.G. Sebald: A Critical Companion*, eds. J.J. Long and Anne Whitehead. Seattle: University of Washington Press, 2004, 155–71.
Dyer, Geoff. "Who's Afraid of Influence?" *The Guardian*, September 22, 2001. <http://books.guardian.co.uk/reviews/generalfiction/0,,555614,00.html>.
Eaglestone, Robert. *Ethical Criticism: Reading after Levinas*. Edinburgh: Edinburgh University Press, 1997.
―――. *The Holocaust and the Postmodern*. Oxford: Oxford University Press, 2004.
Eagleton, Terry. *After Theory*. New York: Basic Books, 2003.
―――. *The Illusions of Postmodernism*. Oxford: Blackwell, 1996.
Eco, Umberto. "Postille a *Il nome della Rosa*" (*Alfabeta* 49, June 1983). Rept[A10]. as a Postscript to *Il nome della Rosa*. Milan: Bompiani, 1984.
―――. *The Role of the Reader: Explorations in the Semiotics of Texts*. Bloomington: Indiana University Press, 1979.
Eder, Richard. "Excavating a Life." Review of *Austerlitz*, *The New York Times*, October 28, 2001. <http://query.nytimes.com/gst/fullpage.html?res=9B0CE2D9153EF93BA15753C1A9679C8B63>.
Elcott, Noam M. "Tattered Snapshots and Castaway Tongues: An Essay at Layout and Translation with W.G. Sebald." *The Germanic Review* 79.3 (Summer 2004): 203–23.
Elekes, Dóra. "A Game of Chests." Review of *The Door*, Hungarian Literature Online. <http://www.hlo.hu/object.33254F4A-E1D1-4DC2-A7A7-482639EE9EE1.ivy>.
―――. "A Passion for Hungarian Fiction: An Interview with Translator Len Rix," *Hungarian Literature Online*. <http://www.hlo.hu/object.2A8D3A10-53C3-4B7E-8313-1836F447119C.ivy>.
Eliot, T.S. *What Is a Classic?* London: Faber & Faber, 1945.
Emmerling, Robert J., Vinod K. Shanwal, and Manas K. Mandal, eds. *Emotional Intelligence: Theoretical and Cultural Perspectives*. New York: Nova Science Publishers, 2008.
Eshel, Amir. "Against the Power of Time: The Poetics of Suspension in W.G. Sebald's Austerlitz." *New German Critique* 88 (2003): 71–96.
Eshelman, Raoul. "After Postmodernism: Performatism in Literature." *Anthropoetics* 11.2 (Fall 2005/Winter 2006). <http://www.anthropoetics.ucla.edu/ap1102/perform05.htm>.
―――. "Performatism in Architecture. On Framing and the Spatial Realization of Ostensivity." *Anthropoetics* 7.2 (Fall 2001/Winter 2002). <www.anthropoetics.ucla.edu/ap0702/arch2.htm>.
―――. "Performatism in the Movies (1997–2003)." *Anthropoetics* 8.2 (Fall 2002/Winter 2003). <www.anthropoetics.ucla.edu/ap0802/movies.htm>.
―――. "Performatism, or the End of Postmodernism." *Anthropoetics* 6.2 (Fall 2000/Winter 2001). <www.anthropoetics.ucla.edu/ap0602/perform.htm>.
―――. *Performatism, or the End of Postmodernism*. Aurora, Colorado: Davies Group, 2008.
Featherstone, Mike, ed. *Global Culture: Nationalism, Globalization and Modernity*. London: Sage, 1990.
Federman, Raymond. *Critifiction: Postmodern Essays*. Albany: State University of New York Press, 1993.
Felman, Shoshana, and Dori Laub. *Testimony: Crises of Witnessing in Literature, Psychoanalysis, and History*. London: Routledge, 1992.
Feuer, Menachem. "Almost Friends: Post-Holocaust Comedy, Tragedy, and Friendship in Jonathan Safran Foer's *Everything Is Illuminated*." *Shofar: An Interdisciplinary Journal of Jewish Studies* 25.2 (Winter 2007): 24–48.
Filler, Shir. "*Reading Lolita in Tehran* Leads to Reading, Writing, Drawing, Painting, Sewing, and Thinking in Saranac Lake, New York," in *Teaching English in the Two-Year College* 33.4 (May 2006): 350–56.
Fine, Robert. *Cosmopolitanism*. London: Routledge, 2007.

Finney, Brian. "Briony's Stand Against Oblivion: The Making of Fiction in Ian McEwan's *Atonement.*" *Journal of Modern Literature* 27.3 (2004): 68–82.
Fink, Guido. "Il calendario impazzito di Yeoshua." *L'indice* 5 (May 1995): 17–18.
Flutsch, Maria. "Girls and the Unconscious in Murakami Haruki's *Kafka on the Shore.*" *Japanese Studies* 26.1 (May 2006): 69–79.
Fokkema, Aleid. "The Author: Postmodernism's Stock Character," in *The Author as Character: Representing Historical Writers in Western Literature,* eds. Paul Franssen and Ton Honselaars. Madison, NJ: Fairleigh Dickinson University Press, 1999, 39–51.
Fokkema, Douwe. *Literary History, Modernism, and Postmodernism.* Amsterdam: Benjamins, 1984.
Fowler, Alastair. *Kinds of Literature: An Introduction to the Theory of Genres and Modes.* Cambridge, MA: Harvard University Press, 1982.
Gabriel, J. Philip. *Spirit Matters: The Transcendent in Modern Japanese Literature.* Honolulu: University of Hawai'i Press, 2006.
Galimberti, Umberto. *La casa di Psiche: Dalla psicoanalisi alla pratica filosofica.* Milan: Feltrinelli, 2005.
_____. *Orme del sacro: Il cristianesimo e la desacralizzazione del sacro.* Milan: Feltrinelli, 2000.
Garloff, Katja. "The Task of the Narrator: Moments of Symbolic Investiture in W.G. Sebald's *Austerlitz,*" in Scott Denham and Mark McCulloh, eds. *W.G. Sebald: History—Memory—Trauma.* Berlin: de Gruyter, 2006, 157–69.
Gascoigne, David. *The Games of Fiction: George Perec and Modern French Ludic Narrative.* Bern: Peter Lang, 2006.
Gasiorek, Andrzej. "Postmodernism and the Problem of History. Julian Barnes," in *Post-War British Fiction: Realism and After.* (London: Edward Arnold, 1995), 158–65.
Geddes, Jennifer L., ed. *Evil after Postmodernism: Histories, Narratives, Ethics.* London: Routledge, 2001.
Gellner, Ernest. *Postmodernism: Reason and Religion.* Routledge: London, 1992.
George, Stephen K., ed. *Ethics, Literature, Theory: An Introductory Reader.* Lanham, MD: Rowman and Littlefield, 2005.
Gessen, Keith. "Horror Tour." *New York Review of Books* 52.14 (Sept. 22, 2005): 68–72.
Gibson, Andrew. *Postmodernity, Ethics and the Novel: From Leavis to Levinas.* London: Routledge, 1999.
Giovannelli, Laura. "I codici infranti: inclusività, riscrittura e metanarratività in 'Flaubert's Parrot' di Julian Barnes." *Strumenti Critici* 2 (May 1995): 271–86.
Gitzen, Julian. "How to Be Postmodern: The Fiction of Julian Barnes and Alain de Botton." *Essays in Arts and Sciences* 30 (Oct. 2001): 45–61.
Glucksmann, André. "The Postmodern Financial Crisis." *City Journal* 19.1 (Winter 2009). <http://www.city-journal.org/2009/19_1_snd-postmodern-financial-crisis.html>.
Goleman, Daniel. *Destructive Emotions and How We Can Overcome Them: A Dialogue with the Dalai Lama.* London: Bloomsbury, 2003.
_____. *Emotional Intelligence.* New York: Bantam Books, 1995.
Greenblatt, Stephen, and Giles Gunn, eds. *Redrawing the Boundaries: The Transformation of English and American Literary Studies.* New York: The Modern Language Association of America, 1992.
Gregory-Guider, Christopher C. "The 'Sixth Emigrant': Traveling Places in the Works of W.G. Sebald." *Contemporary Literature* 46.3 (Fall 2005): 422–49.
Guglielmi, Laura. "Yehoshua: noi ebrei col divieto di sbagliare." Interview with Abraham B. Yehoshua, *Il secolo XIX,* November 7, 2002. <http://www.ilportoritrovato.net/html/biblio yehoshua.html>.
Guignery, Vanessa. "History in Question(s): An Interview with Julian Barnes." *Sources* 8 (Spring 2000): 59–72.
_____. "Julian Barnes in Conversation." *Cercles* 4 (2002): 255–69. <http://www.cercles.com/n4/barnes>.
_____. "Le Narrataire; ou, le lecteur de l'autre côté du miroir dans *Flaubert's Parrot* de Julian Barnes." *Q/W/E/R/T/Y* 11 (Oct. 2001): 167–76.
_____. "'My wife ... died': une mort en pointillé dans *Flaubert's Parrot* de Julian Barnes." *Etudes britanniques contemporaines* 17 (Dec. 1999): 57–68.
_____. "Palimpseste et pastiche générique chez Julian Barnes." *Etudes Anglaises* 50.1 (Jan.–Mar. 1997): 40–52.

Guillén, Claudio. *The Challenge of Comparative Literature*. Translated by Cola Franzen. Cambridge, MA: Harvard University Press, 1993.
_____. *Literature as System: Essays Toward the Theory of Literary History*. Princeton, NJ: Princeton University Press, 1971.
Gussow, Mel. "W.G. Sebald, Elegiac German Novelist, Is Dead at 57." December 15, 2001. <http://query.nytimes.com/gst/fullpage.html?res=9505E7D61E3FF936A25751C1A9679C8B63>.
Hakutani, Yoshinobu. "No Place I Was Meant to Be: Postmodern Japan in Haruki Murakami's Fiction," in *Postmodernity and Cross-Culturalism*, ed. Yoshinobu Hakutani. Madison, NJ: Fairleigh Dickinson University Press; London: Associated University Press, 2002.
Hallet, Wolfgang. "The Multimodal Novel: The Integration of Modes and Media in Novelistic Narration, in *Narratology in the Age of Cross-Disciplinary Narrative Research*, eds. Sandra Heinen and Roy Sommer. Berlin: Walter de Gruyter, 2009, 129–53.
Hamid, Mohsin. "The Pathos of Exile." *Time Magazine*, Special Issue: *The Asian Journey Home*, 162.7, August 18, 2003. <http://www.time.com/time/asia/2003/journey/pakistan_lahore.html>.
Hannerz, Ulf. *Cultural Complexity: Studies in the Social Organization of Meaning*. New York: Columbia University Press, 1992.
_____. "Flows, Boundaries and Hybrids: Keywords in Transnational Anthropology." <http://www.transcomm.ox.ac.uk/working%20papers/hannerz.pdf>.
Hantke, Steffen. "Postmodernism and Genre Fiction as Deferred Action: Haruki Murakami and the Noir Tradition." *Critique* 49.1 (Fall 2007): 3–23.
Hartman, Geoffrey H. *The Longest Shadow: In the Aftermath of the Holocaust*. 1996; New York: Palgrave Macmillan, 2002.
Harvey, David. *The Condition of Postmodernity*. Oxford: Basil Blackwell, 1989.
_____. *The New Imperialism*. Oxford: Oxford University Press, 2003.
Hassan, Ihab. *POSTmodernISM: A Paracritical Bibliography*. *New Literary History* 3.1 (Fall 1971): 5–30.
Hateley, Erica. "Flaubert's Parrot as Modernist Quest." *Q/W/E/R/T/Y* 11 (October 2001): 177–81.
Hay, Simon. "Why Read *Reading Lolita*? Teaching Critical Thinking in a Culture of Choice." *Pedagogy: Critical Approaches to Teaching Literature, Language, Composition, and Culture* 8.1 (Winter 2008): 5–24.
Hidalgo, Pilar. "Memory and Storytelling in Ian McEwan's *Atonement*." *Critique: Studies in Contemporary Fiction* 46.2 (Winter 2005): 82–91.
Hirsch, Marianne. [All]*Family Frames: Photography, Narrative and Postmemory*. Cambridge, MA: Harvard University Press, 1997.
_____. "The Generation of Postmemory." *Poetics Today* 29.1 (Spring 2008): 103–28.
Hobsbawm, Eric J., and Terence Ranger, eds., *The Invention of Tradition*. Cambridge: Cambridge University Press, 1983.
Horn, Bernard. "The Shoah, the Akedah, and the Conversations in A.B. Yehoshua's *Mr. Mani*." *Symposium* (Fall 1999): 136–50.
Horn, Bernard, and Abraham B. Yehoshua. *Facing the Fires: Conversations with A.B. Yehoshua*. Syracuse, NY: Syracuse University Press, 1997.
Horowitz, Sarah R. *Voicing the Void: Muteness and Memory in Holocaust Fiction*. Albany: State University of New York Press, 1997.
Horstkotte, Silke. "Fantastic Gaps: Photography Inserted into Narrative in W.G. Sebald's *Austerlitz*," in Christian Emden and David Midgley, eds. *Science, Technology and the German Cultural Imagination*. Berlin: Peter Lang, 2005, 269–86.
Hsieh, Lili. "Under the Sign of Empire-Transporting Lolita, Surviving WTO, Remapping Taiwan." *Concentric: Literary and Cultural Studies* 31.2 (July 2005): 41–64.
Hudson, Carolyn, and Pamela Smiley. "Obama's Election and the End of Postmodernism." *International Journal of the Humanities* 7.2: 35–46.
Huntington, Samuel. "The Clash of Civilizations?" *Foreign Affairs* (Summer 1993). <http://history.club.fatih.edu.tr/103%20Huntington%20Clash%20of%20Civilizations%20full%20text.htm>.
_____. *The Clash of Civilizations and the Remaking of World Order*. New York: Simon & Schuster, 1996.
Hussein, Aamer. "A Jester among the Jihadis." Review of *The Reluctant Fundamentalist, The Independent*, March 23, 2007. <http://www.independent.co.uk/arts-entertainment/books/reviews/the-reluctant-fundamentalist-by-mohsin-hamid-441392.html>.
Hutcheon, Linda. "Irony, Nostalgia, and the Postmodern." University of Toronto English Language Main Collection, 1998. <http://www.library.utoronto.ca/utel/criticism/hutchinp.html>.

———. *A Poetics of Postmodernism: History, Theory, Fiction*. New York: Routledge, 1988.
———. *The Politics of Postmodernism*. New York: Routledge, 1989.
———. *A Theory of Adaptation*. New York: Routledge, 2006.
———. *A Theory of Parody: The Teaching of Twentieth-Century Art Forms*. New York: Routledge, 1985.
Huyssen, Andreas. *After the Great Divide: Modernism, Mass Culture, Postmodernism*. Bloomington: Indiana University Press, 1986.
———. "Present Pasts: Media, Politics, Amnesia." *Public Culture* 12.1 (2000): 21–38.
Ingersoll, Earl G. "Intertextuality in L.P. Hartley's *The Go-Between* and Ian McEwan's *Atonement*." *Forum for Modern Language Studies* 40.3 (July 2004): 241–58.
Jacobs, Louis. *The Jewish Religion: A Companion*. Oxford: Oxford University Press, 1995.
Jacobson, Dan. *Heshel's Kingdom*. 1998; Evanston, IL: Northwestern University Press, 1999.
Jaggi, Maya. "The Last Word." Interview with W.G. Sebald, *The Guardian*, December 21, 2001. <http://www.guardian.co.uk/education/2001/dec/21/artsandhumanities.highereducation>.
———. "Power and Pity." Interview with Abraham B. Yehoshua, *The Guardian*, June 24, 2006. <http://www.guardian.co.uk/books/2006/jun/24/featuresreviews.guardianreview11>.
———. "Recovered Memories." Interview with W.G. Sebald, *The Guardian*, September 22, 2001. <http://www.guardian.co.uk/books/2001/sep/22/artsandhumanities.highereducation>.
Jahanbegloo, Ramin. *Iran between Tradition and Modernity*. Lanham, MD: Lexington Books, 2004.
———. "Reading Machiavelli in Tehran: Beyond the Theological-Political." <http://jahanbegloo.com/articles/Machiavelli.html>.
Jameson, Fredric. *The Political Unconscious*. 1981; London: Routledge, 2002.
———. "Postmodernism, Or, The Cultural Logic of Late Capitalism." *New Left Review* 146 (July–August 1984), 59–62.
———. *Postmodernism, Or, The Cultural Logic of Late Capitalism*. Durham, NC: Duke University Press, 1991.
Jonas, Hans. *The Imperative of Responsibility: Foundations of an Ethics for the Technological Age*. Translated by Hans Jonas and David Herr. Chicago: University of Chicago Press, 1984.
Joseph-Vilain, Mélanie. "The Writer's Voice(s) in Flaubert's Parrot." *Q/W/E/R/T/Y* 11 (Oct. 2001): 183–88.
Kabdebó, Lóránt. "Heroines of Self-Salvation: The Novels of Magda Szabó." Translated by Elizabeth Szádz. *The Hungarian Quarterly* 34.130 (Summer 1993): 14–38.
Kakutani, Michiko. "And When She Was Bad She Was...." Review of *Atonement*, *The New York Times*, March 7, 2002. <http://query.nytimes.com/gst/fullpage.html?res=9E04E1DD1530F934A35750C0A9649C8B63>.
———. "Book Study as Insubordination under the Mullahs." Review of *Reading Lolita in Tehran*, *The Guardian*, April 15, 2003. <http://query.nytimes.com/gst/fullpage.html?res=9C04E7DC103BF936A25757C0A9659C8B63>.
———. "A Hero with 9/11 Peripheral Vision." *The New York Times*, March 18, 2005. <http://query.nytimes.com/gst/fullpage.html?res=9E01E0DD103CF93BA25750C0A9639C8B63>.
———. "In a No Man's Land of Memories and Loss." Review of *Austerlitz*, *The New York Times*, October 26, 2001. <http://query.nytimes.com/gst/fullpage.html?res=9F07E2DE1331F935A15753C1A9679C8B63>.
Kaplan, Harold. *Democratic Humanism and American Literature*. 1972; New Brunswick, NJ: Transaction, 2005.
Károly, Csaba. "Putting the Manuscript in the Lap of God." Interview with Magda Szabó, *The Hungarian Quarterly* 190 (2008): 98–102. <http://www.ceeol.com>.
Kattoulas, Velisarios. "Pop Master." *Time Asia*, November 17, 2002. <http://www.time.com/time/magazine/article/0,9171,501021123-391572,00.html>.
Katz, Adam. "The Originary Scene, Sacrifice, and the Politics of Normalization in A.B. Yehoshua's *Mr. Mani*." *Anthropoetics* 7.2 (Fall 2001/Winter 2002): 2. <http://www.anthropoetics.ucla.edu/ap0702/sacrifice.htm>.
Kelts, Roland. *Japanamerica: How Japanese Pop Culture Has Invaded the U.S.* New York: Palgrave Macmillan, 2006.
———. "Writer on the Borderline." Interview with Haruki Murakami, *The Japan Times*, December 1, 2002. <http://search.japantimes.co.jp/member/member.html?fl20021201a4.htm>.
Kemp, Peter. "*Atonement* by Ian McEwan." *The Sunday Times*, September 16, 2001. <http://entertainment.timesonline.co.uk/tol/arts_and_entertainment/books/fiction/article2379965.ece>.

Kermode, Frank. "Point of View." Review of *Atonement*, *London Review of Books*, October 4, 2001. <http://www.lrb.co.uk/v23/n19/kerm01_.html>.
Kilbourn, Russell J. A. "Architecture and Cinema: The Representation of Memory in W.G. Sebald's *Austerlitz*," in J.J. Long and Anne Whitehead, eds. *W.G. Sebald: A Critical Companion*. Seattle: University of Washington Press, 2004, 140–54.
Kirby, Alan. "The Death of Postmodernism and Beyond." 2006. <http://www.philosophynow.org/issue58/58kirby.htm>.
Kirn, Walter. "In the Wee Small Hours." Review of *After Dark*, *The New York Times*, June 3, 2007. <http://www.nytimes.com/2007/06/03/books/review/Kirn-t.html?pagewanted=1&_r=1>.
Klein, Naomi. *The Shock Doctrine: The Rise of Disaster Capitalism*. New York: Metropolitan Books/Henry Holt, 2007.
Kohn, Robert E. "Foer's *Everything Is Illuminated*." *Explicator* 65.4 (Summer 2007): 245–47.
Kristof, Agota. *L'analphabète: récit autobiographique*. Geneva: Zoe_, 2004.
Kulbaga, Theresa A. "Pleasurable Pedagogies: *Reading Lolita in Tehran* and the Rhetoric of Empathy." *College English* 70.5 (May 2008): 506–21.
LaCapra, Dominick. *History and Criticism*. Ithaca, NY: Cornell University Press, 1985.
_____. *Writing History, Writing Trauma*. Baltimore: The Johns Hopkins University Press, 2001.
Lai, Amy Ty. "Memory, Hybridity, and Creative Alliance in Haruki Murakami's Fiction." *Mosaic: A Journal for the Interdisciplinary Study of Literature* 40.1 (March 2007): 163–80.
Lanchester, John. "The Dangers of Innocence." *The New York Review of Books* 49.6 (April 11, 2002): 24–26.
Lasdun, James. "The Empire Strikes Back." Review of *The Reluctant Fundamentalist*, *The Guardian*, March 3, 2007. <http://www.guardian.co.uk/books/2007/mar/03/featuresreviews.guardianreview20>.
"LEADALL: Pope Visit to Bethlehem Sets Stage for Political Speeches." *EarthTimes*. <http://www.earthtimes.org/articles/show/268700,leadall-pope-visit-to-bethlehem-sets-stage-for-political-speeches.html>.
Lee, Alison. *Realism and Power: Postmodern British Fiction*. London: Routledge, 1990.
Lee, Hermione. "If Your Memories Serve You Well." Review of *Atonement*, *The Observer*, September 23, 2001. <http://www.guardian.co.uk/books/2001/sep/23/fiction.bookerprize2001>.
Lentin, Ronit. "Postmemory, Received History and the Return of the Auschwitz Code." *Eurozine* 36.4 (2002): 2. <http://www.eurozine.com/articles/2002-09-06-lentin-en.html>.
Lerner, Gad. "Sulle tracce degli scomparsi: viaggio nelle terre della Shoah." *Repubblica*, August 12, 2008, 45.
Levinas, Emmanuel. *Totality and Infinity: An Essay on Exteriority* (1961). Translated by Alphonso Lingis [*Totalité et infini*, 1961]. Pittsburgh: Duquesne University Press, 1969.
Lindberg-Wada, Gunilla, ed. *Studying Transcultural Literary History*. Berlin: Walter de Gruyter, 2006.
Lipovetsky, Gilles. *L'ère du vide: Essais sur l'individualisme contemporain*. 1983, Paris: Gallimard, 1983.
López, José, and Garry Potter, eds. *After Postmodernism: An Introduction to Critical Realism*. London: Continuum, 2001.
Lublow, Arthur. "Arts Abroad; Preoccupied with Death, but Still Funny." *The New York Times*, December 11, 2001. <http://query.nytimes.com/gst/fullpage.html?res=9E05EEDC163FF932A25751C1A9679C8B63>.
Lyotard, Jean-François. *Le Postmoderne explique aux enfants: correspondance 1982–1985*. Paris: Galilée, 1986.
Maalouf, Amin. *In the Name of Identity: Violence and the Need to Belong*. Translated by Barbara Bray [*Identités meutrières*, 1996]. New York: Arcade Publishing, 2001.
MacKinnon, John E. "Crime, Compassion, and *The Reader*." *Philosophy and Literature*, 27.1 (2003): 1–20.
Margalit, Avishai. *The Ethics of Memory*. Cambridge, MA: Harvard University Press, 2002.
Margaronis, Maria. "The Anxiety of Authenticity: Writing Historical Fiction at the End of the Twentieth Century." *History Workshop Journal* 65 (Spring 2008): 138–60.
Martinez, Inez. "Haruki Murakami Reimagining of Sophocles's Oedipus," in *Psyche and the Arts: Jungian Approaches to Music, Architecture, Literature*, ed. Susan Rowland. Hove, UK: Routledge, 2008, 56–65.
Maslin, Janet. "Adrift in a Universe in Flux Like Some FedEx Box." Review of *Kafka on the Shore*,

The New York Times, January 31, 2005. <http://query.nytimes.com/gst/fullpage.html?res=940CE1D8153BF932A05752C0A9639C8B63>.
McCulloh, Mark Richard. "Destruction and Transcendence in W.G. Sebald." *Philosophy and Literature* 30.2 (October 2006): 395–409.
McEwan, Ian. "Jerusalem Prize Acceptance Speech," February 20, 2011. <http://www.ianmcewan.com/bib/articles/jerusalemprize.html>.
McGowan, John. *Postmodernism and Its Critics*. Ithaca, NY: Cornell University Press, 1991.
McGown, Ed. "Genre Bending." Review of *Austerlitz*, *The Observer*, July 14, 2002. <http://www.guardian.co.uk/books/2002/jul/14/wgsebald>.
McKinney, Ronald H. "The Greening of Postmodernism: Graham Swift's *Waterland*." *New Literary History* 28.4 (1997): 821–32.
McLaughlin, Robert. "Post-Postmodern Discontent: Contemporary Fiction and the Social World." *symploke* 12.1–2 (2004): 53–68.
Medick, Doris Bachmann. "Cultural Misunderstanding in Translation: Multicultural Coexistence and Multicultural Conceptions of World Literature." ESSE 7/1996. <http//webdoc.sub.gwdg.de/edoc/ia/eese/artic96/bachman/7_96html>
Mendelsohn, Daniel. *The Lost: A Search for Six of Six Million*. New York: HarperCollins, 2006.
———. "Unforgiven." Review of *Atonement*, Books, *New York*, March 11, 2002. <http://nymag.com/nymetro/arts/books/reviews/5776/>.
Mernissi, Fatima. *Beyond the Veil: Male-Female Dynamics in Modern Muslim Society*. Cambridge, MA: Schenkmann, 1975.
———. *Dreams of Trespass: Tales of a Harem Girlhood*. Reading, MA: Addison-Wesley, 1994.
———. *Scheherazade Goes West: Different Cultures, Different Harems*. New York: Washington Square Press, 2001.
Messina, Dino. "Abraham Yehoshua: perché Israele rimuove la storia." July 1, 2008. <http://lanostrastoria.corriere.it/2008/07/abraham-yehoshua-rimuovere-la.html>.
Metz, Joseph. "'Truth Is a Woman': Post-Holocaust Narrative, Postmodernism, and the Gender of Fascism in Bernhard Schlink's *Der Vorleser*." *German Quarterly* 77.3 (Summer 2004): 300–323.
Milesi, Laurent. "(Double) Dealing with Flaubert's Parrot(s)." *Q/W/E/R/T/Y* 11 (Oct. 2001): 189–95.
Milhouse, Virginia H., Molefi Kete Asante, and Peter O. Nwosu, *Transcultural Realities: Interdisciplinary Perspectives on Cross-Cultural Relations*. Thousand Oaks, CA: Sage Publications, 2001.
Miller, Laura. "'Atonement' by Ian McEwan." <http://dir.salon.com/story/books/review/2002/03/21/mcewan/index.html>.
———. "Crossing Over." Review of *Kafka on the Shore*, *The New York Times*, February 6, 2005. <http://query.nytimes.com/gst/fullpage.html?res=9A02E5DC173BF935A35751C0A9639C8B63>.
———. "Haruki Murakami on the Darkness of the Subconscious, the Aum Cult, Subway Gas Attack and Being an Individualist in Japan." <http://www.salon.com/books/int/1997/12/cov_si_16int.html>.
Miner, Earl. *Comparative Poetics: An Intercultural Essay on Theories of Literature*. (Princeton, NJ: Princeton University Press, 1990.
Minh, Tran Huy. "Haruki Murakami: 'Ecrire, c'est comme rêver éveillé.'" *Magazine Littéraire* 421 (June 2003): 96–102.
Mitchell, David. "Kill Me or the Cat Gets It." Review of *Kafka on the Shore*, *The Guardian*, January 8, 2005. <http://www.guardian.co.uk/books/2005/jan/08/fiction.harukimurakami>.
Moïsi, Dominique. *La Géopolitique de l'émotion*. Paris: Flammarion, 2008.
Morahg, Gilead. "Borderline Cases: National Identity and Territorial Affinity in A.B. Yehoshua's *Mr. Mani*." *AJS Review* 30.1 (2006): 167–82.
———. "The Heritage of the Aqedah in A.B. Yehoshua's *Mr. Mani*," in *Unbinding the Binding of Isaac*, eds. Mishael Caspi and John T. Greene. Lanham, MD: University Press of America, 2007, 187–97.
Moretti, Franco. "Conjectures on World Literature." *New Left Review* 1 (Jan-Feb 2000): 54–67.
———. "More Conjectures." *New Left Review* 20 (Mar-Apr 2003): 73–80.
Moseley, Merritt. "Is There a Novel in this Text? Identities of Narrative in *Flaubert's Parrot*," in *L'Exil et l'allégorie dans le roman anglophone contemporain*, ed. Michel Morel. Paris: Messene, 1998, 35–47.
———. *Understanding Julian Barnes*. Columbia: University of South Carolina Press, 1997.

Mullan, John. "Critical Thinking." Review of *Flaubert's Parrot*, *The Guardian*, September 24, 2005. <http://www.guardian.co.uk/books/2005/sep/24/julianbarnes.gustaveflaubert>.
Murakami, Haruki. "The Novelist in Wartime," February 20, 2009. <http://www.salon.com/books/feature/2009/02/20/haruki_murakami/>.
Napier, Susan Jolliffe. *The Fantastic in Modern Japanese Literature: The Subversion of Modernity*. London: Routledge, 1996.
Negri, Antonio, and Michael Hardt. *Empire*. Cambridge, MA: Harvard University Press, 2000.
Nicol, Bran. *The Cambridge Introduction to Postmodern Fiction*. Cambridge: Cambridge University Press, 2009.
"The Nobel Peace Prize for 2009." <http://nobelprize.org/nobel_prizes/peace/laureates/2009/press.html>.
Nussbaum, Martha C. *Hiding from Humanity: Disgust, Shame and the Law*. Princeton, NJ: Princeton University Press, 2004.
———. *Love's Knowledge: Essays on Philosophy and Literature*. Oxford: Oxford University Press, 1990.
———. *Upheavals of Thought: The Intelligence of Emotions*. Cambridge: Cambridge University Press, 2001.
Oates, Joyce Carol. "Lest We Forget." Review of *Austerlitz*, *The New York Review of Books* 54.12 (July 19, 2007). <http://www.nybooks.com/articles/20399>.
Obama, Barack. "Inaugural Address." January 20, 2009. <http://www.nytimes.com/2009/01/20/us/politics/20text-obama.html?_r=1&pagewanted=print>.
O'Brien, Patrick Karl. "An Engagement with Postmodern Foes, Literary Theorists and Friends on the Borders with History." <http://www.history.ac.uk/ihr/Focus/Whatishistory/obrien.html>.
Osborne, Dora. "Blind Spots: Viewing Trauma in W.G. Sebald's *Austerlitz*." *seminar* 43.4 (November 2007): 517–33.
Ouellet, Pierre. *Hors-Temps: Poétique de la posthistoire*. Montreal: vlb éditeur, 2008.
Oz, Amos. *How to Cure a Fanatic*. Princeton, NJ: Princeton University Press, 2006.
Pàlsson, Gìsli, ed. *Beyond Boundaries*. London: Berg, 1993.
Parey, Armelle. "Ordre et chaos dans Atonement d'Ian McEwan." *Cercles*, Occasional Paper Series (2007): 93–102. <http://www.cercles.com/occasional.html>.
Pateman, Matthew. *Julian Barnes*. Plymouth, UK: Northcote House, 2002.
Pedot, Richard. "Rewriting(s) in Ian McEwan's *Atonement*." *Etudes Anglaises* 60.2 (April–June 2007): 148–59.
Phelan, James. "Narrative Judgments and the Rhetorical Theory of Narrative: Ian McEwan's *Atonement*," in *A Companion to Narrative Theory*, eds. James Phelan and Peter J. Rabinowitz. Malden, MA: Blackwell, 2005, 322–36.
Piason Natali, Marcos. "History and the Politics of Nostalgia." *Iowa Journal of Cultural Studies* 5 (Fall 2004): 10–25. <http://www.uiowa.edu/~ijcs/nostalgia/nostfel.htm>.
Pizer, John. "Goethe's 'World Literature' Paradigm and Contemporary Cultural Globalization." *Comparative Literature* 52.3 (2000): 213–27.
———. *The Idea of World Literature: History and Pedagogical Practice*. Baton Rouge: Louisiana State University Press, 2006.
Pollock, Sheldon, Homi K. Bhabha, Carol A. Breckenridge, and Dipesh Chakrabarty, eds. *Cosmopolitanism*. Durham, NC: Duke University Press, 2002.
Poole, Steven. "Night of the Living Dead." Review of *After Dark*, *The Guardian*, June 9, 2007. <http://books.guardian.co.uk/print/0,,329995257-110738,00.html>.
Postel, Danny. "A Fighting Faith." *The Liberal*, 2008. <http://www.theliberal.co.uk/issue_12/politics/iran_postel.1_12.html>.
———. "Ideas Whose Time Has Come: A Conversation with Iranian Philosopher Ramin Jahanbegloo." <http://www.logosjournal.com/issue_5.2/jahanbegloo_interview.htm>.
———. *Reading Legitimation Crisis in Tehran: Iran and the Future of Liberalism*. Chicago: Prickly Paradigm Press, 2006.
Pratt, Mary Louise. "Arts of the Contact Zone." *Profession* 91 (1991): 33–40.
———. *Imperial Eyes: Travel Writing and Transculturation*. London: Routledge, 1992.
Prendergast, Christopher, ed. *Debating World Literature*. London: Verso, 2004.
Presner, Todd Samuel. "'What a Synoptic and Artificial View Reveals': Extreme History and the Modernism of W.G. Sebald's Realism." *Criticism* 46.3 (Summer 2004): 341–60.

Rastegar, Mitra. "Reading Nafisi in the West: Authenticity, Orientalism, and 'Liberating' Iranian Women." *Women's Studies Quarterly* 34.1/2 (2006): 108–28.
"Reading More Than *Lolita* in Tehran: An Interview with Fatemeh Keshavarz," *Monthly Review*, March 12, 2007. <http://www.monthlyreview.org/mrzine/keshavarz120307.html>.
Ribbat, Christoph. " Nomadic with the Truth: Holocaust Representations in Michael Chabon, James McBride, and Jonathan Safran Foe." *Anglistik und Englischunterricht* 66 (2005): 199–218.
Rix, Len. "Magda Szabo: Acclaimed author of 'The Door.'" *The Independent*, November 22, 2007. <http://www.independent.co.uk/news/obituaries/magda-szabo-acclaimed-author-of-the-door-758994.html>.
Robertson, Roland. *Globalization, Social Theory and Global Culture*. London: Sage, 1992.
Rothenbuhler, Eric W., and Mihai Coman, eds. *Media Anthropology*. Thousand Oaks, CA: Sage Publications, 2005.
Rowe, John Carlos. "Reading *Reading Lolita in Tehran* in Idaho." *American Quarterly* 59.2 (2007): 253–75.
Rubin, Jay. *Haruki Murakami and the Music of Words*. London: Harvill, 2002.
Rushdie, Salman. "The Empire Writes Back with a Vengeance." *Times*, July 3, 1982.
_____. *Imaginary Homelands: 1981–1990 Essays and Criticism*. London: Granta, 1991.
Ryan, Kiernan. *Ian McEwan*. Plymouth, UK: Northcote House, 1994.
Said, Edward. *Culture and Imperialism*. 1993; London: Vintage, 1994.
_____. *Humanism and Democratic Criticism*. New York: Columbia University Press, 2004.
_____. *Orientalism. Western Conceptions of the Orient*. Harmondsworth, UK: Penguin, 1978, 2003.
Saussure, de, Ferdinand. *Course in General Linguistics*. Translated by Roy Harris [*Cours de linguistique générale*, 1916]. Peru, IL: Open Court, 1986.
Scanlan, Sean. "Introduction: Nostalgia." *Iowa Journal of Cultural Studies* 5 Nostalgia: 3–9. <http://www.uiowa.edu/~ijcs/nostalgia/nostint.htm>.
Schlesinger, Philip. "W.G. Sebald and the Condition of Exile." *Theory, Culture & Society* 21.2 (April 2004): 43–67.
Schoene, Berthold. *The Cosmopolitan Novel*. Edinburgh: Edinburgh University Press, 2009.
Scott, James B. "Parrot as Paradigms: Infinite Deferral of Meaning in 'Flaubert's Parrot.'" *ARIEL: A Review of International English Literature* 21.3 (July 1990): 57–68.
Seats, Michael. *Murakami Haruki: The Simulacrum in Contemporary Japanese Culture*. Lanham, MD: Lexington Books, 2006.
Sennett, Richard. *The Corrosion of Character: The Personal Consequences of Work in the New Capitalism*. New York: Norton, 1999.
Seymenliyska, Elena. "Labours of Love." Review of *The Door*, *The Guardian*, October 29, 2005. <http://www.guardian.co.uk/books/2005/oct/29/featuresreviews.guardianreview29>.
Shepherd, Tania. "Towards a Description of Atypical Narratives: A Study of the Underlying Organisation of *Flaubert's Parrot*." *Language and Discourse* 5 (1997): 71–95.
Shone, Tom. "White Lies." Review of *Atonement*, *The New York Times*, March 10, 2002. <http://query.nytimes.com/gst/fullpage.html?res=9405E5D81231F933A25750C0A9649C8B63>.
Sicher, Efraim, ed. *Breaking Crystal: Writing and Memory after Auschwitz*. Urbana: University of Illinois Press, 1998.
Simons, Herbert W., and Michael Billig, eds. *After Postmodernism: Reconstructing Ideology Critique*. London: Sage Publications, 1994.
Simonsen, Karen-Margrethe, and Jacob Stougaard-Nielsen, eds. *World Literature, World Culture: History, Theory, Analysis*. Aarhus, DK: Aarhus University Press, 2008.
Smith, Charles Saumarez. "Another Time, Another Place." Review of *Austerlitz*, *The Observer*, September 30, 2001. <http://www.guardian.co.uk/books/2001/sep/30/travel.highereducation>.
Smith, Sidonie, and Julia Watson. *Reading Autobiography: A Guide for Interpreting Life Narratives*. Minneapolis: University of Minnesota Press, 2010.
Smith, Samuel R. "Distributed Culture and the Rise of the Network Age." <http://www.intelligentagent.com/archive/Vol3_No1_polisci_smith.html>.
Snoj, Vid. "World Literature against the Background of the Other." *Interlitteraria*, Issue 11 (2006): 41–49. <http://www.ceeol.com>.
Spivak, Gayatri Chakravorty. *Death of a Discipline*. New York: Columbia University Press, 2003.
Steiner, George. *After Babel: Aspects of Language and Translation*. New York: Oxford University Press, 1975.
_____. *What Is Comparative Literature?* Oxford: Clarendon Press, 1995.

Stephanides, Stephanos, ed. *Cultures of Memory/Memories of Culture*. Nicosia, CY: University of Nicosia Press, 2007.
Stierstorfer, Klaus, ed. *Beyond Postmodernism: Reassessments in Literature, Theory and Culture*. Berlin: Walter de Gruyter, 2003.
Strecher, Matthew C. *Dances with Sheep: The Quest for Identity in the Fiction of Murakami Haruki*. Ann Arbor: University of Michigan, Center for Japanese Studies, 2002.
_____. "Magical Realism and the Search for Identity in the Fiction of Haruki Murakami." *Journal of Japanese Studies* 25.2 (Summer 1999): 263–98.
Summers-Bremner, Eluned. "Reading, Walking, Mourning: W.G. Sebald's Peripatetic Fictions." *Journal of Narrative Theory* 34.3 (Fall 2004): 304–34.
Suter, Rebecca. *The Japanization of Modernity: Murakami Haruki between Japan and the United States*. Cambridge, MA: Harvard University Press, 2008.
Taberner, Stuart. "German Nostalgia? Remembering German-Jewish Life in W.G. Sebald's *Die Ausgewanderten* and *Austerlitz*." *The Germanic Review* 79.3 (Summer 2004): 181–202.
Tal, Kalí. *Worlds of Hurt: Reading the Literatures of Trauma*. Cambridge: Cambridge University Press, 1996.
Tani, Stefano. *The Doomed Detective: The Contribution of the Detective Novel to Postmodern American and Italian Fiction*. Carbondale: Southern Illinois University Press, 1984.
Taylor, Chloë. *The Culture of Confession from Augustine to Foucault: A Genealogy of the "Confessing Animal."* New York: Routledge, 2009.
Tennstedt, Antje. "L'Illusion d'une communication orale dans *Die Ausgewanderten* (1992) et *Austerlitz* (2001) de W.G. Sebald." *Cahiers d'Etudes Germaniques* 47 (Autumn 2004): 33–43.
Tonkin, Boyd. "W.G. Sebald: The Gentle Ghosts of a Tragic History." *The Independent*, April 13, 2002. <http://www.independent.co.uk/arts-entertainment/books/features/w-g-sebald-the-gentle-ghosts-of-a-tragic-history-750564.html>.
Torgovnick, Marianna. *The War Complex: War World Two in Our Time*. Chicago: The University of Chicago Press, 2005.
Ullmann-Margalit, Edna. "Between Basis and Roots: Religious Fundamentalism, Radicalism, and {PRIVATE} Women." *Dones Mediterrànies*. <http://www.mediterraneas.org/article.php3?id_article=387>.
Updike, John. "Subconscious Tunnels: Haruki Murakami's Dreamlike New Novel." Review of *Kafka on the Shore*, *The New Yorker*, January 24, 2005. <http://www.newyorker.com/archive/2005/01/24/050124crbo_booksl>.
Valenta, Markha G. "Islam as the New Frontier: America at Work in the World." *RSA Journal* 17/18 (2006/7): 71–100.
Venturi, Robert, Denise Scott Brown, and Steven Izenour. *Learning from Las Vegas*, eds. Kester Rattenbury and Samantha Hardingham. 1972, Abingdon, UK: Routledge, 2007.
Vermeulen, H., and C. Govers, eds., *The Anthropology of Ethnicity: Beyond Ethnic Groups and Boundaries*. Amsterdam: Het Spinhuis, 1994.
Vickroy, Laurie. *Trauma and Survival in Contemporary Fiction*. Charlottesville: University of Virginia Press, 2002.
Wallace, David Foster. "E Unibus Pluram: Television and U.S. Fiction." *Review of Contemporary Fiction* 13.2 (Summer 1993): 151–94.
Walters, Tim. "'Nabokov' as Both String and Hole in the Postmodern Net of Flaubert's Parrot." *Q/W/E/R/T/Y* 11 (Oct. 2001): 197–203.
Washburn, Dennis Charles. *Translating Mount Fuji: Japanese Fiction and the Ethics of Identity*. New York: Columbia University Press, 2007.
Waters, Malcolm. *Globalization*. London: Routledge, 1995.
Wattanagun, Kanya, and Suradech Chotiudompant. "The Quest and Reconstruction of Identity Is Haruki Murakami's *Kafka on the Shore*." *Manusya Journal of Humanities* 12:1 (2009): 26–39. <http://www.manusya.journals.chula.ac.th/files/essay/Kanya_26-39.pdf>.
Welch, Patricia, "Haruki Murakami's Storytelling World." *World Literature Today* 79.1 (Jan.–Feb. 2005): 55–59.
Welsch, Wolfgang. "Transculturality — The Puzzling Form of Cultures Today," in *Spaces of Culture: City, Nation, World*, eds. Mike Featherstone and Scott Lash. London: Sage, 1999.
White, Hayden. *Metahistory: The Historical Imagination in Nineteenth-Century Europe*. Baltimore: The Johns Hopkins University Press, 1973.
Whitehead, Anne. *Trauma Fiction*. Edinburgh: Edinburgh University Press, 2004.

Whitlock, Gillian. "Autographics: The Seeing 'I' of the Comics." *Modern Fiction Studies* 52.4 (Winter 2006): 965–79.
Wiesel, Elie. "The Holocaust as Literary Inspiration," in *Dimensions of the Holocaust*, ed. Elliot Lefkovitz. Evanston, IL: Northwestern University Press, [A14], 5–19.
Williams, Richard. "Marathon Man." *The Guardian*, May 17, 2003. <http://www.guardian.co.uk/books/2003/may/17/fiction.harukimurakami>.
Woolf, Virginia. "Craftsmanship," in *The Death of the Moth and Other Essays*. <http://ebooks.adelaide.edu.au/w/woolf/virginia/w91d/chapter24.html>.
———. "The New Biography" (1927), in *Selected Essays*, ed. David Bradshaw with a biographical preface by Frank Kermode. Oxford: Oxford University Press, 2008, 95–100.
Wylie, John. "The Spectral Geographies of W.G. Sebald." *cultural geographies* 14 (2007): 171–88.
Yehoshua, Abraham B. "An Attempt to Identify the Root Cause of Antisemitism." *Azure* 32 (Spring 2008). <http://www.azure.org.il/article.php?id=18>.
———. *Antisemitismo e sionismo: una discussione*. Translated by Glauco Felici. Turin: Einaudi, 2004.
———. "*Mr. Mani* and the *Akedah*." *Judaism* (Winter 2001): 61–65. <http://findarticles.com/p/articles/mi_m0411/is_5_49/ai_73180736>.
———. *The Terrible Power of a Minor Guilt: Literary Essays*. Translated by Ora Cumming [*Koḥah ha-nora shel ashmah ḳeṭanah: ha-heḳsher ha-musari shel ha-ṭeḳst ha-sifruti*, 1998]. Syracuse, NY: Syracuse University Press, 2000.
———. "The Zionist Revolution: Is It Continuing?" *CCAR Journal* 54.2 (2007): 123–45.
Young, James Edward. *Writing and Rewriting the Holocaust: Narrative and the Consequences of Interpretation*. Bloomington: Indiana University Press, 1988.
Ziegler, Heide, ed. *The End of Postmodernism: New Directions Proceedings of the First Stuttgart Seminar in Cultural Studies, 04.08.-18.08.1991*. Stuttgart: M & P Verlag fur Wissenschaft und Forschung, 1993.
Zilcosky, John. "Lost and Found: Disorientation, Nostalgia, and Holocaust Melodrama in Sebald's *Austerlitz*." *Modern Language Notes* 121.3 (April 2006): 679–98.

Index

Adorno, Theodor 131
Aeschylus 112
Afghanistan 14, 22
Ahmed, Akbar S. 21; *Posmodernism and Islam* 22
Akedah 72–74, 76
Al Ahram 148
Al Aida (refugee camp) 15
Alexander, Jeffrey 124
Alterity 9–10, 60, 72, 125; *see also* difference; identity; otherness
Améry, Jean 97, 101, 134
Amis, Martin 24; "The Last Days of Muhammad Atta" 23
Anderson, Benedict 8; *Imagined Communities* 8
Anderson, Paul Thomas 177n; *Magnolia* 177n
anti-Semitism 67, 72–74, 79–80, 102
Antwerp 98–100
Appadurai, Arjun 13; *Modernity at Large* 13
Appiah, Kwame Anthony 6
Arab-Israeli conflict 7, 9, 15; *see also* Palestine question
Arendt, Hannah 151
Aristotle 157; *Poetics* 157
Auerbach, Erich 167n; *Mimesis* 167n
Aum Shinrikyo 110
Auschwitz 21, 32, 131, 133
Austen, Jane 83–84; *Northanger Abbey* 83–84
Auster, Paul 113
Austria 103

Bala 103
Balfour Declaration 67, 69
Band, Arnold J. 73, 81
Barakat, Hoda 16, 23; *The Tiller of Waters* 16, 23

Barenboim, David 9
Barnes, Julian 12, 19, 34, 41, 51 44, 46–51, 169n, 172n; *Cross Channel* 50; *England England* 169n; *Flaubert's Parrot* 19, 34, 36, 41, 44, 47, 50, 158; "The Rebuke" 172n
Barthes, Roland 46–47; "The Death of the Author" 46
Baudrillard, Jean 29
Bauman, Zygmunt 12, 28, 38, 102; *Modernity and the Holocaust* 38, 102
Bavaria 12, 97
The Beach Boys 121
bearing witness *see* witnessing
The Beatles 121
Beaumont, Matthew 29
Bechhofer, Susie 106
Beckett, Samuel 30, 168n
Beirut 16, 23, 163
Belgium 101, 108
Bendelack, Steve: *Mr. Bean's Holiday* 154–155
Benedict XVI, Pope 15
Ben-Gurion, David 75
Benigni, Roberto 132; *Life Is Beautiful* 132
Benjamin, Walter 100
Ben-Zvi, Yitzhak 75
Berger, Alan L. 137
Bergson, Henri 82
Berlin 15
Berlin Wall 15, 19, 21, 59, 125
Bhabha, Homi 5, 8, 12, 30; *Nation and Narration* 8
Bible 68, 70–71, 73–74, 77
Bin Laden, Osama 22
biography 9, 17, 36, 41–42, 44, 46–47, 49–51, 68
Bloom, Allan 10–11; *The Closing of the American Mind* 10

Index

Bloom, Harold 10–11; *The Western Canon* 11
Bolter, Jay David 163
Bonaparte, Marie 104
Booth, Wayne C. 37
Borges, Jorge Luis 113
Borowski, Tadeusz 134
Bosnia 26
Bowen, Elizabeth 94; *The Heat of the Day* 94
Brautigan, Richard 121
Brockmeier, Jens 95
Brontë (family) 43
Brontë, Charlotte 32; *Jane Eyre* 32
Brooks, Neil 28; *The Mourning After* 28
Brussels 102
Buber, Martin 173*n*
Buddha 49
Burn, Stephen J. 29, 32; *Jonathan Franzen and the End of Postmodernism* 29
Buruma, Ian 22; *Occidentalism* 22
Burwell, Catherine 151
Bush, George W. 22, 29, 148

Cahoone, Lawrence 18
Calvino, Italo 31–32; *If on a Winter's Night a Traveler* 31
Canada 151
Cannes 154–155
canon 7–8, 10–11, 25, 139, 176*n*
Capote, Truman 121
Capra, Fritjof 112
Caravaggio, Michelangelo Merisi da 99
Carter, Angela 170*n*; *The Bloody Chamber* 170*n*
Caruth, Cathy 129, 161
Cavarero, Adriana 99
Chekhov, Anton 121
Chozick, Matthew Richard 176*n*
Cleave, Chris 25
close reading 8, 10, 113
Coetzee, J.M. 25; *Foe* 25
Cold War 7, 19, 21–22
Colet, Louise 50
Collado-Rodriguez, Francisco 137
comparatism 9–10, 66, 110, 148, 167*n*
comparative literature *see* comparatism
Conrad, Joseph 12
Cosmopolitanism 5–6, 9, 98, 107, 149, 167*n*
Cotiudompant, Suradech 122
Crete 67, 77–80
Croisset 43, 49, 51
cultural memory 42, 67, 100, 125
Cunningham, Michael 24; *Specimen Days* 24
Cyprus 1, 15–16; Republic of Cyprus 15
Czech Republic 103

Dabashi, Hamid 148
Dalai Lama 13
Damrosch, David 7
DeLillo, Don 24; *Falling Man* 24

Dennett, Daniel Clement 23, 169*n*; *Breaking the Spell* 23
DePaul, Amy 150–151
Derrida, Jacques 39
De Saussure, Ferdinand 152
Deutsche Demokratische Republik (DDR) 169*n*
diaspora 66, 72, 74–75, 97, 105, 125, 146–48, 173; *see also* exile; expatriation
Dickens, Charles 121
difference 6, 19, 28, 66, 72, 81, 125, 145; *see also* alterity; identity; otherness
distant reading 10
Dostoyevsky, Fyodor 121
Dublin 56
Dunkirk 90
Dyer, Geoff 83

Eaglestone, Robert 38, 157; *Ethical Criticism* 38
Eagleton, Terry 27, 39; *After Theory* 39; *The Illusions of Postmodernism* 27
East Anglia 12
Ebadi, Shirin 146–148, 151, 178*n*, 179*n*; *The Golden Cage* 146, 151; *Iran Awakening* 146, 178*n*
Eco, Umberto 31, 46, 113
ecumene 5, 9, 81
Eder, Richard 98
Egypt 68, 75
Eichmann, Adolf 35, 115
Eisner, Will 164; *Contract with God* 164; *The Plot* 164
Eliot, T.S. 5–6, 115, 168*n*; "What Is a Classic?" 5
Elvis (Elvis Aaron Presley) 121
Emmaus 51
emotions 13–16, 27, 32, 34, 36, 43, 47, 51–52, 54–58, 60, 64, 66, 90, 93, 97, 100, 107, 122, 127–128, 130, 132, 133, 135, 146, 155–158, 161, 165, 174*n*
Eshel, Amir 97
Eshelman, Raoul 39, 132, 156
Esther, Book of 74
ethics 13–14, 17, 30, 33–39, 55–56, 62, 83, 96, 115, 125, 137, 156–157 *see also* morality
Ethics, Literature, Theory 37
Euphrates 68
Euripides 112, 169*n*
Europe 5, 10, 15, 44, 99, 103, 106, 125, 159
exile 74, 96–98, 105, 141, 147, 167*n*; *see also* diaspora; expatriation
Exodus, Book of 68
expatriation 23, 35, 63, 97–98, 147–148, 158; *see also* diaspora; exile

fake 43, 62, 87; *see also* forgery
fantastic 111, 126, 176*n*, 178*n*; *see also* fantasy; magic realism; realism

fantasy 13, 105, 148; *see also* fantastic; magic realism; realism
Felman, Shoshana 161
Fens 45
Feuer, Menachem 178*n*
Fine, Robert 167*n*
Fink, Guido 72
Fitzgerald, F.S. 139, 145; *The Great Gatsby* 145
Flaubert, Gustave 36, 41–44, 46–51, 121; *Bouvard and Pecuchet* 47; *Dictionary of Commonplaces* 47–48; *Madame Bovary* 46, 48, 145, 172*n*; "A Simple Heart" 48
Foer, Jonathan Safran 11, 13, 24, 35, 39, 124, 126–128, 130–131, 136–137; *Extremely Loud and Incredibly Close* 24; *Everything Is Illuminated* 36, 39, 124, 126, 130–132, 134, 136–137, 158, 162
Folman, Ari 164; *Waltz with Bashir* 164–165
Ford, Ford Madox 82, 92, 168*n*; *The Good Soldier* 82
forgery 86–87; *see also* fake
Forster, E.M. 94; *Howard's End* 94; *A Passage to India* 94
Foucault, Michel 100
Fowles, John 31, 83; *The French Lieutenant's Woman* 31, 83
France 89, 125, 162
Freud, Sigmund 67, 111
fundamentalism 8, 24, 144, 150, 153

Gabriel, Philip 110, 121
Gaia 6
Galicia 178*n*
Galimberti, Umberto 38
Gaza 15, 17, 165
Genesis, Book of 68, 70–72
Germany 77, 79, 97–98, 103, 132–133, 163, 167*n*
Gibson, Andrew 38; *Postmodernity, Ethics and the Novel* 38
Giovannelli, Laura 46
globalization 6, 8–9, 28, 37, 100, 104
Glucksmann, André 29
Goethe, Johann Wolfgang von 9–10, 43; *West-Eastern Divan* 9
Goleman, Daniel 13, 157; *Destructive Emotions* 13; *Emotional Intelligence* 157
Gospel of Luke 61
graphic memoir *see* graphic narrative
graphic narrative 17, 24, 27, 146, 163–165
graphic novel *see* graphic narrative
Great Britain 11–12, 76, 97, 102–103, 106, 147; *see also* United Kingdom
Greece 15, 80
green line 1, 14–17
Greenblatt, Stephen 8, 10
Greenwich 103–104

Grusin, Richard 163
Gulf Wars 14, 22
Gunn, Giles 8, 10

Haifa 66
Hakutani, Yoshinobu 110
Hallet, Wolfgang 164
Hamid, Mohsin 24–25; *The Reluctant Fundamentalist* 24
Hannerz, Ulf 9
Hardt, Michael 28; *Empire* 28
Hartley, L.P. 93; *The Go-Between* 93
Hastings 44
Haworth 43
Hay, Simon 149
Hebron 73
Hegel, G.W.F. 151, 167*n*
Hellas 78
Heraklion 67
Herbert, Juliet 50
Herder, Johann Gottfried 6
Hirsch, Marianne 34, 136
historiographic metafiction 25, 45
history 13–14, 20, 27, 32, 35, 44–46, 55, 59, 66, 73–78, 81, 96–97, 100, 102–103, 129, 137, 141, 147, 149–150, 156, 159, 161, 165, 174–175
Hobsbawm, Eric J. 45; *The Invention of Tradition* 45
Holocaust 7, 27, 32–35, 38, 72, 95, 98–99, 101–102, 124, 129, 131–132, 136–137, 157–158, 161
Holocaust fiction 36, 132, 178
Horn, Bernard 66
Horowitz, Sarah R. 161
Hosseini, Khaled 23; *The Kite Runner* 23; *A Thousand Splendid Suns* 23
Hungary 12, 19, 55, 60
Huntington, Samuel 11, 16, 21–22; *The Clash of Civilizations* 16, 21
Hutcheon, Linda 18, 25–26, 32, 45
Huyssen, Andreas 27

identity 2, 7–9, 10–11, 13, 19–20, 24, 27–28, 35, 66–67, 69, 72, 74–75, 79–81, 89, 96, 104, 106, 110, 122, 124–125, 134, 137, 140, 142–144, 147–148, 162, 165, 168*n*, 173, 176; *see also* alterity; otherness; difference
imagination 13–14, 20–21, 22, 35, 39, 41, 46–47, 66, 83–84, 89, 92–95, 110, 114–115, 120, 128–129, 136, 140, 143–144, 146, 152, 155, 158, 169*n*
India 9
Iran 139–140, 145–146
Iraq 139, 141
Iron Curtain 19
Irony 19, 26, 32–33, 37, 39, 41–42, 46–48, 50, 83–85, 120, 155; *see also* parody

irresponsibility 25, 153; *see also* responsibility
Iser, Wolfgang 30
Israel 9, 15–17, 21, 35, 66–68, 72–73, 75, 81, 125, 163
Istanbul 167*n*

Jacobson, Dan 108; *Heshel's Kingdom* 108
Jahabengloo, Ramin 151; "Reading Machiavelli in Tehran" 151
James, Henry 39, 43, 50, 82, 92–94, 113, 139, 145, 168*n*; "The Aspern Papers" 50; "The Birthplace" 43; *The Golden Bowl* 93; The Real Right Thing" 50; *What Maisie Knew* 94
James, William 169*n*
Jameson, Fredric 26–27, 32; "The Cultural Logic of Late Capitalism" 26
Japan 112, 114–115
Jauss, Hans Robert 31
Jerusalem 11, 15, 18, 66–69, 72–73, 75–76
Jordan 69
Joyce, James 30, 82, 168*n*

Kabul 23
Kafka, Franz 177*n*; "In the Penal Colony" 116; "Letter to His Father" 177*n*
Kakutani, Michiko 89, 148
Kant, Immanuel 151, 167*n*
Katz, Adam 73
Kermode, Frank 92, 174*n*
Keshavarz, Fatemeh 149; *Jasmine and Stars* 149
Khatami, Mohammad 148
Khomeini, Ruhollah 36, 140–141
Khuri, Elias 23, 163; *Gate of the Sun* 23, 163
Kirby, Alan 28
Knossos 78
Kosovo 27
Kristof, Agota 12; *L'Analphabète* 12

LaCapra, Dominick 27, 45
Las Vegas 169*n*
Lawrence, D.H. 168*n*; *Lady Chatterley's Lover* 94
Lebanon 16, 75, 80, 163
Lebanon War 75, 164
Lee, Allison 49
Lehmann, Rosamond 94; *Dusty Answer* 94
Lentin, Ronit 132
Leopold of Belgium, King 99
Levi, Primo 97, 99, 134
Levinas, Emmanuel 18, 38
Liège 101
liquid modernity 12, 28
literature of the Holocaust *see* Holocaust fiction
Lithuania 108

Littel, Jonathan 132; *The Kindly Ones* 132
Llanwddyn 108–109
London 24, 85, 90, 103, 104, 106, 108
Lublin 125
Lynch, David 114; *Mulholland Drive* 114
Lyotard, Jean-François 21; *The Postmodern Condition* 21

Maalouf, Amin 162
MacArthur, Douglas 114
magic realism 35, 111, 126, 178*n*; *see also* fantastic; fantasy; realism
Majdanek 125
Mansfield, Katherine 30, 82, 168*n*
Mantes 50
Margalit, Avishai 14; *The Ethics of Memory* 14; *Occidentalism* 22
Margaronis, Maria 173*n*
Marx, Karl 167*n*
Mayer, John 157
McEwan, Ian 12, 18, 24, 35, 83–87, 90, 92–94, 125, 159, 165; *Atonement* 35, 83, 90, 92–94, 127, 158, 160, 174*n*; *Black Dogs* 125–126, 159; *Saturday* 24
McInerney, Jay 24; *The Good Life* 24
McLaughlin, Robert 155; "Post-Postmodern Discontent" 155
Mecca 71
memory 7, 13–14, 20, 27, 32–34, 85, 96, 98, 100, 104, 116, 124, 126, 128–29, 131–32, 135–37, 141, 157–61, 164–65
Mendelsohn, Daniel 85
Mernissi, Fatema 148; *Beyond the Veil* 148; *Dreams of Trespass* 148; *Scheherazade Goes West* 148
Miami 127
Mihaileanu, Radu 132; *Train of Life* 132
Miller, Laura 113, 177*n*
Moaveni, Azadeh 146–147, 178*n*; *Honeymoon in Tehran* 146; *Lipstick Jihad* 146–147
Moïsi, Dominique 13; *Geopolitics of Emotion* 13
Monet, Claude 43
Morahg, Gilead 80–81
morality 37–40, 55, 130, 134–136; *see also* ethics
Moretti, Franco 9–10
Moseley, Merritt 171*n*
Mossadegh, Mohammad 141, 147
multimodal novel 163
Munich 107
Murakami, Haruki 11, 13, 17–18, 35, 39, 110–116, 119–120, 122–123, 159, 168*n*, 176*n*; *Hear the Wind Sing* 110; *Kafka on the Shore* 35, 39, 110–115, 121–122, 159; *Underground* 110
myth 8, 12–13, 18–19, 27, 34, 36, 39, 46, 53, 57–58, 64, 68, 70, 72–75, 77–81, 99–100, 105, 109, 111, 114, 126, 137, 169*n*

Nablus 69
Nabokov, Vladimir 12, 139, 143; *Lolita* 143, 145, 152
Nadar (Gaspard-Félix Tournachon) 43
Nafisi, Azar 1, 11, 23, 139–152, 178*n*; *Reading Lolita in Tehran* 23, 35, 139, 141, 146, 148–152; *Things I've Been Silent About* 141
Napoleon 103
Negri, Antonio 28; *Empire* 28
Nelson, Prince Roger 120
Némirovsky, Irène 30
New York 21, 23–24, 29, 56, 58, 133
Nicosia 14–15
9/11 14, 21–25
9/11 novel 24
nostalgia 26, 32, 36, 39, 65, 93, 118
Nussbaum, Martha 38, 55–56, 157; *Love's Knowledge* 37; *Upheavals of Thought* 55, 157

Obama, Barack Hussein 16, 22, 29, 33
Odessa 127
Offenbach, Jacques 107
otherness 25–26, 79, 81, 125; *see also* alterity; difference; identity
Oulipo 32

Pahlavi, Mohammad Reza 140, 147
Palestine 70, 81
Palestine question 7, 14, 20, 23, 67–70, 75, 78, 81, 163, 165; *see also* Arab-Israeli conflict
Pamuk, Ohran 162; *Snow* 162
Parey, Armelle 174*n*
Paris 103, 108
parody 26, 47, 83, 98, 119, 154; *see also* irony
Partisan Review 177*n*
Pater, Walter 10, 30
Perec, Georges 31–32; *A Void* 31; *W, or the Memory of Childhood* 32
performativity 2, 6, 13, 17–18, 36, 39, 94, 122, 156
Pest 64
Pizer, John 6
Plato 157
Poe, E.A. 104–105; "The Man of the Crowd" 104
pogroms *see* anti-Semitism
Poland 67, 125
Pollock, Sheldon 5
Polonski, David 164; *Waltz with Bashir* 164–165
post-9/11 novel 24
Postel, Danny 151; *Reading Legitimation Crisis in Tehran* 151
postmemory 34, 136; postmemory fiction 34, 136
postmodernism 7, 10, 17–22, 24–36, 39, 41, 45–47, 49, 82–83, 123, 132, 155–156, 168*n*, 170*n*

post-postmodernism 29
Post-Western Europe 19
Prague 106–107, 130
Presley, Elvis Aaron 120–121
Prince (Prince Roger Nelson) 120
Princeton 24
Proust 98
pseudo-modernism 28
psychoanalysis 67, 76, 82, 112, 114, 161
Pynchon, Thomas 31, 113; *The Crying of Lot 49* 31
Pyrenees 108

Queneau, Raymond 32
Qur'an 71

Radcliffe, Ann 84
Rahimi, Atiq 23; *Le Retour imaginaire* 23; *A Thousand Rooms of Dreams and Fear* 23
Rákosy, Mátyás 55
Ramallah 69
Ranger, Terence 45; *The Invention of Tradition* 45
Rastegar, Mitra 149
realism 13, 29, 31, 48, 82–83, 92, 98, 102, 110, 116, 126, 130, 132, 137; *see also* fantastic; fantasy; magic realism
relativism 5, 8, 17–18, 22, 35, 49–51
relics 43, 49
remediation 128, 163–164
Renegotiating Ethics in Literature, Philosophy, and Theory 37–38
Rennes 12
responsibility 6–7, 30–39, 72, 83, 107, 115–116, 119–120, 131, 134–135, 147, 154, 156, 158, 165; aesthetic 30; ethical 30; free-floating 38; *see also* irresponsibility
Rhys, Jean 32, 168*n*; *Great Sargasso Sea* 31
Rix, Len 64
Robertson, Roland 8
Rome 87
Rothenbuhler, Eric W. 25
Rouen 42, 47, 50–51
Rowe, John Carlos 150
Ruanda 27
Rushdie, Salman 24–25, 152; *Midnight's Children* 25; *Shalimar the Clown* 24
Russia 103

Sabra and Shatila 165
Sacco, Joe 165; *Palestine* 165
Said, Edward 2, 9, 11, 22, 156; *Humanism and Democratic Criticism* 156; *Orientalism* 22
Salovey, Peter 157
Satrapi, Marjane 146–147, 164; *Persepolis* 146, 164–165
Schlink, Bernard 132, 160–161, 172*n*; *The Reader* 132–134, 160, 172*n*

Index

Schopenhauer, Arthur 54
Schubert, Franz 120
Schwarz, Delmore 177n; "In Dreams Begin Responsibilities" 177n
Seats, Michael 114
Sebald, W.G. 12–13, 34–35, 95–96, 98–99, 101, 105–108, 175n; *Austerlitz* 34, 95–100, 105, 135, 158, 162, 175n; *The Emigrants* 96, 98; *The Rings of Saturn* 175n; *Vertigo* 175n
Seine 43
self-referentiality 29–31, 92, 145, 154–155
self-reflexivity *see* self-referentiality
Shah, Saira 148; *Beneath the Veil* 148
Shakespeare, William 43, 152; *Hamlet* 87
Shikibu, Murasaki 113; *The Tale of Genji* 113
Sicher, Efraim 96, 124
simulacrum 25, 33
Singapore 12
Sodom 71
Sōseki, Natsume 119; *I Am a Cat* 119
South Africa 108
Soviet Bloc 19
Soviet Union 127
Spiegelman, Art 24, 34, 162, 164–165; *In the Shadow of No Towers* 23, 165; *Maus* 34, 164–165
Spitzer, Leo 167n
Spivak, Gayatri Chakravorty 9; *Death of a Discipline* 9
Stein, Gertrude 168n
Steiner, George 9
Stratford-upon-Avon 43
Strecher, Matthew 111
Suter, Rebecca 168n
Sweden 59
Swift, Graham 45; *Waterland* 45
Switzerland 12, 98
Szabó, Magda 12–13, 19, 33–34, 39, 52, 54–56, 58–60, 64, 151; *The Door* 12, 18–19, 32–33, 38, 52, 56, 59, 64, 151, 158

Taberner, Stuart 107
Takamatsu 112, 120
Tal, Kalí 36
Tehran 139–140, 142, 150
Tel Aviv 75
Terezín (Theresienstadt) 107–108
terrorism 14, 21, 23–24, 29
testimony 17, 27, 97–98, 139, 157, 161–162, 165; *see also* witnessing
Thousand and One Nights 144
Tokyo 110, 112, 120
Toth, Josh 28; *The Mourning After* 28
trauma 7, 25, 27, 33–37, 54–55, 58, 76, 86, 93, 98, 104–105, 115, 122, 124, 129, 134–137, 157–165
trauma fiction 34, 36, 157, 161
Trenet, Charles 155; *La Mer* 155

Tripoli 12
Truffaut, François 120
Turkey 15
Ukraine 126, 130, 137
Ullmann-Margalit, Edna 153
United Kingdom 15, 19; *see also* Great Britain
United States 9, 11, 24, 127, 140–142, 147–149, 151, 155, 167n
Updike, John 24; *Terrorist* 24

Vickroy, Laurie 34, 157, 161
Virgil 64; *Aeneid* 57
Vonnegut, Kurt 121

Wales 103, 106, 108
Wallace, David Foster 155
Washburn, Dennis Charles 115
Wattanagun, Kanya 122
Weimar 43
Welsch, Wolfgang 6
Weltliteratur 9; *see also* world literature
West Bank 15, 165
West-Eastern Divan (orchestra) 9
White, Hayden 45, 49; *Metahistory* 45
Whitehead, Anne 105
Whitlock, Gillian 147, 165
Wiesel, Elie 124, 134
Wilde, Oscar 10, 30–31, 38, 94; *The Picture of Dorian Gray* 30
William the Conqueror 44
witnessing 27, 34, 44, 49, 85, 88–89, 93, 97, 100, 128–29, 135–37, 149, 157–58, 161, 165; *see also* testimony
Wittgenstein, Ludwig 176n
Wolf, Christa 19, 169n; *Medea* 19
Woolf, Virginia 30, 46, 82, 94, 153; *The Waves* 94
world literature 2, 6, 7, 10, 168n; *see also* Weltliteratur
World War I 77, 85, 108, 145
World War II 5, 7, 26, 34, 39, 44, 51, 55, 67, 76, 89–90, 115, 127, 160
World Wars 18, 93

Yeats, W.B. 115
Yehoshua, Abraham B. 1, 11, 13, 35–36, 66–68, 70–71, 73, 75, 80–81; *Mr. Mani* 1, 35, 66–67, 70, 72–73, 75, 80–81; *The Terrible Power of a Minor Guilt* 36
Yugoslavia 125

Zafón, Carlos Ruiz 176n; *The Shadow of the Wind* 176n
Ziegler, Heide 29, 155; *The End of Postmodernism* 29
Zilcosky, John 175n
Zionism 67, 74–75, 80, 140, 173n

www.ingramcontent.com/pod-product-compliance
Lightning Source LLC
Chambersburg PA
CBHW032058300426
44116CB00007B/790